LOUIS BAMBERGER

BRANDEIS SERIES IN AMERICAN JEWISH
HISTORY, CULTURE, AND LIFE

Jonathan D. Sarna, Editor
Sylvia Barack Fishman, Associate Editor

For a complete list of books that are available in the series,
visit www.upne.com

Linda B. Forgosh
   Louis Bamberger: Department Store Innovator and Philanthropist
Gary Phillip Zola and Marc Dollinger, editors
   American Jewish History: A Primary Source Reader
Vincent Brook and Marat Grinberg, editors
   Woody on Rye: Jewishness in the Films and Plays of Woody Allen
Mark Cohen
   Overweight Sensation: The Life and Comedy of Allan Sherman
David E. Kaufman
   *Jewhooing the Sixties: American Celebrity and Jewish Identity —
   Sandy Koufax, Lenny Bruce, Bob Dylan, and Barbra Streisand*
Jack Wertheimer, editor
   The New Jewish Leaders: Reshaping the American Jewish Landscape
Eitan P. Fishbane and Jonathan D. Sarna, editors
   Jewish Renaissance and Revival in America
Jonathan B. Krasner
   The Benderly Boys and American Jewish Education
Derek Rubin, editor
   *Promised Lands: New Jewish American Fiction on
   Longing and Belonging*
Susan G. Solomon
   *Louis I. Kahn's Jewish Architecture: Mikveh Israel
   and the Midcentury American Synagogue*
Amy Neustein, editor
   Tempest in the Temple: Jewish Communities and Child Sex Scandals
Jack Wertheimer, editor
   *Learning and Community: Jewish Supplementary Schools in the
   Twenty-first Century*
Carole S. Kessner
   Marie Syrkin: Values Beyond the Self

LOUIS BAMBERGER

DEPARTMENT STORE INNOVATOR AND PHILANTHROPIST

LINDA B. FORGOSH

BRANDEIS UNIVERSITY PRESS

Waltham, Massachusetts

Brandeis University Press

An imprint of University Press of New England

www.upne.com

© 2016 Brandeis University

All rights reserved

Manufactured in the United States of America

Designed by Richard Hendel

Typeset in Utopia and Transat by Passumpsic Publishing

Library of Congress Cataloging-in-Publication Data

Names: Forgosh, Linda B., author.

Title: Louis Bamberger: department store innovator and
    philanthropist / Linda B. Forgosh.

Description: Waltham, Massachusetts: Brandeis University Press, 2016 |
    Series: Brandeis series in American Jewish history, culture, and life |
    Includes bibliographical references and index.

Identifiers: LCCN 2016004971 (print) | LCCN 2016017453 (ebook) |
    ISBN 9781611689815 (cloth: alk. paper) | ISBN 9781611689822 (epub,
    mobi & pdf)

Subjects: LCSH: Bamberger, Louis, 1855-1944. | Jews—New Jersey—
    Newark—Biography. | Jewish businesspeople—New Jersey—
    Newark—Biography. | Philanthropists—New Jersey—Newark—
    Biography. | Department stores—New Jersey—Newark—
    History. | Newark (N.J.)—History.

Classification: LCC F144.N653 B3646 2016 (print) |
    LCC F144.N653 (ebook) | DDC 338.092

[B]—dc23

LC record available at https://lccn.loc.gov/2016004971

5 4 3 2 1

CONTENTS

ACKNOWLEDGMENTS

The suggestion to write the biography of Louis Bamberger came from Oscar Lax, a longtime member of the Jewish Historical Society of New Jersey, who claimed that no such history existed and that honoring Louis Bamberger's legacy was long overdue. Preliminary research told me that Lax was right: Bamberger was not only a leading American and New Jersey philanthropist, but also a major, if underappreciated, Jewish American figure.

Two other individuals influenced my decision to write the Bamberger biography. The first is Warren Grover, a well-respected historian, author of *Nazis in Newark*, and cofounder of the Newark History Society. Usually in the throes of his own research, Warren copied Bamberger-related articles and sent them to me.

The second individual is Dr. Edward Shapiro, who was my mentor in graduate school. Shapiro recommended me for my job at the Jewish Historical Society. He is an important and influential historian in the field of American Studies. Dr. Shapiro provided an outline of topics that he felt needed to be covered to make the Bamberger biography a serious work by a serious historian. I owe my enthusiasm for history to years of listening to him lecture.

In addition, I cannot adequately express my gratitude to my editor, Stephanie Golden, for her invaluable contributions to the preparation of this book. She is a consummate professional and, lucky for me, proved to be a genuine pleasure to work with.

Researching Bamberger's life and times began with a special projects grant awarded from the New Jersey Historical Commission. The grant covered trips to Baltimore, Princeton, Huntington, Long Island, the Jersey shore and Avon-by-the-Sea, Washington, DC, and New York City and weekly trips to Newark.

Efforts to locate Bamberger family members began with Andrew Schindel, who came to the Jewish Historical Society looking for information about his great-grandfather Abraham Schindel. I recognized the Schindel name as being related to Bamberger through marriage. It was Andrew who put me in touch with Ellen Bamberger De Franco, Louis Bamberger's great-niece, and her son, John Schindel. Ellen supplied names and addresses for the remaining members of the Bamberger and Fuld families. Ellen, a published author in her own right, answered every question I asked. Her descriptions of Sunday dinners at Louis Bamberger's home in South Orange or her recollections of attending Bamberger's private funeral are in an exhibit of Bamberger photographs and memorabilia.

John Schindel went through the collections of newspaper articles, family photographs, and memorabilia saved by his mother and sent them to me. His attention to detail was constant, ongoing, and invaluable to this history. Private collections from the Bamberger and Fuld families tell the story of a man with a vast array of interests, whose personal wealth permitted him to engage with the world on his own terms.

De Franco suggested I contact her nephew, the late Edgar "Ed" Bamberger Bing, who lived at the Jersey shore in Avon-by-the-Sea, and her niece Mildred "Bunny" Levine, whose family spent summers at Avon. A close friend, Barbara Langella, checked her local phone book and found the listing for Bing. I called and left a voice message and Ed Bing returned my call immediately. The next thing I knew I had an invitation to visit the "Bamberger compound," a series of three houses facing the Shark River, to see where Louis Bamberger and the Bamberger clan gathered every summer to escape the New Jersey heat. On one of my trips to Avon, I sat at Louis Bamberger's desk. It was the same desk that had been in Bamberger's office in Newark, made doubly historic as this was where Albert Einstein sat scribbling his formulae and equations during his visits to Avon.

Ed Bing, his wife, Cheryl Wild, and Mildred and her husband, Mark Levine, came to Newark to hear me speak about the life and times of Louis Bamberger to a gathering of several hundred volunteers, who were celebrating the Newark Museum's one hundredth anniversary. Newark Museum was a gift to the City of Newark from Louis Bamberger and a perfect subject for a spring afternoon. Their presence lent an air of authenticity to Bamberger's story.

Information about Bamberger's partner and brother-in-law, Felix Fuld, came from Fuld's great-niece and great-nephew, Jackie and David Berg. David Berg shared his father Felix's personal papers and generously scanned family photographs. Jacqueline Berg inherited a run of valuable store employee newsletters for L. Bamberger & Co.'s peak years from 1921 to 1929 and sent me copies.

Direct appeals to send in a "Bamberger memory" were published in the *New Jersey Jewish News*, Newark's *Star-Ledger*, and in Jac Toporek's weekly Weequahic e-mail newsletter. One particular article, "History Expert Seeks Bamberger Memories," written by the *Star-Ledger* reporter Susan Lake, produced hundreds of responses.

The article, "A Retail Giant Recalled," by *New Jersey Jewish News* reporter Robert Wiener, prompted a call from the Macy's executive Edward J. Goldberg, senior vice president of government and consumer affairs and diversity vendor development at Macy's East in New York City. Goldberg, who spent a considerable portion of his career working at Bamberger's, arranged for me to do research in Macy's archives, where I was ably assisted by Scott Byers, Robin Hall, Bob Rutan, Nolan F. Hines, and Michael H. Johnson.

Four research institutions—the New Jersey Historical Society, the Newark Public Library, Newark Museum, and the Institute for Advanced Study—provided significant information for this biography. The most rewarding time was spent at the New Jersey Historical Society reading weekly editions of the *Newark Sunday Call* (1914–1941). Happily the trio of Maureen O'Rourke, Douglas Oxenhorn, and James Amemasor never seemed to mind that the library floor was littered with "snowflakes" that fell from the pages of very fragile newspapers. This went on for more than a year. I was sorry to see the end of my research at the New Jersey Historical Society, as my experience there was so positive.

The Newark Public Library has copies of the *Newark Evening News* on microfilm. The paper chronicles Bamberger's years in Newark. With assistance from Brad Small, George Crawley, Deirdre Schmidel, and William Dane, I was given access to copies of Bamberger's *Charm* magazine. I saw the page from the Gutenberg Bible given to the library by Louis Bamberger, and was directed to a series of articles entitled "Knowing Newark," written by the late Newark historian Charles Cummings.

I spent time in the archives of the Newark Museum, of which I am a longtime member, with Ulysses Dietz, senior curator and curator of decorative arts, who furnished me with an entire list of items donated to the museum by the Bamberger family. Archivist Jeffrey Moy compiled information about Bamberger from the museum's minutes for the years 1909–1944. Others from the Newark Museum to be thanked are Merle Lomrantz, Diana Bella, Olivia Arnone, Carole Bozzelli, Beverlee Kanengeiser, and Heidi Warbasse.

Erica Mosner, an archivist at the Institute for Advanced Study, was indispensable. She pulled numerous boxes containing correspondence between Bamberger and the institute's director at that time, Abraham Flexner. Mosner methodically copied and annotated hundreds of pages of correspondence and sent them to me. She must be thanked for answering all e-mail requests promptly and in great detail.

Additional archivists and research institutions to be thanked include Jennifer Brathovde and Lewis Wymann, Library of Congress; Ellen Kastel, Ratner Center for the Study of Conservative Judaism, Jewish Theological Seminary; Adina Anflick, American Jewish Historical Society; Laura Ruttum, manuscripts specialist, New York Public Library; Joan Adler, executive director, Straus Family Society archives; Jonathan Roscow, Jewish Museum of Maryland; Douglas Eldridge and Elizabeth Del Tufo, Newark Preservation and Landmarks Committee; Jac Toporek's weekly Weequahic e-mail newsletter; Phil Yourish, executive director, Weequahic Alumni Association; Tim Crist, copresident, Newark History Society; Robert Steinbaum, associate dean for advancement, Rutgers School of Law–Newark; Doug Eldridge, former president, Newark Preservation and Landmarks Committee; Stephen P. Wolsky and Robert A. Blum, Mountain Ridge Country Club; James Lecky, Branch Brook Park Alliance; Jeffrey Bennett, East Orange Library; Sandra L. Warren, East Orange Veterans Hospital; the late Frank Korczukowski, who unearthed the story of the SS *Bamberger*; Gail Malmgreen, director, Newark History Project; and Joanne La Greca, Rosehill Crematory, Linden, New Jersey. Lillian Dabney sent me newspaper articles; Harvey Weissbard sent a copy of the Bamberger's Restaurant menu; and Edward J. Goldberg donated Bamberger memorabilia. John Elwood provided photographs of the working farm and gardens on the Bamberger estate; Laurence Leonard forwarded a scan of a professional photograph of Bamberger's billiard room; and John and Mary Carnahan provided information about Bamberger's custom-built Estey organ.

Capturing the flavor of Newark's Bamberger era belongs to those who lived the history. More than two hundred individuals responded to requests to send in a "Bamberger memory" to remind us of what it was like to shop or work at L. Bamberger & Co. Their memories were used to help shape the content of this book. They are: Mary Rigby

Abernathy, Estelle Agisim, Cyrene Aksman, Anne Alexander, Palma Antonaccio, Mary Arcadipane, Katherine Atalla, Betty Barrett, Celeste Bateman, Margie Bauman, Frank Bellina, Sophia Bellina, Abner Benisch, Carol Bernstein, Mendel Bernstein, George Bersh, Anita Goldstein Blutinger, Howard Botnick, Lacy Brannic, Marian Braverman, Marcia Brous, Harriet Buono, Susan Calantone, Jane Cates, Edith Churchman, Judy Churgin, Bernard S. Cohen, Winifred Kessler Conley, Carol Jenkins Cooper, Charles Cooperstein, Grace Jubb Corbet, Grace Coutant, Lillian Dabney, Ruth Dargan, Janet B. Davidson, Sheldon Denburg, Diane Bash Deo, Barbara Wigler Dinnerman, Bernard Dlugash, Joseph Dombroski, Gloria Dougherty, Florence Drinkard, Gail Meyer Dunbar, Beatrice Epstein, Ginny Fagerstrom, Farrell Fand, Sheila Stein Farbman, Gretchen Fisher, Sara Friedman Fishkin, Laurie Fitzmaurice, Marcia Prince Freedman, Jane Biber Freeman, Lillian Freundlich, Stephen Frank, Esther Frieder, Gloria Fulton, Walter Galinder, Marlene "Pinky" Gold Gamble, Geraldyne Gardner, Sy Gelbard, Larry Geller, Louise Gersten, Frank Ghiselli, Peter Gilman, Patrick Gilmore, Philip Glucksman, Evelyn Gold, Sis Gold, Barry Goldberg, Edward Jay Goldberg, Marvin Goldberg, Harry Goldman, Dave Gorowitz, Barry Grabelle, Barry Graver, George Green, Phyllis Miller Green, Lory Greenbaum, Michael Gross, Faith Lurie Grossman, Sayde Grossman, Elaine Hagaman, Ben Halper, Irving Halper, Sam Halper, Linda Halperin, Alice Hannoch, David Harris, Carol Wodnick Harrison, Sanford Harwood, Joyce Haskins, Jean Gorowitz Helfman, Libby Friedman Heller, Nancy Leon Herman, Syma Herzog, Anna Heyman, Nate Himelstein, Myra Lieberman Hoffman, Margaret H. Hooper, Larry Horn, Marty Horn, Robert G. Huntington, Ronnie Olszewski Illig, Leila Deutsch Jacobsen, Victoria Jennings, Delores E. Johnson, Karen A. Johnson, Joel Kampf, Ben Kanter, Margaret Karass, Rita Karmiol, Donald Karp, Audree Kiesel, Bonnie Fand Klane, Peter Kolben, Angela Kolbinger, Dorothy Kosec, Harold Krauss, Janice Kriegman, Elaine Hersh Krusch, Judy Kulick, Oscar Lax, Gordon Leavitt, Thelma "Teddy" Leff, Phyllis Levin, Min Levine, Stephen B. Levitt, Gloria Yates Lewis, Elaine Lieb, Clark Lissner, Sylvia Longo, Herb Lutsky, Harry Lutzke, Anna Madris, Susan Maiella, Mary Sherot Mandel, Arlene Marantz, J. Marciano, Al and Marjorie Marcus, Ida Marech, Diane Nikel Martin, Kelly Marx, Mina McAllister, Thom McCloud, Margaret McCray, Wilbur McNeill, Edith Maas Mendel, Marie Menkes, Alida G. Michelson,

Gary N. Miller, Joan Stein Miller, Philip Mintz, Susan Mintz, Fan G. Mulvaney, Jerilyn Mulvaney, Joan Odes, Helen Palonsky, Katherine Petrallia, Wilma Bernhaut Pitman, Leslie Pumphrey, Scott Rajoppi, Margie Ramirez, Georgia Crawley Ransome, Rosemary Rello, Catherine Reynolds, Milton Riegel, Louise Rosen, Marilyn Kurman Rosen, Marie Rotondo, Arlene Glickenhaus Rubenstein, Kate Rubenstein, Jack Rudowsky, Raymond Rudy, Catherine Reynolds, Rose Ruesch, Rose Ann Russo, Eleanor Sacco, Steve Sacco, Marcia Heiss Samuels, Barbara Gruber Savino, Evelyn Jentis Schachtel, Sy Schaefer, Beverly Scharago, David Schechner, Richard Schlenger, Beatrice Schneider, Marilyn Schurer, Rona Leichter Seidel, Harold S. Shapiro, Paul Shapiro, and Seymour Shapiro, Roberta Singeltary, Joan Frieder Smith, Loretta Gudell Soloway, Bertha C. Sossin, Susan Sparks, Dore Denburg Stark, Dorothy Strand, Pamela Scott Threets, Corinne Tinsky, Jac Toporek, James R. Trotto, Jane Wallerstein, Sandra B. Warren, Connie Warshoff, Sam Wasserson, Andy Warren, Luella Watkins, Harvey Weisbard, Michael Weisman, Myrna Jelling Weisman, Jerry Wichinsky, Margie Wichinsky, Cheryl Wild, who sent me photos of Bamberger's desk, Daisy Williams, Lew Wymisner, Phil Yourish, George Zeevalk, and Nina "Jennie" Zerbino. Sincere apologies go to those whose names were inadvertently omitted.

Thanks to the staff at the Jewish Historical Society of New Jersey, Jill Hershorin and Irene Segal, and former Jewish Historical Society employees Susan Rivkind and Jennifer McGillan, who helped craft the successful grant application to the New Jersey Historical Commission that supported my research. The IT expert Yair J. Vinderboim provided assistance with saving and storing information in electronic files. Yair was indispensable to the writing of Mr. Bamberger's life and times. He listened to me read each chapter until, in his opinion, I had gotten it right. I am also indebted to the Jewish Historical Society of New Jersey's officers and board of trustees for their ongoing support of my efforts to tell Bamberger's story; the editor in chief of the *New Jersey Jewish News*, Andrew Silow-Carroll, for agreeing to read portions of the manuscript; and Lauren Hayes of Bradley Funeral Homes, whose records from March 25, 1944, confirm that Bamberger's ashes were picked up for eventual "burial" by his nephew, Edgar Bamberger.

My children, David and Beth, have to be thanked. David spurred me on when he asked, "Well, what chapter are you on?" Beth took time from her busy work schedule to come to hear me speak about the Bamberger history and checked my progress regularly, as we speak almost nightly. My daughter-in-law, Lisa Gil, with my granddaughter Willow Sofia in tow—and her brother Sullivan has to be mentioned—photographed badges of Bamberger's Aero Club exhibited at the Smithsonian's Air and Space Museum and reported her findings. My work ethic is from my mother, Laura Moggs Berman, and my godmother, Minna Golodner.

None of my friends or family escaped the life and times of Louis Bamberger, including my family: Lee and Jeffrey Forgosh, Marjorie and Neil Forgosh, "Uncle" David Forgosh, Frances G. Marsh, Gary and Mary Ann Marsh, Alida G. Michelson, and Joy and Alan Rockoff; and my friends: Arlene and Richard Bookbinder, Barbara and Jack Langella, Rabbi Herman and Renee Savitz, Evelyn and Herman Schachtel, Yael and Mike Weinstein, and Linda Willner. To all, my sincere thanks.

This book was published with the generous support of the Jewish Federation of Greater MetroWest NJ, Warren Grover, Robert R. Max, Jane and Dr. Victor Parsonnet, Jean Rich, Ilene and Robert Cowen, Bonnie and Jim Shrager, Susan and Lawrence Lubow, the Vinder and Rogers families, Ellen and Robert G. Rose, Carol and Robert Marcus, Hal and Elaine Braff, Ethel and Robert Singer, Linda Willner, Howard Kiesel, David Schechner, Sanford Hollander, and Norbert Gaelen.

Once again, my sincere thanks to all.

LOUIS BAMBERGER

INTRODUCTION
"ONE OF NEW JERSEY'S MOST ENLIGHTENED PERSONALITIES"

On March 11, 1944, flags in Newark, New Jersey, were lowered to half-mast to mark the passing of "first citizen" and "adopted son" Louis Bamberger, one of America's great merchant princes. Bamberger, founder and owner of L. Bamberger & Co., New Jersey's largest department store, had died peacefully in his sleep at age eighty-nine. The next morning, a private service was held for family and close friends at Bamberger's home in South Orange. Among those present was Albert Einstein, who had become friendly with Bamberger after joining the faculty of the Institute for Advanced Study in Princeton, an institution created and wholly funded by Bamberger. Later that day, a service at Temple B'nai Jeshurun, Newark's oldest and most prestigious Reform congregation, was attended by an estimated twelve hundred mourners, who heard civic and religious leaders describe Bamberger's philanthropic activities as "legendary" and extol his life as manifesting the "indelible marks of human greatness." To enable all New Jerseyans to participate in the mourning, the Board of Trustees of Newark Museum (an institution that had been presented by Bamberger as a gift to his city) published the "Memorial Service for Louis Bamberger" in its entirety. Bamberger himself had wanted no public memorials or cemetery headstone. Why this outpouring of public emotion on the death of a department store magnate? Perhaps because Bamberger had done his best to stay out of the public eye, historians of the great department stores have paid scant attention to him. Yet he was a figure of considerable importance, not only in Newark and New Jersey but also as a man who helped create modern America.

It is rare to meet a city dweller who does not have some memory or story to tell about his or her hometown department store—not to mention a lively interest in its owners. Universal interest in the department store as a public institution and in those who owned and operated it underlies the success of Public Broadcasting's 2013 Masterpiece Theater television series *Mr. Selfridge*, about the flamboyant owner of a major London-based department store, whose career began in Chicago at Marshall Field. Harry Gordon Selfridge was an acquaintance of Bamberger, and the two stayed in touch when he moved to London.

While Bamberger was a shrewd, tremendously successful businessman and astonishingly generous philanthropist, he was something of a mystery throughout his career because of his shyness and reticence. He shunned the limelight, even as he built his business into one of the major department stores in the country and became a multimillionaire, catapulting himself from modest beginnings in Baltimore into the ranks of the elite circle of German Jews who owned such stores as Macy's and Bloomingdale's in New York, Filene's in Boston, Kaufmann's in Pittsburgh, and F. & R. Lazarus in Columbus. He left no business records, kept no diaries, remained a bachelor, and kept his private life and rationales for his business decisions to himself. His closest companions were his sister Caroline, known as Carrie, and her husband Felix Fuld, with whom he lived and traveled. He hosted regular family gatherings in his relatively modest Georgian brick home in South Orange; and he spent summers at the Jersey shore, also with family, autumns in New York City at the Hotel Madison during the concert season, and winters at the Hotel Biltmore in Phoenix. The air of secrecy surrounding Bamberger's private life and his unwillingness to grant interviews fueled public curiosity about him. He discovered that there were benefits to being reclusive: when he spoke everybody listened.

All three Newark papers published obituaries of Bamberger, and even the *New York Times*, which unlike the others had not been dependent on his advertising, editorialized that L. Bamberger & Co. "might be called a public utility under unofficial control." In his novel *American Pastoral*, written forty-three years after Bamberger's death, Newark native Philip Roth recalled him as a "powerful personage as meaningful to local Jews as Bernard Baruch was meaningful to Jews around the country for his close association with FDR." And yet historians have shown little or no interest in the one-hundred-year history (1892–1992) of L. Bamberger & Co., or the life of its founder and owner, though in fact Bamberger's life has a significance that extends well beyond Newark and New Jersey.

Three separate components of Bamberger's career made him remarkable: the building of his business, his role as patron of the arts, and his enduring philanthropic legacy, the second two being made possible by his enormous success as a businessman. During his thirty-six-year career in Newark, Bamberger oversaw five expansions of his store, culminating in the impressive final addition in 1929 that created a total of sixteen floors aboveground and four floors below, making Bamberger's the sixth-largest department store in America. (The others were Macy's and Abraham & Straus in New York, Wanamaker's in Philadelphia, Marshall Field's in Chicago, and Hudson's in Detroit.) That the others were located in large cities made L. Bamberger & Co.'s growth in a small city such as Newark doubly impressive. Bamberger's faith in Newark was not always shared by his fellow merchants, who worried because Newark sat in the shadow of New York City. This did not bother Bamberger. He was never afraid of competition from the New York stores and said so frequently.

In 1892, the year L. Bamberger & Co. opened for business, America was entering what could be described as the golden era of the twentieth-century department store. Small dry goods firms that sold limited selections of handmade goods were being replaced by a new generation of enterprising merchants who added new wings to make space for the larger quantities of mass-produced goods now being manufactured in the nation's factories. Department stores nationwide thrived because they had lots of ready-made goods to stock their inventories. In Bamberger's time, Newark was the fourth-largest manufacturing center in America, and its industries fed Bamberger's store, to their mutual advantage.

Store owners such as Bamberger needed to devise a system to distribute mass-produced quality goods and then figure out a way to entice their consumers to buy them. Their answer was to build taller buildings with more light, wider aisles, and better ventilation. Advances in technology had made it possible to control the movement of goods and people in large numbers. Bamberger's took the lead in 1912, when it was among only a half-dozen stores in the country to install "moving stairways," escalators that enabled shoppers to reach the upper floors more quickly and cheaply than did elevators.

Many companies that had grown in a helter-skelter manner built their first major stores in the period from 1900 to World War I. This includes Macy's (1902), Marshall Field's (1902–1907), Wanamaker's (1911), Bamberger's, Filene's (1912), and many others. Department stores were a by-product of what historians refer to as the Progressive Era, a period of relative peace and prosperity associated with rising incomes, when technological innovations convinced store owners that the time was right to build.

Bamberger's department store came of age in the 1920s. This was a period of vigorous, vital economic growth marked by the availability of increasing conveniences for the middle class—the vacuum cleaner, electric refrigerators, washing machines, and irons—with department stores such as Bamberger's acting as agents convincing America's consumers they could indeed have it all. Shoppers were introduced to new customer services never seen before in a retail establishment, such as restaurants, tearooms, counter service, restrooms, a branch of the local public library, a branch of the local post office, free home delivery, wrapping services, convenient store hours, information booths, travel services, and innovative merchandise displays. For the Newark historian Charles Cummings, in "the opulent atmosphere it offered to shoppers, the practical education it provided on the availability and uses of new products, and in the opportunities the department store afforded for socialization of the growing middle class, department stores such as Bamberger's were key links in establishing the culture of consumption in 20th century America."[1]

Department stores both contributed to and benefited from the growth of America's middle class. They hired women at good wages as clerical workers (typists, clerks, and telephone operators) and then capitalized on these women's ability to buy more goods. A considerable portion of Bamberger's revenue came from his own employees, who received store discounts. An expanding city such as Newark offered Bamberger's store many advantages, including improved transportation systems that made it convenient to go "downtown" to shop. However, it wasn't Newark's lower-middle-class workers whom Bamberger wanted to attract. They became important only after he decided in 1922 to add a bargain basement. Until then his store targeted middle- and upper-middle-class women whose husbands' incomes qualified them to make purchases using the store's credit card. Credit card holders were automatically added to a list of eighty thousand households who received Bamberger's *Charm* magazine for women. *Charm* reflected

America's emerging culture of consumption. America's best-known writers, including Malcolm Crowley, Herman J. Mankiewicz, and Gilbert Seldes, contributed to it. Picasso designed several of its covers, and the wife of a former governor wrote the travel column. Bamberger monitored its content himself.

Most of the founders of twentieth-century department stores, particularly those located in large cities, were first- and second-generation German American Jews. They included such names as Bloomingdale; Abraham and Straus, the Straus family who owned Macy's, Gimbels, and Altman's; and the Goodman family, who owned Bergdorf Goodman's in New York. They began as peddlers and eventually became owners not only of lavish stores, but also of factories that manufactured ready-to-wear clothing and many other private-label household items. Collectively they transformed the very scope and definition of shopping with their state-of-the-art department stores, which to contemporary observers seemed like cathedrals and palaces of consumption. They were agents of mass marketing, distributors of quality goods to the masses, and inventors of endless innovations. Bamberger knew them all, and they knew him. Yet none was more innovative than he.

While there were many reasons why Bamberger's became such a successful operation, several were particularly important. First, its motto "The Customer Is Always Right" won more friends than it lost money for the store. Second, the store had a liberal policy of allowing for refunds, which was almost unheard of at the time. L. Bamberger & Co. stood behind the merchandise it sold. Dissatisfied customers received refunds and exchanges without a fuss. "Nothing," said Bamberger, "helped to build the store more than this policy."[2] If a customer had a complaint, Bamberger wanted to hear about it directly. When the teenager Philip Mintz, sent to Bamberger's to buy a particular item on sale, was told by the clerk that they were "sold out," he demanded to speak to Mr. Bamberger himself. Bamberger listened and assured him that he personally would take care of the problem. The next day a personal representative from the store delivered the item to Mintz.[3] Bamberger treated his customers as he wanted to be treated, and they repaid him with their continued loyalty.

Bamberger was a leader in sponsoring classes to train his workers. He took pride in his efficient, well-trained, and courteous sales staff, and he insisted that everyone working for Bamberger's had to enroll in the store's salesmanship classes. The course was repeated every six weeks and ended with a graduation party, with Bamberger on hand to congratulate the graduates. He was also among the first to give his employees every opportunity to advance their careers. Through an arrangement with Rutgers University, employees could take courses in salesmanship, the graphic arts, public speaking, art history, accounting, or any subject that would make for a well-rounded salesperson. Bamberger created unique financial arrangements for his employees. When the company went public, he allowed them to purchase shares, which resulted in increased employee loyalty. Upon his retirement and the sale of the store, he gave away more than $1 million to longtime employees.

Like other large retailers, Bamberger's instituted charge accounts. Customers with these accounts were expected to remain loyal for a long time. Bamberger's got its first charge customer through a chance meeting in the store's aisles between Bamberger and Jenny Bachman, whose family had sold Bamberger the parcel of land at the corner of Washington and Market Streets on which the store had been built. It was raining, and Bachman had come downtown without an umbrella. Bamberger insisted that she buy one, send him a check at the end of the month, and become his first charge customer.[4] The story suggests that Bamberger's real strength lay in the way he built a great business one customer at a time.

Bamberger was responsible for numerous other "firsts." His store was the first to feature a fashion show using live models and the first to install little red phones, the "Red Phone" service, at the ends of the counters so that customers could pick up a receiver and ask questions at any time regarding anything pertaining to the store. Bamberger's also created Newark's first toll-free telephone service, which ran between Newark and towns in suburban Essex County, in 1915. It invented the annual Thanksgiving Day parade, which it held in Newark as early as 1924; Charles F. Cummings maintained that Macy's actually "stole" Newark's original parade, and there is sufficient evidence to suggest that he was correct.[5] Bamberger's customers didn't have to leave Newark to find out what was new in fashion overseas. Bamberger's was among the first to establish buying offices in Paris, Vienna, Frankfurt, Berlin, Japan, and London.

Bamberger himself felt that two innovations in particular were his most important. The first was his willingness to take a chance on an in-house radio station, making L. Bamberger & Co. the first department store in America to do so. It turned out to be a successful marketing strategy, and WOR 710 still broadcasts today from New York. The second was Bamberger's airplane delivery service. Forced to find alternative ways to move merchandise, Bamberger decided to conduct experimental flights in order to expedite deliveries. His was among the first, if not the first, department store in America to use the airplane to receive and deliver goods.

In addition to the obvious requirement of hard work and long hours, the real difference between those who built big department stores and those who did not was boldness and lots of advertising. Bamberger's advertised every day of the week. Its customers relied on another of Bamberger's innovations — a daily weather report, a tradition that started in 1904. Bamberger was a consummate promoter in other ways as well. In 1936, for the first time in its history, New York's Metropolitan Opera moved an entire production, including scenery and costumes, across the Hudson River to hold a sold-out performance in Newark. The credit went to Bamberger, whose store was also the first in America to sponsor music scholarships. The winners always had a source for sheet music and pianos, since both items were sold in the store's music department.

Bamberger also used high-profile personalities to promote his business. Shoppers who bought sheet music in the store's piano department lined up to have it autographed by the popular composer Irving Berlin. They could see and buy a line of clothing designed for Bamberger's by the world-renowned aviatrix Amelia Earhart. She also spoke at Newark's YM-YWHA, and Bamberger funded her appearance. A photograph in the *Newark Evening News* featured Albert Einstein and his wife in the store. Einstein had accompanied her on a shopping expedition to purchase a new invention, the ballpoint pen, as a gift for their son-in-law. Perhaps Bamberger's most spectacular promotional stunt was to bring an Eskimo family and live reindeer from Alaska and put them on display in the store's Christmas windows. Although one Santa Claus might have been sufficient to please shoppers, Bamberger's had three.

Louis Bamberger had no interest in politics. He never ran for public office, though he once agreed to serve as a state representative on the Republican ticket, but he knew that such an "honor" was only a ploy to get him to contribute to a campaign. Bamberger—like his fellow store owners—exerted an indirect influence on politics through advertising, to which L. Bamberger & Co. devoted a major portion of its profits. Advertisements provided a stream of revenue that made it possible for a newspaper editor to report the news of the day unencumbered by politics or rivalries among politicians. In this way department stores were partially responsible for promoting American democracy.

This account of L. Bamberger & Co.'s growth in size and influence relies on four sources: decades of advertisements in Newark's high-circulation newspapers; access to Bamberger family collections; a full run of the store employee newsletter, *Counter Currents* (1918–1929); and several hundred reminiscences by individuals who had vivid memories of the store and its owner.

Bamberger's advertisements went all out to convince shoppers that when compared to prices in Newark's other department stores, Plaut's and Hahne's, Bamberger's offerings were not to be beat. Persistent efforts to locate remaining Bamberger relatives yielded access to primary sources such as private family papers, which provided information about Bamberger's life outside the store, and *Counter Currents* was a trove of information about the store's inner workings. For example, the newsletter documents Bamberger's idea of educating his workers about the city they earned their living in, which might be considered another innovation to be added to his list of accomplishments. If someone wanted to know what life in Newark was like during World War I, learn about Thomas Edison's latest invention, or find out what the opening of the Hudson Tubes meant for transportation between Newark and New York, they would find it there. Above all, *Counter Currents* conveys what it was like to work at a store headed by a man who viewed his employees as his family. It was Bamberger's enormous business success that enabled him to become a philanthropist. He was the only wealthy man in Newark to donate a major cultural institution to that city—the Newark Museum. In response, Newark's City Commission adopted a resolution describing him as Newark's "first citizen." While some praised him for advancing Newark's reputation as a compassionate city, others claimed that he shared his fortune because it was good for business. A friend of Julius Rosenwald, owner of Sears in Chicago, told Rosenwald that he had heard it said that Rosenwald's own philanthropy was nothing more than self-advertisement.

Rosenwald's response, "I'm too good a businessman for that . . . I know how to buy publicity much cheaper," could just as well have come from Bamberger.[6]

Records indicate that Bamberger sat on as many as thirty volunteer boards. He never served as an organization's president but did agree to be listed as "honorary" president of several charities and social service agencies. Infinitely more important was his work to ensure that the city's social service agencies, including institutions established by Newark's Jews such as Newark Beth Israel Hospital and the YM-YWHA, remained solvent. He accomplished this by insisting in 1922 that Newark establish a Community Chest, such as already existed in cities such as Chicago, Cleveland, and Baltimore, that would organize and regulate citywide fundraising for all these agencies.

Although Bamberger supported Newark's YM-YWHA (or "Y"), Beth Israel Hospital, summer camps for children, and other social agencies, much of his philanthropy focused on culture and the arts. When Bamberger's first opened for business, Newark was dominated by industry and manufacturing and lacked a museum, concert hall, or public library. In 1923 Bamberger announced his intention to give Newark its first and only fine arts museum, the Newark Museum. The reason for his "unprecedented gift," he stated, was to "thank the citizens of Newark for making his store a success." He went on to use his influence to make his city a center for the performing arts. He brought world-class soloists and symphony orchestras to its concert halls, sponsored open-air concerts in the city's parks, and created a branch of the public library in his department store. This kind of philanthropy, which convinced customers that their department store was an institution that enriched their lives, was certainly good for business. He may have had other motivations, but there can be no doubt that Bamberger sincerely wanted to do good.

But beyond his local philanthropy, Louis Bamberger will be remembered for his decision to use his fortune in an unexpected way. In 1930 — after he had sold his store to the Straus brothers, owners of Macy's, and had more time to devote to philanthropy — he and his sister, Carrie Fuld, agreed to become the sole benefactors of the Princeton-based Institute for Advanced Study. This educational experiment, which required a $5 million endowment, remains a private institution designed to foster research by scientists and scholars in various fields — history, mathematics, economics, astronomy, art history, and physics. The IAS's policies of researchers having no classes to teach, unlimited time to do research, and guaranteed salaries all date to Bamberger's time. The institute also created a connection between Bamberger and Albert Einstein, who became the first head of its mathematics department. By the time Einstein had settled in and taken up his teaching assignments, he and Bamberger had begun a decadelong friendship that few knew about.

Paul Rich, the owner of Rich's department store in Atlanta, remarked that "the significance of the merchant-prince-as-public-benefactor was nowhere in America more importantly illustrated than at Bamberger's."[7] Rich had Bamberger's endowment of the Institute for Advanced Study in mind. In his opinion, Bamberger's willingness to fund an untried educational experiment because it would advance the cause of education in America put Bamberger, as a public benefactor, in a league of his own. Rich may also have been biased toward Bamberger. As a young man out of school, he spent time learning the retail business at Bamberger's and developed a great admiration for him. Bamberger kept an open-door policy for the sons of fellow store owners just as he did for his customers. He was always willing to teach those interested in learning the business; however, he was not a team player. In 1929 Louis Kirstein of Filene's and Fred Lazarus Jr. of F. and R. Lazarus in Columbus, Ohio, were preoccupied with bringing many stores under the umbrella of Federated Department Stores. But Bamberger chose not to tell them of his plan to sell his store and did not offer them shares in his business. They considered this secrecy reprehensible, accusing him of having "gone over to their archenemy, Macy's."[8] But this behavior was characteristic. He alone decided where to locate his store and he alone made the decision to sell it. He appeared to operate on Benjamin Franklin's theory that three could keep a secret as long as two of them were dead.

Department store owners often hired professional historians to write their store's history. It was a form of promotion and viewed as "good for business." Sometimes the historian was hired by a second or third generation of merchants with an eye to the future and a desire to preserve their family's legacy. Bamberger never had children, so there was no second generation to follow in his footsteps. In any case one can argue that Bamberger needed no historian to promote his legacy. The Bamberger name was so ingrained in the minds of New Jersey shoppers that the owners of Macy's, which bought L. Bamberger & Co. in 1929, retained it until 1986. Louis Bamberger was never part of Macy's expansion to the suburbs, but Macy's called these branch stores Bamberger's. Shoppers there knew the name and believed that the shopping experience they had had in Newark would follow them to the suburbs. For as long as memory holds the building located at 131 Market Street in downtown Newark will continue to be referred to as Bamberger's.

When Bamberger died, he left the bulk of his estate to the Institute for Advanced Study. He never considered establishing a foundation; he didn't believe in them because he thought the boards of directors they created were more interested in preserving the status quo than in funding new ideas. Besides, he had no desire to perpetuate his name. In Newark there is not so much as a street sign with Bamberger's name on it. Everything we know about Bamberger suggests that he agreed with Andrew Carnegie's famous quote, "The man who dies rich, dies disgraced." Perhaps Louis Bamberger's greatest quality was his philosophy of distributing the bulk of his wealth while he was still living. It seemed that he made money in order to be benevolent and to be able to help those in need.

Long after Louis Bamberger's death, hundreds of individuals, in states up and down the Eastern Seaboard from New Jersey to Florida, as well as in California and even Alaska, have retained personal memories of themselves or family members working or shopping at "Bam's" until its doors closed in 1992 and it left Newark for good. Edward Jay Goldberg, senior vice president of government and consumer affairs at Macy's East, who honed his management skills working at Bamberger's, described the Bamberger building as his "home away from home with the ghost of Louis Bamberger haunting every office and hallway throughout the building." He added, "You could sense just how important LB was to the city."[9]

Bamberger remained chairman of the board of L. Bamberger after the sale to Macy's until 1939, when he retired from the business. At a gathering of the full board on December 6, 1942, Bamberger did something that was unusual for him: he made a few predictions about Newark's future. "The future of Newark is bright," he told a reporter covering the event, and "its nearness to New York is a help, not a handicap."[10]

Bamberger was convinced New York's shoppers would use mass transit to make the trip to Newark to take advantage of his store's better prices and comparable fashions.

Years before, on a visit to Selfridge's in London, Bamberger had defended his decision to build in Newark to Gordon Selfridge, who had asked, "How is it that in a city of Newark's size, just a stone's throw from New York, you have built up so big a business?" "I gave him the only reason I knew," Bamberger said. "The folks in Newark made it possible."[11] Bamberger could have made this comment at any point in his career. More precisely, however, he might have said that Newark made it possible for him to be the master of his own operations. Operating in a small city, where he could be a "big fish in a little pond," suited Bamberger. His loyalty to Newark reflected Bamberger's personality. Yet he was astute enough to see the big picture.

Bamberger, "one of Newark's and New Jersey's most enlightened personalities," as Charles Cummings put it, built an empire from scratch and demonstrated what it was to be a self-made man. Yet his great gifts remain little known outside his city. In a 1999 letter to the *New York Times*, responding to an article about the Institute for Advanced Study, Chatham, New Jersey, resident Louis Schindel — the son of Abe Schindel, a longtime L. Bamberger manager — suggested that "we might take a closer look at Louis Bamberger, whose fortune built the institute" and who deserved more recognition. This book does just that.

1

BALTIMORE ROOTS, 1855–1887

No one was better prepared for a career in retail than Louis Bamberger. He was raised in a family of dry goods merchants and shopkeepers. His mother and her parents were the Hutzlers who founded Baltimore's famous department store. He was expected to go into the family business and learn about the rigors of owning a retail business from the ground up—not just from family members, but also from his parents' friends, whose enormous fortunes made during the Civil War as manufacturers and pioneers of Baltimore's garment industry made them excellent teachers.

Born on May 15, 1855, Louis Bamberger was the third child of German Jewish immigrants Elkan and Theresa Hutzler Bamberger. The Hutzler family had settled in East Baltimore's immigrant neighborhood in 1838 to live among peddlers and small-scale merchants like themselves. They owned a general store that moved across town to Howard Street in 1858 to join dozens of small dry goods dealers, many of whom were German Jewish immigrants, who helped establish Baltimore's retail center. Elkan Bamberger, whose last name was originally Karlindig,[1] arrived in New York City in 1840. He did what many other Jewish immigrants from Germany were doing: he found work as a peddler. The job lasted only two months before he and his three brothers moved south in search of business opportunities. When Elkan discovered that Baltimore was home to a small population of successful German Jewish merchants who, like himself, were from Bavaria, he opened a dry goods business and stayed.[2] By the end of the Civil War, the Bamberger and Hutzler families had become successful merchants and pillars of Baltimore's Jewish community; by the 1870s they were able to move to more prosperous neighborhoods.

Baltimore in Louis Bamberger's time was a border town situated midway between North and South, linked by sea to Europe and by rail to all parts of the country, with a fairly good supply of raw material and cheap labor. Its chief industry was ready-to-wear clothing, which the invention of the sewing machine in 1846 made possible and huge government orders during the Civil War made popular. In letters to family and friends in Germany, Baltimore's Jewish merchants described their businesses as having grown into major enterprises. They invited their correspondents to join them.[3]

Germany's Jews didn't need much convincing. A rise in German nationalism, marriage restrictions that prevented Jews from establishing households, increased antisemitism and pogroms provoked by the revolutions of 1848–1849, and a desire to avoid military conscription left these Jews little choice but to leave. Tailoring was one of the few livelihoods they had been free to pursue, and they were long accustomed to making their living either as peddlers or by clustering in cities and towns where they became experts in the clothing trades. Thus they arrived in Baltimore equipped with skills specific to an urban economy.[4]

Their move to Baltimore was well timed. By the 1850s Baltimore's Jewish merchants had achieved a measure of economic stability. Using their expertise as tailors and dressmakers, hat makers, and furriers and tanners, they opened factories that manufactured ready-to-wear clothing, military uniforms, hats, umbrellas, shoes, and luggage, all of which was a perfect fit for Baltimore's Civil War economy. As a result the city's German Jews, including Bamberger's family, prospered.

Louis Bamberger spent his formative years socializing with and learning about the retail business from these merchants. Henry Sonneborn, whose firm dominated the South in the manufacture and sale of men's clothing, became the owner of the largest menswear factory in the world. Sonneborn lived in the same neighborhood as Bamberger's Hutzler uncles and was a guest in Bamberger's home. So were Moses Wiesenfeld, who became one of the leading wholesale clothiers in the country, and fellow German Levi Grief, who launched what for a time was the second-largest men's clothing company in America. Sociable visits naturally included conversations about business. Bamberger sat and listened. It isn't often that someone as successful as Bamberger could claim that his career was determined by what he heard in his parents' living room.

The move to Baltimore was a good one for Elkan Bamberger, who claimed that business enabled him to save enough money to pay the passage for his father, Isaac, to leave Schopfloch, his hometown in Bavaria, for a new life in Baltimore.[5]

Elkan's good fortune continued. He met and married Theresa Hutzler in 1850 and left his clothing business to his brothers in order to work for his father-in-law Moses Hutzler's dry goods business. The first floor of Hutzler's store sold laces and imported fabrics. The second floor was shared by three generations of Hutzlers, all of whom lived together. This was where Louis Bamberger was born and grew up.[6]

Recalling Bamberger's youth, his sister Lavinia wrote: "My brother was born above the store owned by our grandfather, Moses Hutzler. It was situated at the corner of Howard and Clay Streets, on the site of the present great department store of the Hutzler Brothers Company. But my first memories of him are in a spacious house on Lombard Street, a member of an enormous family. I remember the house with front parlor, back parlor, "Green Room," and a beautiful garden, teeming with life and a happy family atmosphere. In this house I remember my brother for his quiet kindness and gentle qualities that he showed all his life."[7] It was here that Bamberger was raised as one of seven children. He had five sisters and an older brother. Although he had little in common with his brother, in later years, no matter how busy Louis was, he always made time for his sisters, who traveled the world with him as sociable companions.

Bamberger was only three years old when his uncle, Abram Hutzler, decided to leave his father Moses's business to open his own general store, which he called M. Hutzler & Son. He used his father's name because he was too young to get credit on his own.[8] Abram invited his two brothers, Charles and David, to join him in the business. This was the start of Hutzler Brothers department store, where Louis Bamberger got his first job. Abram set an example for the young Bamberger who, when the time was right, started a retail business of his own.

There was nothing special about Louis Bamberger as a youngster. He didn't play a musical instrument, although he loved music, and he was not an outstanding student. He was a listener, not a talker. Painfully shy, he frequently kept to himself. If Bamberger was described as a serious youngster, it was because he was raised during serious times. He was six years old in 1861 when the Civil War broke out—old enough to grasp the effect the war had on his family's business and their lives in Baltimore. His Hutzler uncles' business was disrupted when fighting erupted on a street adjacent to their store.[9] The business took a year to recover, long enough for the majority of Baltimore's Jewish merchants to determine that they must steer clear of politics. Their only interest was in profiting from demands for clothing manufacture, including uniforms for soldiers on both sides of the fight.

Bamberger's parents, however, broke ranks: they decided to speak in favor of abolition. In danger of being attacked by proslavery supporters, the couple fled Baltimore by horse and wagon. They spent six weeks in Philadelphia before they returned home.[10] If what children see at home influences the adults they become, it is reasonable to credit Bamberger's later outspoken advocacy for social justice, the causes he backed with his considerable influence and money, to his parents' strong moral code.

Indeed, life in Baltimore prepared Louis Bamberger to be a philanthropist. In his time all successful Jewish businessmen were active in charities and synagogue work. Their names were on the rosters of both Jewish and non-Jewish charitable institutions. The United Hebrew Benevolent Society of Baltimore and Ladies Sewing Society played leading roles in providing help for the needy there.[11] Baltimore's nonsectarian Hebrew Hospital, originally only ten rooms, grew as the city's population increased. It always had beds for non-Jews.[12] Other organizations supported by Bamberger's family included the Baltimore Hebrew Benevolent Society and Orphan Asylum, the first YM-YWHA in America, and the Harmony Circle, a social club that was disbanded during the Civil War and reorganized under the leadership of David and Charles Hutzler.[13]

Few realize that Newark's modern-day Jewish institutions and volunteer organizations are modeled after those of Baltimore. When Bamberger moved to Newark, he discovered that there was no Jewish hospital and no "Y," so he and his brother-in-law and business partner Felix Fuld made sure there were funds for both. When Bamberger agreed to oversee the building of a new home for Newark's Jewish orphans, he traveled to Baltimore to see what that city's Jews had built for its homeless youngsters.[14] The first executive director of Newark's "Y" was Rabbi Aaron G. Robison, who was originally from Baltimore. Bamberger convinced Robison to leave his job as executive director of New York's Ninety-Second Street "Y" and used his influence to get Robison's daughter, Hope, into college. The Baltimore connection also benefited long-tenured Rabbi Joseph Leucht, who served Newark's predominantly German congregation, Temple B'nai Jeshurun, of which Bamberger was a member. Leucht, originally from Bavaria, spent nine years in Baltimore before moving to Newark.[15]

From the time he was a child to the time he decided to leave Baltimore, there is nothing to tell us that Bamberger wanted to live anywhere but with his parents. As long as he was single, there was nothing to be gained by living alone. Unfortunately, he kept no diaries to tell us how he occupied his free time. Conveniently for Bamberger there was sufficient entertainment at home. His father had half-sisters with a reputation for being "tip top," who attracted visits from Baltimore's most eligible bachelors. As one suitor who enjoyed the fine musical entertainment in Bamberger's home put it, "I only regret that there are not more of them, their likes are scarce."[16] Louis was continuously surrounded by relatives brought over from Germany by his parents and grandparents. His sister Lavinia described her German relatives as a boisterous, good-natured group of aunts, uncles, and cousins who enjoyed socializing with one another.

When Bamberger resettled in Newark thirty years later, he showed the same devotion to family that he had seen in his parents' home. After his brother-in-law's death, he continued to provide Fuld's German relatives with papers and money for passage to America. Bamberger gave them jobs and comfortable housing and welcomed them to his home. Most notably, the "Berg Boys"—Fuld's nephews, Bertram and Felix— had successful careers working at the Bamberger store.

Growing up in Baltimore had other pluses. Related through business, marriage, or community activities to Baltimore's prominent German Jewish families, Bamberger's family was close to the Szolds, whose most famous member was Henrietta Szold, founder of Israel's world-renowned Hadassah Hospital, and to Dr. Harry Friedenwald, a noted educator, medical historian, and ardent pioneer in the Zionist movement, whose brother Aaron married Bamberger's aunt Bertha.[17] Many years later Friedenwald wondered how it was possible for his cousin Louis, who had no more than a few years of formal schooling, to become the wealthiest man in Newark and recipient of honorary degrees from institutions of higher learning.[18] Bamberger's lack of higher education was not unusual among German Jews of his time. German Jews in America expressed middle-class values and thought education was important, but they generally did not encourage their sons to go to college, preferring to have them join the family firm.[19]

Baltimore's public schools were so overcrowded that parents were unwilling to endanger the health of their children by sending them there. A considerable number of Jewish boys from well-to-do families attended the two private non-Jewish schools in the city.[20] Bamberger attended the F. Knapp German and English Institute, open to children of all faiths, even though parents who sent their boys to Knapp's risked the criticism that they were *Chazir Fresser* (pork guzzlers).[21] But the teachers were woefully underpaid, discipline was a problem, and corporal punishment was not unheard of. Unwilling to put up with teachers who made life unpleasant for him, Bamberger complained until his parents gave him permission to leave school to go to work.[22] He was fourteen and considered a young adult by the standards of the day. At the time, not completing high school was not unusual either. Bamberger went to work for his Hutzler uncles at their dry goods store, then a concern of moderate size. His first duties were to sweep out the store and to be a general errand and utility boy at a salary of four dollars per week.[23] He was treated more like a stranger than a family member, and his on-the-job training focused on exactly what an apprentice in a retail business was expected to know. Bamberger's friend Julius Rosenwald, who became the owner of Sears, had a similar experience; but he was a better negotiator than Bamberger, for he earned the grand sum of five dollars a week for the privilege of working for his uncles in their New York City clothing business.[24] Hutzler's was the beginning of Bamberger's career as a retail merchant, the place where he spent his time waiting until he could take his future into his own hands.

Bamberger's willingness to work for his Hutzler uncles paid off. Baltimore was where he met Felix Fuld, who was working as a salesman for the Chesapeake Rubber Company.[25] His father, Ludwig Fuld, a partner in the Wall Street banking firm of Sternberg, Sinn, and Fuld, had arranged for the job. A year later illness forced Felix to return to New York City, but in the meantime he had become acquainted with Bamberger's family. Both men moved in the same social circles, so when Bamberger relocated to New York, it was only a matter of time before they met again.[26]

Bamberger spent three uneventful years working at Hutzler Brothers. At seventeen he decided to leave and join his brother Julius in their father's business, E. Bamberger & Co. This was a small notions business that sold mainly laces, fine fabrics, and fancy goods. Elkan soon sold his business to his sons and retired. The two brothers decided to form a partnership, but after fifteen years in business realized that they were not a good fit. Bamberger sold his part of the business to Julius. Julius, who was not a merchant at heart, retired early and moved to Europe. When he became too sick to live alone, he accepted an invitation to live with Bamberger and their sister Carrie and her husband, Felix, at their home in South Orange, New Jersey. He died in 1926 and was buried in the family plot in the B'nai Jeshurun Cemetery in Elizabeth.[27]

The brothers' breakup in 1887, when Louis was thirty-two, freed him to move to New York City to take a job as a resident buyer for two wholesale firms, Kann's of Washington and Rosenbaum's of California.[28] According to Lavinia, his parting remarks to her were in the spirit of the "elder brother fashion of those times"; he advised her that she "must always be tolerant of other people. I should always be kind and thoughtful and then people would like me! He certainly lived by that precept himself!"[29]

In 1888, one year after Bamberger left for New York, Hutzler Brothers opened a new five-story state-of-the-art building.[30] The timing raises the question of Bamberger's relationship with his uncles. The new Hutzler building, so ornate that it was dubbed a "palace," was built while Bamberger was living at home and working nearby. There must have been ongoing conversations in his parents' home about his uncles' plans to expand the business, but it seems that these plans did not include Bamberger, or for that matter his father. They were members of the same family but were never connected in business.

Presumably his uncles were aware that Louis's later success far exceeded any expectations they had had of him; his uncle Abram Hutzler left bequests of $20,000 each for Bamberger's sisters, but only $1,000 for Louis, saying he believed Louis "was rich enough."[31] The Hutzlers socialized and spent summers in Maine with fellow department store owners, the Sangers from Dallas and the Gimbels of Philadelphia, whose "cabins" rivaled summer homes in Newport.[32] But Bamberger was never asked to join them.

What did make an impression on Bamberger was his Hutzler uncles' aggressive plans to expand their business by buying buildings and property adjacent to their original department store. Bamberger came to understand that, in order to succeed, a retail business had to keep pace with customers' demands for new and more modern goods and services. In later years he bought land in downtown Newark, long before he needed it, in order to ensure the future of his business.

Bamberger could have spent a lifetime working at Hutzler's, but knew that he had little chance of ever being promoted to management. His well-known shyness prevented him from speaking up. Instead he used his time as a low-level employee to learn what he could about the retail business. He studied the methods of department stores located in cities across America, some founded as far back as the 1840s.

The origins of the department store go back to a time when there was scarcely a village in any state of the Union that did not have a "Jew storekeeper" and his family.[33] These storekeepers had been itinerant peddlers who made their way across America looking for towns that needed a local merchant. When they found one, they opened a small general store and settled down. Jewish peddlers sold thread, lace, ribbons, knives, bonnets, jewelry, and various other items—exactly as the Bamberger family did when they came to America. Department stores developed from these origins in different regions of the country, suggesting that peddling was one of the best possible ways to learn merchandising.

Bamberger's pursuit of a career in retail was perfectly timed. The first forty years of American department store retailing, 1850–1890, were a time of tremendous growth and success. During this period America's retail merchants began a slow transition from dry goods businesses and specialty stores to department stores. These were the years when Bamberger lived and worked in Baltimore. He witnessed and participated in this transformation.

According to the department store historian Jan Whitaker, the term "department store" first appeared in a *New York Times* story in July 1888.[34] Historian Robert Hendrickson claims that the phrase was first used in 1887 when a New York establishment advertised itself as "H. H. Heyn's Department Store."[35] Coincidentally, 1887 was the year Bamberger left Baltimore for New York City.

By 1892, when Bamberger was ready to open his Newark store, the department store had a firm foothold in America.[36] Coast to coast, American shoppers, primarily in cities, had become accustomed to the idea of finding everything they needed under one roof. Bamberger read store advertisements, more than likely visited start-up department stores on the East Coast, and subscribed to the influential trade magazine *Dry Goods Economist*. Throughout his career Bamberger could tell you what almost any store in the country was doing in a particular department at any time. One obituary mentioned that he had made a study of the lives of men at the helms of larger enterprises, looking for the common denominator that elevated them to their leadership positions.[37]

The Baltimore historian Michael Lisicky gave Hutzler Brothers credit as the first department store in America to institute a one-price policy.[38] Bamberger must have known, however, that his Hutzler uncles were not pioneers in instituting this or any other customer-friendly policies. A survey of early department stores in the 1840s and 1850s, including Gimbels, Macy's, and F. & R. Lazarus (whose owner Simon Lazarus's motto was "Ohio's great one price house, that price the lowest, and the same to one and all")[39] reveals that a one-price policy (meaning that there was no haggling) was already standard practice. So was a standard returned-goods policy that allowed for refunds to assure customers that the store's merchandise was reliable. When Bamberger opened his business in Newark, he took pains to credit another department store owner, John Wanamaker, as the originator of these ideas, though he said he was the first to institute the refund policy in Newark.

Wanamaker got the ideas of exchanging unsatisfactory merchandise and refunding cash from Aristide Boucicaut, the Frenchman believed to be the founder of the first department store, Le Bon Marché in Paris. It is not hard to imagine how Boucicaut's store policies got Hutzler's or Bamberger's attention in Baltimore. Many American merchants sent observers overseas to study the great original in Paris.[40] Ideas, like immigrants and tourists, crossed the Atlantic and were readily copied. Years later Bamberger employees stationed in Paris during World War I used their furlough time to visit Le Bon Marché and reported their findings back to Bamberger. New York and Baltimore may have been the garment manufacturing capitals of America in Bamberger's time, but Paris styles set fashion trends, then as now.

Leaving Baltimore was not as life altering for Bamberger as one might imagine. It was no longer the city he had grown up in, but now a city of two worlds. The first consisted of the earlier generation of wealthy uptown German Jews who had become bankers, jobbers, department store owners, and clothing manufacturers, and whom Bamberger had known all his life.[41] The second world was Baltimore's deteriorating downtown, which now was full of bawdy houses, all-night poolrooms, low-class dance halls, debasing movie shows, and hotels that accepted transients, all of which did little to enhance the city's civic life.[42] Sweat-shops proliferated and union strikes by needle workers made it hard to do business. A growing demand for a better grade of clothing forced department store owners to get involved in the production process, which Hutzler Brothers did by reserving two floors in their new store for in-house manufacturing.[43]

Bamberger also had private reasons for wanting to leave Baltimore. His parents, who were founders of Baltimore's Temple Har Sinai, wanted him to become active in synagogue life, but he apparently had no interest in doing so. The fact that he was already in his thirties and not married raised eyebrows and put social pressure on him. This alone was sufficient reason to leave Baltimore.

Bamberger was an ideal candidate for an arranged marriage. He was welcome in polite, influential German Jewish society and presumably received invitations to meet the daughters of successful Jewish busi-nessmen like himself. He was not a handsome man, nor a great conver-sationalist, and did not make friends easily. But none of these qualities would have stopped some woman from being interested in the lifestyle he offered. The question of his sexuality remains open and was the subject of some speculation later. In any case, Bamberger remained a bachelor. The cliché that we should not judge a book by its cover applies to Bamberger. His looks and demeanor belied his strength of character. Motivated not only by social pressure but also by his determination to succeed, he left for New York.

2

BUILDING AN EMPIRE,
1892–1911

On December 13, 1892, Louis Bamberger, Felix Fuld, Louis Frank, three sales people, one errand boy, and one delivery horse named Finnegan opened a small business on Market Street in Newark, selling merchandise purchased at a deep discount from a firm that had gone bankrupt. The horse was carefully selected, since buying it used up Bamberger's last dollar.[1] Their timing coincided with the Panic of 1893 and the opening of the Chicago World's Fair, the acclaimed World's Columbian Exposition showcasing the country's growing economic and industrial strength. Millions of Americans viewed exhibits of new inventions, products, and appliances that were eventually made available in Bamberger's department store.

Faced with a dip in the economy, Bamberger did not change his mind or alter his determination to start his own business. He was firmly convinced that economic downturns were inevitably followed by upswings, and he always wanted to be prepared for the upswings. "The year I came here—December 1892, and we opened the store on the thirteenth too, was one of the panic years," Bamberger recalled, but "I still stuck with my plan."[2] His persistence paid off. The opening of L. Bamberger & Co. coincided with the start of the era in which large department stores flourished in cities all around the country. Louis Bamberger's career as Newark's and New Jersey's undisputed merchant prince spanned these years, 1890 to 1940.[3]

From 1890 through 1892, Bamberger had weighed the pros and cons of opening a retail business in Newark. After three years of working and living in New York, where he established contacts in the retail industry, he quit his job as a buyer in the wholesale business to get into retail, where more money could be made. Opening a business in New York was not a realistic proposition. He lacked sufficient hands-on experience and the capital for such a venture. So he considered Newark as a possible location. Returning to Baltimore was no longer an option. He would never expose himself to the ridicule of having to admit to his family that he was unsuccessful.

It is clear that Bamberger's decision to explore Newark as a site for his business was not random or capricious. Louis Bamberger was not a man to make snap decisions. He did his homework and learned that in the 1840s Newark's German Jews had opened the forerunners of the city's modern department stores. The first to open was Hart and Dittlebach, on the corner of Broad and West Park Street, which sold "everything that ladies wore except shoes and hats."[4] Ullman and Isaacs opened a rival store on Broad and New Streets, and Klein and Thalheimer was located on Broad Street near Williams. Broad Street was thus established as Newark's most desirable business location.[5] These stores dominated until 1870, the year Newark was introduced to its first full-service department store, Isaac Fox and L. Simon Plaut's "Bee Hive." One of Plaut's first errand boys was Benjamin Altman, the future owner of B. Altman's department store in New York City.[6]

Bamberger waited two years for the right location, and he eventually opened his business not on Broad, but on Market Street, which intersected Broad. He stuck to temporary work, which gave him the time he needed to research what Newark had to offer its merchants. He wanted to know who lived there, what municipal services were provided to local businesses and city residents, and if there was competition from other retail merchants.[7] The more he learned about Newark, the more he was convinced that the opportunities which existed in New York City were also present in Newark, albeit on a somewhat smaller scale, in proportion to the city's population. According to historian Clement Price, Newark in Louis Bamberger's time was the "City of Opportunity" and one of the nation's most vital cities.[8]

Bamberger missed out on his first choice, a building on Market Street. The retail firm Hill and Cragg had rented it before he was financially ready to make an offer. Four months later Hill and Cragg declared bankruptcy. Not knowing when a second chance might arise, Bamberger purchased the firm's stock and rented two floors of the six-story building, the Ballantine building, from which to sell it.[9]

Examining the stock, which consisted of "holiday goods, ladies' and gents' furnishings, linens and embroideries, jewelry, and handkerchiefs," Bamberger realized he had bought far more merchandise than his experience as a wholesale agent would enable him to handle.[10] Under pressure, he sent for his brother-in-law Isadore Hammerslough in Baltimore and instructed him to go to New York and sell the overstock to a prospective buyer.[11] When Hammerslough reached New York, he learned that the prospect had left for Boston.

At this point Bamberger enlisted the aid of his brother-in-law Louis Frank, who was married to his sister Carrie. He dropped by Felix Fuld's home in New York and left a calling card with the instruction "See me at 147 Market Street, Newark."[12] Fuld found the note three days later and went directly to Newark, where he found Bamberger in shirtsleeves organizing the store's newly purchased merchandise. Fuld pitched in and the business opened the next day. Two months later, Felix was invited to join the Bamberger partnership. Bamberger was already exhibiting his ability to inspire those around him, including Fuld, who confided to a reporter years later that he had been unsuccessful in business before his partnership with Bamberger.[13]

Bamberger's strategy of starting his business by buying merchandise at deep discounts for resale was not new. He followed the example of William Filene, who in 1868 had purchased an entire wholesale business at a bargain price during one of the financial crises caused by the Civil War.[14] Filene, who was a risk taker, left his original location in bustling New York City and opened a business in Boston in 1881. His willingness to take a chance on an untried city was a model for Bamberger's search for the right location to open his own business in another untried city. Filene had what Bamberger did not have—two sons to help him. Edward and Lincoln Filene assumed management of the store in 1891, a year before Bamberger opened his. In 1908 Edward Filene opened Filene's Basement, the automatic-bargain annex for which his store became famous.[15] His mantra "money back if not satisfied" was echoed in department stores across America, including L. Bamberger & Co.

Most of the large department stores had opened decades earlier, so Bamberger had ample time to study the way the owners ran their businesses. For example, the Strauses started R. H. Macy in 1842 and grew it into what became "the world's largest store"—motivating Bamberger early on in his career to purchase an entire block of land, piece by piece, until his own store became the largest in New Jersey. He studied the reasons for Macy's success, including the importance of selling at fixed, marked prices and advertising vigorously.[16]

Macy's rival, Gimbel Brothers, was also founded in 1842, by Adam Gimbel, who began his career as a peddler. In fact, the German Jews who founded most of America's "great stores" had started out as peddlers.[17] Historian Leon Harris describes the children who inherited their family's department store businesses and denied that their predecessors were ever peddlers. They thought it was bad for businesses to publicize these humble beginnings. "Years later," Harris writes, "the social pecking order among rich Jews in communities all across America was frequently determined by who had first ceased peddling and opened a shop, no matter how modest, even if the time difference was a matter of months."[18] In 1842, when Gimbel ran an advertisement proclaiming "Fairness and Equality to All Patrons," his business was nothing more than a trading post on the Wabash River in Indiana.[19] Even then he recognized that his "pioneering fixed-price policy" would earn customer loyalty, a point not lost on Bamberger.

Rich's in Atlanta, Georgia, opened in 1867 with a policy of taking back *everything* a customer bought, including items sold in its store but purchased elsewhere.[20] This was Bamberger's policy, too. His sales staff was dismayed when customers returned such merchandise, but were instructed by an in-store memo from Bamberger not to ask questions.[21] Their job was to generate goodwill even if it meant taking a loss.

Politicians and economists began to acknowledge that the great stores were the economic engine that helped build modern-day America, and store owners quickly grasped the fact that they and their stores wielded influence that could extend as far as the White House. For example, in 1941 Fred Lazarus Jr. convinced FDR and Congress to pass legislation that established Thanksgiving as the fourth Thursday in November, enabling department stores to extend the Christmas shopping season by an extra week.[22] When the stock market collapsed on October 29, 1929, and workers and important executives alike faced the prospect of losing everything they owned, Julius Rosenwald, owner of Sears, Roebuck and Company and the wealthiest Jew in America, saved hundreds of people from immediate bankruptcy by purchasing their shares in his company. The headline and story in the *Chicago Herald and Examiner*, "Rosenwald Aids Workers Caught in Stock Market," helped restore public confidence and inspired praise from business leaders and public officials throughout America, including Henrietta Szold, the founder of Hadassah Hospital, who wrote: "Such acts demonstrate that moral heights can be reached in our condemned commercial era as in the eras glorified by historians."[23]

Like his fellow magnates, Bamberger needed financial backing in order to go out on his own. Julius Rosenwald bought into Richard Sears's business with money from his brother-in-law Aaron Nusbaum. Theirs was a rancorous and ultimately unsuccessful partnership, and Rosenwald had to buy Nusbaum out, much as Bamberger had bought out his brother before leaving Baltimore. The idea of "drifting" and waiting for something to happen to propel his future forward was anathema to Bamberger. He knew what he wanted and was prepared to do what it took to succeed. His soft-spoken manner might have lulled people into thinking that he would make allowances for errors; but in fact he expected excellence in all things related to his business, and his store managers and employees were prepared to follow his lead. Without sons to assist him, he did the next best thing by taking his nephew, Julius's son, Edgar, under his wing and teaching him the business.

Bamberger realized that he needed a cash infusion and that meant acquiring partners, so he, Frank, and Fuld pooled their resources. Bamberger's share was $45,000, Fuld contributed $25,000,[24] and Frank borrowed an undisclosed amount of money from his uncle, Max Liveright, a successful Philadelphia businessman.[25] The three were equal partners in the department store, which was known as L. Bamberger & Co. Years later Bamberger confessed to reporters, "You may be interested to know that the first time I considered selling was in 1893 immediately after the successful sale of the stock I had purchased from Hill and Cragg. . . . I had a chance to sell the business, but I decided I wouldn't because it had opportunities."[26] So it did.

It was Bamberger who made the decision to locate their business at 147–149 Market Street in downtown Newark, rather than on Broad Street, which in 1892 was Newark's main shopping thoroughfare.[27] "Market Street," he said, "was not an attractive street; there were many saloons; and the [surrounding] dry-goods shops were mainly of the type that showed their goods on the sidewalk."[28] Bamberger intended to open a department store that catered to the carriage trade. Sidewalk displays would not fit its image. He therefore added a touch of class to the streetscape by putting up a tasteful sign in black with gold letters over the store entrance that read "L. Bamberger & Co."[29] The original store—a full-grown department store for its day—consisted of two floors and a basement of approximately 40 by 150 feet.[30] The location might not be ideal, but Bamberger believed that if a store had something to offer, shoppers would come.

The emergence of the American department store in the mid-nineteenth century was just as important to America as the mall became after World War II. For the first time in shopping history there existed a "palace for the American consumer." Gone were the endless searches for the right type of item in a dozen small shops and the haggling over prices on unmarked items. When Bamberger's opened, people for the first time had already begun to refer to the "big stores."[31] Small individually owned businesses fought a losing battle against department stores, which stocked the same items for greatly reduced prices. Customers appeared to like the change from compartmentalized dry goods shops to stores that sold just about everything under one roof, and millions of people shopped in them. Even if many Americans were too poor to shop at department stores and probably visited them only on rare occasions, by 1900 almost everyone agreed that, like them or not, department stores were here to stay.[32]

By the time Bamberger arrived in 1892, dictionaries had begun to include a new word—"downtown"—to refer to a city's retail hub.[33] Newark was New Jersey's financial hub, home to ten banks, five savings institutions, and eleven insurance companies.[34] In 1892 the Prudential Insurance Company completed a new building for its four thousand employees conveniently located next door to Bamberger's. Prudential's employees shopped at Bamberger's, and so did workers from the banks and corporate headquarters within walking distance.[35]

Bamberger arrived at the beginning of Newark's skyscraper era; the Fireman's Insurance Company building, at sixteen stories, was the city's first skyscraper.[36] The new courthouse and city hall, the Broad and Shubert movie theaters, Newark's growing legal profession, publishing and printing industry, jewelry industry, and other related businesses contributed to Bamberger's favorable impression of the city.[37]

It was important that his store be close to residential neighborhoods. Newark was a walking city, and Bamberger counted on local residents for steady foot traffic; the automobile was not yet a significant factor. One by-product of America's Second Industrial Revolution (1870–1910) was the growth of an affluent bourgeois middle class that lived primarily in cities. They demanded "service and style" from department store

owners and got it. Newark's wealthy financiers, merchants, and industrialists, whose custom was to walk to work, built fine homes along the
streets surrounding the nearby Washington and Military Parks, so the
store's location on Market Street was convenient for them.

Store owners established merchant associations and served on
boards of trade. Bamberger was active in the Market Street Merchants'
Association. Members campaigned to keep the streets clean, insisted
that the city provide electricity for sufficient lighting, and requested
that events for Christmas holiday shopping be coordinated among
all the city's stores. According to historian William Leach, "By clustering together they could function like an irresistible unified magnet of
selling power."[38]

Department stores reflected a growing urban society that included
large numbers of immigrants, who packed into cities like Newark, attracted by factory jobs. They provided the workforce needed to build
Newark's infrastructure.[39] Bamberger watched from the sidewalk in
front of his store as city workers laid sewers, buried electric cables,
ripped up old trolley tracks and replaced them with new ones.[40] Advances in urban transportation allowed masses of people to travel to the
city center. Bamberger's drew customers from nearby suburban towns
and newly developed residential neighborhoods in Essex County. They
came to shop, but also to admire the window displays made possible
by new glass technology. Indeed, Bamberger's store was made possible by many technological advances—steel construction for truly tall
buildings, electric lights that replaced gas lamps and decreased the risk
of fire, electric ventilators to clean the air inside, and escalators and
elevators that escorted shoppers to high floors.

In 1894, an about-to-fail crockery business located in the basement
beneath Bamberger's store came on the market and he bought its stock.
He later purchased a shoe business in the same way, and so his new
concern became a department store.[41] By 1898 L. Bamberger was using
all six floors of the original building, and the landlord was convinced
to enlarge the building "to the extent that its nature permitted." By
1907 there was no room left to expand; so a narrow strip was acquired
on Halsey Street from Bank Street south, and a six-story addition was
added to the existing store.[42] It, too, was not sufficient to meet Bamberger's constant demands for more space. Next came an eight-story
store on the northwest corner of Market and Halsey Streets followed by

two major expansions, in 1922 and in 1929, which made Bamberger the owner of a department store empire.

Bamberger hired prominent Newark attorney John Hardin to negotiate each expansion, later land purchases, and other business-related contracts. He and Bamberger became lifelong friends—a testament to Hardin, for Bamberger did not cultivate friendships. Hardin discovered that the normally shy Bamberger had a way with children. He recalled one Christmas when his wife took their oldest son downtown to "check out" Bamberger's toy department. The next day the boy asked his mother to take him downtown again so he could play with Mr. Bamberger. "I told that to Mr. Bamberger and he never forgot it."[43] Hardin added that Bamberger "was by all odds one of the best friends I ever had and as a friend and client I valued him more than any other man I ever came in contact with."[44]

In 1893 Bamberger's staged a grand opening. Shoppers were greeted by salesmen "in fierce looking mustaches, saleswomen in 'mutton-leg sleeves,' items displayed on table tops, and a hanging display of 'made up' neckties."[45] An orchestra played in the background as the customers explored the aisles. The festivities also included a promenade concert. The store at this time did not have beautiful spacious aisles as it did later, but shoppers were invited to experience "a perfect flood of beautiful colorings, novel effects and exquisite designs."[46] The advertisement for this event was so exceptional that it was repeated in 1929 in celebration of the fifth and last addition to Bamberger's flagship store.[47]

The next day, Newark resident Arthur Reinhart came seeking a job and was hired for the wash goods section. He was the forty-ninth employee to join the three partners.[48] After thirty-five years of working at Bamberger's, he could still remember when he had to whistle through a pipe to attract a stock boy's attention upstairs and then call through the pipe to order merchandise. Sales checks were sent back and forth by a cord-and-basket arrangement suspended from the ceiling. "In particularly cold weather the cords contracted and the little baskets occasionally fell off, tumbling on customers' heads and causing lawsuits."[49] In 1928 Bamberger reminisced about the "Good Old Days" when on Thanksgiving, Christmas, and New Year's the sales force received only half a day off, and hours were from morning until midnight. There were no summer vacations and no ventilating system, and the old-fashioned gas lighting made the store very hot. Errand boys delivered packages.

Nor were there lunchrooms, so some of the salespeople brought their lunches. Newark was so small that those who lived in the neighborhood went home to eat. Maybe, Bamberger suggested, the "good old days" were not so good.[50]

Customers were far more patient in the early days of department stores. Bamberger once recalled a customer who came late in the evening to buy a pair of white gloves to wear to the theater. He waited on her. The gloves had a special clasp with a little spring attached to a push button. Another salesperson showed her how to put them on. The next morning when the store opened, the lady was waiting outside, still wearing her white gloves. It seems she hadn't been able to get them off—had to wear them to bed that night—and came in not for a refund but to find out how to remove them.[51]

After four years in business, and still considered a newcomer, Bamberger was praised by the *Newark Sunday Call* for "displaying much enterprise . . . [he] has bounded into the front rank with rapidity. His department store is now one of the great business institutions of the city."[52] Market Street came alive with shoppers who made Bamberger's store their destination, "talking about the remarkable values which this little shop of Mr. L. Bamberger offered and the service it gave."[53]

Driving Bamberger's continued optimism was the best barometer of a great city—an increasing population. In 1891, Newark's population was 181,000.[54] By 1900 it had grown to over 246,000, which meant 65,000 more potential shoppers.[55] In 1912, when Bamberger opened a new eight-story store, Newark's population of over 347,000 made it the fourteenth-largest city in the United States.[56] By then Bamberger's was known for catering to the "carriage trade" of solidly middle- or upper-class shoppers.[57] Newark had still another component necessary for a department store to succeed: large-circulation newspapers. Well established when Bamberger opened for business, they included the *Newark Evening News*, founded in 1883, and the *Newark Sunday Call* and *Star Eagle*, both established in 1872.[58] Wallace M. Scudder's *Newark Evening News* had a circulation of eight thousand in 1883 and thirty thousand in 1893, the year of Bamberger's grand opening.[59]

Bamberger placed his first ad, for the initial inventory of merchandise bought from Hill and Cragg, in the *Newark Sunday Call* for December 11, 1892. It read: "These goods must be sold regardless of cost. All Goods Offered at a Great Sacrifice."[60] The ad did its job. The entire stock sold in four days, and more had to be ordered. The store's rapid growth demonstrated the value of Bamberger's continuous advertising throughout the year. He was following the advice of John Wanamaker, believed to be the founder of the first American department store, who said, "The time to advertise is all the time."[61] Bamberger's advertising was on a scale that Newark had never seen before.[62]

The value of large-circulation newspapers was inestimable; how else did a merchant attract shoppers? By 1900 the *Call*'s readers enjoyed columns on sports, the theater, fashion, food, women's news, and spots of interest in the city accessible by walking or by train or trolley.[63] Bamberger, who spent his entire career devising ways to attract shoppers to Newark, relied on the fact that newspapers promoted events and points of interest to their readers to bring potential shoppers downtown. Increased newspaper circulations in Newark and the suburbs indicated that business was good and getting better.

It is not likely that department store owners thought much about the larger impact of their high-volume advertising. They were interested in only the foot traffic the ads brought to their stores. In fact, though, their advertising played a role in advancing democracy and public debate in America.[64] Since American newspapers received most of their income from retail advertisers, editors were able to remain relatively independent, free to report the news impartially.[65] As one retailer noted, "The newspaper of today is largely the creation of the department store."[66]

In addition to newspapers, between 1890 and 1915 there was a growing outdoor advertising industry that included countless posters, signboards, billboards, and electrical images.[67] Bamberger put no faith in easily removed posters. Instead, L. Bamberger's first motto, "The Always Busy Store," was painted on the risers of the steps of Newark's buses and trolleys, reminding customers to shop there as they climbed aboard. In 1910 one-third of the store's horse-drawn wagons were replaced by a fleet of one hundred sparkling-clean, electric-powered delivery trucks painted in Bamberger's trademark colors of green and gold. The trucks were visible proof that Bamberger's was a modern store which kept pace with technology.

Before a full-time advertising man was hired, Felix Fuld was in charge of advertising. It was Fuld who insisted on advertising policies that eventually became standard with Newark publishers.[68] Over time readers got accustomed to finding Bamberger's advertisements in the same spot in every issue.[69] Eventually, Bamberger's competitors, Hahne's and Plaut's, asked to have their advertisements appear on the same pages each time, with a guarantee that their ads would be near Bamberger's to make it easier for customers to compare prices. Bamberger's policy was to match his competitors' prices, "even if it meant taking a loss."[70]

Since Newark had a large German-speaking population, Bamberger also placed ads in German-language papers, including the weekly *Orange Volksbote*, covering Orange and its vicinity.[71] Determined to attract shoppers from the suburbs, particularly towns bordering Newark, he placed attractive ads in each town's local newspaper encouraging shoppers to board a trolley car or train for downtown Newark, where they would be welcomed by Bamberger's well-trained, courteous sales staff and find exceptional bargains. These advertisements had another result. Once Bamberger's name became known, he began receiving requests for charitable donations. He considered this the price of doing business, and usually responded by sending a check.

Louis Hannoch, manager of the *Newark Sunday Call*, loved to tell the story of how he demanded that Bamberger pay for his advertisements in advance because he wouldn't take any chances on the credit of an unknown merchant. The *Call* had a "cash-and-carry" policy, and Hannoch made it a practice to drop by Bamberger's store each Monday to collect for Sunday's advertisement until he realized Bamberger's credit could be trusted; then he asked for monthly payments. Bamberger turned the tables on him, however, announcing that he planned to stick with the established routine, which suited him just fine. It appeared that Bamberger had a stubborn streak and wasn't satisfied until he got the upper hand. Only thirty years later did Bamberger learn why he had had to pay cash, and both men shared a good laugh over ancient history.[72]

How did a partnership among three men who were so completely different in temperament and style become so successful? Louis Bamberger was shy and reclusive, Fuld was outgoing and gregarious, and Frank had leadership qualities. Bamberger hired Frank to be his partner because his sister Carrie was married to him, and in the end, was not sorry that he had done so.[73] In addition to buying merchandise for the store, Frank had become the head of a campaign to raise funds for Newark's first Jewish hospital. His reputation as a community leader was good for business.

Bamberger and Fuld, who were bachelors, agreed to live with Louis and Carrie Frank in a boardinghouse at 6 West Park Street to be close to the store.[74] This unusual arrangement continued in one form or another for the rest of their lives. Each morning, at 8 A.M., the partners met in rented office space adjacent to their boardinghouse. This is where they opened the mail and discussed each letter. If a letter contained a complaint, Bamberger answered it personally.[75]

The importance of Felix Fuld to the Bamberger partnership cannot be overstated. Fuld was always keen to investigate anything new: new products, new technology, and new ways to build the business. He was a "great story-teller, hardy hand-shaker, and overall outgoing affable man."[76] His gregarious personality, in stark contrast to Bamberger's reserved demeanor, made him stand out in a crowd, which often prompted casual observers to give him the lion's share of credit for the success of L. Bamberger & Co. But the impression that Bamberger was too shy to be an effective manager was quite wrong. "Louis Bamberger," according to company treasurer Frank I. Liveright, "was quiet and retiring with an aversion for the limelight, but nonetheless he dominated the firm."[77] The name of the store was L. Bamberger & Co., and Louis Bamberger always made the decisions.

The partnership lasted thirty-seven years, until Fuld's death in 1929. In 1910 Louis Frank died, and three years later Carrie married Felix, making him and Louis brothers-in-law as well as business partners. The threesome, affectionately known as the Bamberger-Fuld Clan, lived together in a modest brick Georgian-style home on a thirty-five-acre estate in South Orange, the subject of never-ending curiosity in Newark society. Bamberger lived with his sister and her husband because he preferred not to live alone. He was accustomed to living with family; he enjoyed having them around and they him. Their closeness prompted observers to refer to Bamberger and Fuld as a modern-day Damian and Pythias, after characters in Greek mythology who were willing to sacrifice their lives for one another in the name of loyalty and friendship.[78]

Bamberger's great-niece, Ellen Bamberger De Franco, described Bamberger's "modest size bedroom, with a single bed, one chest of drawers, and no artwork on the walls," which she saw on one of her family's Sunday evening visits to his home in South Orange.[79] Her account of this almost monastic room confirms that Bamberger had no interest in luxurious lifestyles. A delegation of officials from the Institute for Advanced Study, who visited his home after his death, was startled to discover that there wasn't even a dishwasher. He was a quiet man with simple tastes. After he moved to Newark, he continued to visit his parents and other sisters, and they reciprocated with frequent visits to South Orange.

In 1921 Bamberger built two houses in Avon, a town on the Jersey shore. One was for himself, Carrie, and Felix and one was for his Baltimore sisters Pauline and Lavinia. His nephew Edgar built a third house for himself.[80] In 2012, when Hurricane Sandy destroyed towns and businesses located along the Jersey shore, Bamberger's house survived. According to his great-niece, Mildred Levine, he had had the foresight, and the knowledge that came from watching contractors dig the foundations at his store's building sites, to install a huge pipe to transport water from under his house directly into the Shark River.[81]

Avon was where the normally shy Bamberger relaxed and revealed a keen sense of humor, and where Edgar's daughter, Ellen De Franco, got to know her Uncle Louis. He was "sweet, kind and interested in us kids," she said, and he gave her money for a car when she graduated from Wheaton College. Her Aunt Carrie was "nice, and gave us some of her jewelry when she got too old to go out to symphonies," while her Uncle Felix was "sweet and full of fun with us children and the only gregarious relative we had."[82] She remembered Fuld romping on the lawn at Avon with her sisters.

Despite rags-to-riches tales about store founders who accumulated capital as shop clerks or itinerant peddlers, in fact few, if any, made it to the megastore level without financial backing from relatives.[83] In return it was customary to keep the business in the family. Accordingly, Bamberger agreed to hire his partners' relatives, although not before he had mentored them to make sure each learned the business before being promoted to management.

The first relative Bamberger hired was Louis Frank's cousin, Frank I. Liveright, whose father, Max, had provided the start-up loans mentioned previously to ensure a place for his son in Bamberger's business.[84] Bamberger didn't need to mentor Liveright, who had owned a store in Danville, Illinois.[85] He was slotted in as Bamberger's controller, a position he held for thirty-five years. Because funds were tight, Liveright had to go to Philadelphia every three months with notes for his father to endorse. Nevertheless—and despite warnings that the store's location on Market Street was too far off the beaten track—when the first year's figures were tallied, L. Bamberger & Co. had respectable sales of $265,000.[86]

Abraham (Abe) Schindel began working as a bundle wrapper for Bamberger in 1900 at age fourteen. He rose through the ranks to become superintendent of building operations, a position he held until 1929, the year Bamberger sold his store to Macy's. In 1912, when a new building was erected, he was in charge of plans and construction. He also supervised a 1922 addition that included a delivery service station and the furniture warehouse and oversaw the building of Newark Museum.[87] He was responsible for anything that had to do with machinery, including selecting and purchasing Louis's and Felix's cars— Rolls Royces, because Schindel had described them to Bamberger as reliable.[88] Ruth and Abe Schindel named one of their three sons Louis Elkan in honor of Bamberger and his father. Another son, Morton Schindel, married Bamberger's great-niece Ellen Bamberger, making Abe and Ruth Schindel part of Bamberger's extended family. The couple quickly learned that being related to Bamberger opened doors to Newark society.

Bamberger's nephew, Edgar Sutro Bamberger, his brother Julius's son and the last male to carry the Bamberger name, lived in neighboring West Orange. He was the son Louis never had. In addition to his official store duties as vice president of merchandise, Edgar was expected to learn the entire business so Louis could travel at will and to be on hand to represent his uncle at public events. By all accounts Edgar met and exceeded his uncle's expectations. His career in retail started after his graduation from Johns Hopkins in 1904. He left Baltimore for a job at Wanamaker's in New York City, where he was a bundle wrapper and salesman. He started work at Bamberger's in 1907 and stayed until 1931.[89] Edgar convinced Bamberger to pay for the store's start-up radio station WOR and then served as its president and head of operations.

By building a loyal team of managers, Bamberger was able to turn his attention to promoting his business, at which he excelled. He considered his creative use of advertising a critical factor in his success and esteemed no one more than the man whose job it was to create store promotions and brand the Bamberger name, Walter S. Moler. Moler worked at L. S. Plaut & Co. for eighteen months before coming to L. Bamberger & Co. in 1911. He became merchandise manager and director of publicity and advertising and remained there until his death in 1928.[90] Moler wrote copy, produced posters, oversaw employee etiquette, and coordinated window displays with merchandise. He kept pace with changes in department store advertising techniques as described in publications such as *Women's Wear Daily* and the *Dry Goods Economist*, whose reporters also covered Bamberger's on their beat.[91] The *Dry Goods Economist* was a trade journal for the textile industry that provided instruction in retailing methods from 1852 onward, showing merchants and managers how to display and sell their merchandise effectively. Through its editors' encouragement, thirty-seven stores formed a dry goods trade association named the National Retail Dry Goods Association; Bamberger's was a member.

A tremendous growth spurt in their businesses led department store owners to pay attention to their workers. Bamberger's store hours were from 8 A.M. to 6 P.M. weekdays and 8 A.M. to 10 P.M. on Saturdays.[92] On Sunday mornings the partners cleaned up the store. From December 1 to Christmas, hours were every day until 10 P.M., and the store didn't close until the last customer was served.[93] Long after he retired, Frank Liveright wrote, "The store hours were long, the work was hard, yet I think all of us, from top to bottom, were from the start caught up with the awareness that each individual's efforts were valued and appreciated. Employees didn't seem to mind the long hours as eventually it became known that it was almost impossible to hire an employee away from the firm."[94]

Nevertheless, workers needed something more to make them feel that this grind was worth the effort. Thus department store owners, in an effort to establish worker loyalty, started to make a big show of treating their clerks better. For example, leading stores began to refer to employees as "associates." Bamberger's employees were called co-workers, a term introduced by Felix Fuld. Even when the workforce numbered in the hundreds, the Bamberger partners knew each worker and his or her family, found time to visit sick employees in the hospital, and sent wedding gifts to longtime employees. Each time Bamberger stopped to say hello to an employee or inquired as to a family member's health contributed to his reputation as a caring employer.

L. Bamberger & Co. also established the "L. Bamberger & Company's Employees' Mutual Aid Association." On February 11, 1897, co-workers met to inaugurate this association, whose purpose was "to create funds to assist members in sickness or distress."[95] The treasury was started with a $100 gift from the firm. Dues depended on a worker's salary, but were never sufficient to cover the cost of benefits. Louis Bamberger made up for the shortfalls by transferring company money to restore the fund whenever it was necessary.

Other strategies to encourage loyalty included the practice of reviewing a worker's employment records yearly. The custom of hiring a person for a year's trial before awarding permanent employee status meant that no employee could be fired on a passing whim.[96] After the review each year, good employees were rewarded. Thus Bamberger employees felt secure. The firm also believed that loyal employees deserved vacations; and as early as 1900 every employee was granted a one-week vacation with pay, something most businesses did not do even for favored employees.[97] Bamberger's employees were paid well by department store standards. "Sales girls earned $5 and $6 a week plus commissions and girls and boys as young as 13 earned $1 to $2 a week while they learned the business."[98] Twenty-five dollars a week for a "floorwalker" who supervised an entire store aisle was considered a princely salary in the early 1900s, and the floorwalkers certainly looked like princes in elegantly tailored Prince Albert coats. Seventy years after Bamberger's passing, Felix Fuld's great-niece, Jackie Berg, described Bamberger's as "a family business" co-owned by two caring partners and staffed by a "family" of loyal co-workers.[99]

"I know," Liveright wrote, "that Mr. Bamberger was the most ethical man I've ever met, and it was he who built the employee, customer and supplier loyalty that became company hallmarks."[100] Bamberger insisted that no advantage be taken of any individual who worked for the firm. This included his suppliers. "You must never, never take advantage of a supplier," he insisted.[101] The concern for suppliers began in the 1890s with the shift from dry goods to finished garments, or what came to be known as ready-to-wear.[102] Larger stores bought apparel directly from the manufacturer. Small manufacturers with a single account risked going out of business if a store demanded an exclusive deal and then switched sources.[103] Former Bamberger employee Seymour ("Sy") Grossman explained that when an invoice and merchandise came in, the order was to pay the bill within three days. "Mr. Bamberger knew that any company who wanted to do business with L. Bamberger & Co.

would honor any claim for shortages. Because of this, the company had the best credit in the whole industry."[104] It also meant that when scarce times came, Bamberger's had first call on merchandise.

The Bamberger name was its stock-in-trade. Its trademark logo, designed by the store's advertising department, was used on packaging, signage, stationery, labels, and lettering on delivery trucks. L. Bamberger & Co. had a private label, "Elbeco," which linked the parts of the abbreviation "L. B. Co." into one word; according to Abraham Schindel, the name was created in 1901.[105] In 1919 Elbeco was replaced by the full name L. Bamberger & Co. to satisfy some executives who felt Elbeco was not very distinctive.[106]

L. Bamberger & Co. was the first department store in Newark to feature foreign-made items.[107] As early as 1904 it sent representatives to visit factories and warehouses in Europe. While Bamberger opened accounts with local manufacturers, it was Fuld's job to scout European markets; by 1914 Bamberger's had buying offices in all the principal centers of Europe, including Frankfurt, Berlin, Bremen, Vienna, Paris, and London. Fuld was in Europe when World War I broke out. He was among the many travelers stuck in Europe, in a war zone no less, without access to cash or credit, making it nearly impossible to pay for hotel bills and steamship tickets, until the American Express office in Rotterdam obtained safe passage for him and others to New York aboard the steamship *Nieuw Amsterdam*.[108] One of the first signers of a letter of appreciation to American Express from its customers served in Rotterdam in 1914 was Felix Fuld.[109]

As time passed, the store sent other managers and buyers on trips to look at what other stores were doing and see what new products might interest Bamberger's customers. It is still possible to find ladies' evening bags with the Bamberger label, including European country of origin, in pristine condition.[110]

Newarkers' seemingly inexhaustible needs for clothing, bedding, household goods, and all manner of things drove sales to $2 million in 1908. Claiming it was not their nature to stand still, the Bamberger partners made plans to build a larger, more modern department store. These plans were dealt a blow when Louis Frank died unexpectedly on a trip to Lucerne in fall 1910. Bamberger and Fuld immediately bought Frank's share of the business and incorporated a new firm with Bamberger as president, Fuld as vice president and treasurer, and Liveright as secretary.[111] The building plans went ahead, and three successive issues of the *Newark Sunday Call* in December 1910 reported the details of the "handsome new store" that Bamberger was building. Louis Bamberger's store had occupied three sites: first, the 147–149 Market Street location; second, the northeast corner of Halsey and Market Streets; and third, in 1912, when the firm moved across Halsey Street to open what became Bamberger's flagship building located at 131 Market Street.

Like department stores in cities around America, Bamberger's grew both vertically and horizontally using whatever means necessary to control available real estate.[112] In fact, these stores were empires in the making. Bamberger continually kept an eye on how other department store owners expanded their businesses. All became caught up in real estate deals as land values shot up. Store owners "worked day and night to get possession of the full block of real estate that fronted their downtown store."[113] Bamberger followed suit. Even before ground was broken for his first multistory department store, he was busy buying up land in the heart of downtown Newark, even though he had no immediate use for it. Always preparing for the future, he insisted that his attorney, John Hardin, secretly buy the land to avoid a future price war. Hardin did this through a privately owned company known as Chester Realty Company. The company kept a separate set of books for Bamberger and Fuld's real estate holdings.[114]

Bamberger insisted on adhering to a strict building schedule. His architect, Jarvis Hunt of Chicago, filed detailed plans and specifications for an eight-story building with the city's building department. Hunt's design called for a skeleton steel structure providing approximately 405,000 square feet of selling space at a cost of approximately $2 million. The ground breaking was on February 18, 1911.[115] At the same time Bamberger gave orders to build two tunnels under Halsey Street to facilitate the movement of stock between the basements of the new and old buildings.[116] Excavation, which included tearing down small stores and houses on the property, started the next day. Charles Nisenson, who owned a hat store on Halsey Street, refused to acknowledge that his lease had expired and would not move.[117] In response Bamberger took unusually strong action. According to Liveright, "One night, when the streets were dark, we broke open the store, moved the hats out into the street and tore down the building. Then we excavated the plot. The next morning Nisenson discovered a deep hole where his store had been when he locked up the night before and decided to sue."[118] However, court records do not mention this suit. Instead, they document a case titled "District Court, D., New Jersey, in re Charles Nisenson," which had been filed on November 15, 1912, that had nothing to do with Bamberger. It was about bankruptcy proceedings filed against Nisenson for breach of promise of marriage and sale of jewelry that didn't belong to him. In any case, stores that were on land Bamberger had purchased for the new store, including Nisenson's, were demolished on February 25, 1911. Bamberger thus put those around him on notice that he was capable of playing hardball.

A workers' strike lasting from mid-August to mid-September caused another delay. At last, on November 3, 1911, a crowd of onlookers watched as Louis Bamberger, with Felix Fuld at his side, drove in the first rivet for the new store.[119] After two years of construction, the new L. Bamberger & Co. department store took up all but thirty-five feet of the frontage on Market Street between Halsey and Washington Streets. The new store officially opened on October 15, 1912. Visitors to Newark accustomed to shopping at Bamberger's were surprised to see that the store had "jumped across Halsey" into a building that was soon affectionately dubbed the "Great White Store." White was perhaps the most common exterior finish found on department stores.[120] L. Bamberger & Co. was clad with a light terra-cotta that stood out amid the surrounding dark red and brown buildings. It was the largest, most elegant retail establishment in downtown Newark.[121]

Another critical component of building a department store empire was membership in influential organizations. Accordingly, during the construction Bamberger, along with 656 prominent New Jersey business leaders and mayors, signed a petition calling for the formation of a statewide chamber of commerce and then accepted an offer to be a signer of the chamber's incorporation papers. Joining him at the signing were inventor Thomas Edison, Prudential Insurance president John F. Dryden, and founder of the Public Service utility corporation Uzal H. McCarter. Having given the occasion some thought, Bamberger brought a red-ink rubber Bamberger's stamp and used it next to his signature. One hundred years later, in 2011, New Jersey Chamber of Commerce officials noted that Bamberger's signature was one they didn't have to struggle to read.[122]

Bamberger had his own reasons for promoting the Chamber of Commerce. Through its members' combined energies, the group influenced real estate taxes, zoning, street improvements, and public transportation serving their properties. Fellow merchants were encouraged to join, since their businesses also brought foot traffic to Newark.

Bamberger's new store was just a few blocks from the busy intersection of Broad and Market Streets, known as the Four Corners. This was the heart of the city's central business district, near a point where all public transportation facilities converged. An iconic photograph in the archives of the Newark Public Library shows a uniformed policeman mounted on a platform and gesturing wildly with his hands, trying to tame the congestion caused by a bottleneck of trolleys, automobiles, and an occasional horse and wagon that threatened to prevent pedestrians from crossing the street to reach Bamberger's front entrance.

The opening of the new store coincided with the opening of railroad service through the Hudson Tubes (a pair of tunnels under the Hudson River) to Newark on November 26, 1911. With transportation to New York made easy, the question on the minds of Newark's merchants was how Newark could compete with the biggest market in the world. Bamberger told a reporter for the *American Magazine* that he had no such fears. "We argued that we could always hold the trade, not by appealing to people to buy in their home town but by giving them everything New York could give in as good a way—and a little more if possible."[123] Bamberger recognized the implications of the Hudson Tubes for his store. Suddenly he had a larger market to draw from and that, he said, "was why we decided to put up our new store, to be ready when the tubes were finished, so that we could give the people a beautiful store as well as good merchandise." It was also why his shoppers could expect even greater expansion in the near future.[124]

3

THE GREAT WHITE STORE, 1912–1921

Bamberger's publicity department got the job of alerting the public that the "old" Bamberger building was closing and a newer, more modern eight-story building was about to open. They hired a bugler to stand at the entrance and play "Taps" at precisely 10:00 P.M. on the day when the doors to the old store closed for the last time. The sound of the bugle, heard throughout downtown Newark and in nearby neighborhoods, was reported in the city's newspapers the following day. The lyrics, "All is well, safely rest," were meant to signify that a new chapter in L. Bamberger & Co.'s remarkable history was about to begin, and to assure shoppers that Newark's leading department store would reopen the following week.[1] This gambit was typical of the novel techniques that made the store successful.

That same night workers piled hundreds of boxes of merchandise onto flatbeds and handcarts and into trucks in preparation for the move to the new store directly across the street.[2] It took twelve to fourteen hours to transfer the stock[3] and three days to arrange merchandise in the various departments in preparation for a grand opening the likes of which Newark had never seen. The last items to be transferred were special pouches filled with jewelry. This job was supposed to be done by armed security guards. Amid the distractions of movers and handcarts, no one noticed that Mr. Bamberger had stayed behind watching and waiting patiently for the last guard to disappear from sight, at which time he crossed the street with the jewelry in his pockets![4]

The opening of the new Bamberger store on October 16, 1912, was a major event in Newark's business and civic life. That same year the store placed a large clock on the building's exterior. The "Bamberger clock," suspended two stories above street level on the corner of Halsey and Market Streets, became one of Newark's most famous landmarks.[5] It was the idea of Walter Moler, the publicity director. Louis's nephew

Edgar Bamberger, however, suggested that the store begin to advertise the phrase "Meet me under the clock at Bamberger's," and the idea caught on.[6]

Bamberger's was not the first department store to feature a clock. In 1897 Marshall Field had installed a clock that was immortalized by Norman Rockwell on a 1945 cover of the *Saturday Evening Post*. Handsome, ornate clocks on American department stores—for example, Rich's in Atlanta, Ayer's in Indianapolis, Kaufmann's in Pittsburgh, Meier and Frank in Portland, Oregon, and Filene's in Boston—were symbols of elegance and prosperity and were among the many services such stores offered the public-at-large.

Bamberger's clock, which was square, echoing the shape of the building, with ornate finials on the top, became more than a timekeeper; it was a destination. It was where you met your boyfriend or girlfriend, parent, business associate, or future spouse to decide what movie to see or where to dine in downtown Newark.[7] While you waited, you had time to window-shop, which was the store's intention. The idea of devising creative tactics to get customers to "watch the window" came from Frank Baum, better known as the author of *The Wizard of Oz*. Baum's magazine, *The Show Window*, helped transform window-shopping into a leisure activity.[8] More than one Bamberger shopper was lured into the store to make a purchase because of something featured in the display windows. The thousands of ties sold by Bamberger's in response to an enormously popular window that showed ties selected by men paired with those chosen by their wives illustrated the power of window displays to sell goods.[9]

By 1912 advertising had changed drastically, from copy in tiny type confined to half-columns and page corners into full pages of display advertising. Bamberger's hired the noted artist Arthur J. Elder, who created four eye-catching full-page advertisements recalling the twenty years since Bamberger had opened his business on Market Street, during which time "the little store became a big store and the big store became bigger." The ads appeared in papers within a fifty-mile radius of Newark.

Even by current standards these ads were worthy of awards for their understated elegance and subtle message to the consumer. One, entitled "The Greater Bamberger Store," described the store's remarkable growth. It showed two trees united under a bower of lemon leaves and joined at the bottom by an elaborate system of intertwining roots. The trees formed a frame for an image of the new store in the distance. Another, "Through the Vista of Years," contrasted modern-day Newark with the city at the time of its founder Robert Treat and the colonists who settled on the banks of the Passaic River in 1666, presenting the opening of the "Great White Store" as an opportunity to unite the past with the present. A third ad, "The Greater Store as a Fashion Centre," promised that the new store would be new in everything—its construction, its interior fittings, and its stock.

That same year, Wanamaker's presented an enormously popular fashion show it called "The Garden of Allah," based on a popular novel of the same name. The novel was credited with having single-handedly inspired "perhaps the most popular of all merchandising themes in the years before World War I—the oriental theme."[10] Crowds vied for tickets for a chance to see a parade of thirty models dressed in turbans and harem-style pants circulate throughout the store's first-floor arcade. Bamberger's then proceeded to exploit the same theme. The public obsession with Arab fashions inspired another Bamberger ad, "The Magic of the New Store," whose artwork evoked the mystery of the "Orient." It was captioned: "The greater [Bamberger] store has cast its spell over New Jersey—admiration runs riot. Those who have not yet made a tour of the new Bamberger building can form no adequate idea of its splendors or *its usefulness as a public institution*" [emphasis added]. It is noteworthy that the ad did not mention any goods for sale; it just conveyed the message "Greater Bamberger's is yours—come and enjoy it!" Bamberger's strategy, like that of other store owners, was to offer incomparable service in exchange for customer loyalty. With this series of exceptional ads, Moler set the bar high for those who followed.

Residents of Newark and of towns in suburban Essex County, greater northern New Jersey, and as far west as Morristown were invited to "spend the day" getting acquainted with Bamberger's new store. Subsequent advertisements proclaimed that the inauguration of the new store was too important a function to miss. Concluding that Bamberger's was "in for the long haul," Newark's shoppers paid it the compliment of nicknaming it "Bam's," a moniker that stayed with the store for eight decades.

Elected officials and other dignitaries were invited to tour the new store in advance of the general public.[11] Then a curious public took

Bamberger up on his offer and came to the opening. No souvenirs were given out, "but the public took care of that itself," as Frank Liveright recalled.[12] Those who ate at the store's restaurant that day took most of the cutlery stamped "Bamberger's" and the crockery with the Bamberger monogram. When Bamberger and Fuld heard of the losses, they were amused. Both felt these lifted items would bring them nothing but goodwill.[13]

Shoppers discovered that the store had installed a moving stairway called the Reno escalator; Bamberger's was among a half-dozen stores in the entire country that had them.[14] Some customers came in just to look at the escalator. Some were afraid to ride its slanted wooden steps, and others walked out so unnerved that they forgot what they had come to purchase. Escalators permitted merchants to distribute "quick sellers" even more widely throughout their stores. The Bamberger management team claimed that their use increased profits by allowing the store "to place the staple, year-round 'sellers' on the second and third floors, relieving the congestion of departments on the main floor."[15]

In 1915 another technological innovation allowed those who wanted to check the store's hours of operation to call its newly announced permanent telephone number, Market One—a name suggesting that Bamberger's was the "First Market" a shopper should be thinking about.[16] Bamberger's had come far from the time it had one secretary and one phone on the outside wall of its main office. By 1919 the store had a phone order department staffed by a dozen operators available to take orders from customers day and night. Bamberger's strategy of providing superior customer service led even further: it was the first department store to install a "red phone" service throughout the store so customers could ask questions about anything. These phones were also connected to the mail-order room.[17]

The opening of the new store was important to Newark for numerous reasons. Merchants would get increased foot traffic, manufacturers would profit from orders for their products, local tradesmen would be kept busy with repairs, and new merchants would be encouraged to open businesses in the city. This is why, in the period leading up to Bamberger's opening, merchant associations in downtown Newark removed unsightly billboards and eliminated pushcart vendors. The idea was to make Newark look more attractive.

The Down Town Club, famous for its white-glove service and the best menu in town, opened in the Bamberger building in 1913 with access through a private entrance on the side of the building. Its original membership list included Louis Bamberger and Felix Fuld, among other prominent citizens. According to Newark banker Donald Karp, the city's businessmen used the club to entertain their clients over lunch or dinner.[18] Former Bamberger executive Edward J. Goldberg recalled that the daily guests were a "who's who" of Newark society at the time, including businessmen, the judiciary, politicians, and real estate barons.[19]

The year 1913 saw the first issue of *Counter Currents*, a monthly newsletter costing two cents, "by and for employees of L. Bamberger & Co."[20] The masthead read: "A little magazine published monthly by the co-workers of the store family of L. Bamberger & Co. for the purpose of keeping in touch with each other and perpetuating pep." Fuld defined "pep" as the "fuel that metaphorically feeds the furnace of the Great White Store . . . It supplies it with new ideas, stands for efficiency, eliminates waste and pushes it on. Therefore get into the 'pep' line and you will never get into the bread line."[21]

The first department store "house organ" is credited to Sears Roebuck. *The Skylight*, created in 1901 and edited and written by Sears employees, was so successful that by 1915 more than sixty such papers were being published by department stores around the country.[22] L. S. Plaut in Newark, also known as "The Beehive," had *Honey-Comb Briefs*. At Bamberger's, concerns about the costs of printing and high-quality paper were dismissed once management realized that there was no other way to keep in touch with a workforce that now numbered in the thousands.

Bamberger and Fuld relied on *Counter Currents* to offer New Year's greetings and encouragement to co-workers to keep up the good work. "Our ideal is to do away with this feeling of strangeness as far as possible, to make every co-worker feel at home with us from the beginning."[23] This was accomplished through a network of "sponsors," who acquainted new workers with the store's numerous departments.[24] Anything management wanted its employees to know about day-to-day operations was reported in *Counter Currents*, whose central message was that every employee was part of one big [happy] family.

Store executives and division superintendents got their fair share

47

of coverage, but employee photographs were featured as well. Covers were the work both of in-house talent and of professional artists and illustrators who also created covers for the *Saturday Evening Post*, *McClure's*, and other national magazines. Bamberger's hired Howard Chandler Christy, who was famous for illustrations featuring the "Christy Girl," similar to the more familiar "Gibson Girl."[25] Christy was also famous for World War I Liberty Loan posters. He was a perfect choice for Bamberger, who chaired Newark's war bond and Liberty Loan drives.

Fellow store magnates recognized that the employee newsletters were useful because they provided information and generated worker loyalty. Management praised individual workers' accomplishments, hoping that others would follow their example. Bamberger's sent *Counter Currents* to department stores throughout America and received compliments in return. A letter came from R. H. Macy saying that *Counter Currents* "is the best department store house organ published."[26] The owner of Ed Shuster & Co. in Milwaukee wrote, "I don't know of any retail store in the country where the people employed get as much of a share in the operation and results of the business as at Bamberger's," a comment that was naturally reprinted in *Counter Currents*.[27]

The newsletter reported all kinds of unusual statistics. Ten thousand wet umbrellas had to be looked after while customers shopped; twenty-five hundred co-workers ate in the co-workers' restaurant during the December Christmas rush; and an order for clothes that had to be shipped from the men's department to a gentleman in Sumatra in the Dutch East Indies demonstrated how Bamberger's reputation for customer service reached beyond America's shores.[28]

Starting in 1913, Bamberger's sponsored the first of three exhibits featuring "things Newark makes." Each was part of a branding and promotion strategy to convince shoppers that L. Bamberger & Co. was a public institution dedicated to Newark's progress. The first was titled "Made in Newark."[29] The second, in 1914, was called "The Great Industrial Fair."[30] Visitors compared it to a World's Fair.[31] The honor of opening the exhibit was awarded to the president of the United States, Woodrow Wilson. Western Union had run a special wire from Bamberger's to the White House. Bamberger's advertisement on this occasion read, "The President, who has always manifested a lively interest in the industrial development of Newark, has graciously consented to open the 'Made in Newark' exposition and at promptly 2 o'clock Tuesday afternoon, he will press a button which will galvanize into action every piece of machinery throughout the store."[32]

In 1915, approximately 335,000 people—equal to three-quarters of the city's population—attended the third Bamberger storewide exposition, which featured 123 items manufactured in Newark.[33] Residents were informed, "There are very few Newarkers who realize what a wonderful manufacturing city they are living in."[34] This exhibit was spread over all but the main floor, a deliberate tactic to entice shoppers to the visit the upper floors.

Beyond these highly publicized, successful expositions, Bamberger did something even more out of the ordinary to promote his business. Against Fuld's better judgment, he directed his publicity department to run an advertisement promoting the store's "First Annual Poultry Exhibition" in the sixth-floor auditorium.[35] Holding poultry shows—which the store did for seventeen years—seems quite inconsistent with Bamberger's desire to appeal to middle- and upper-class shoppers. But this is what separated Bamberger from other promoters. He was willing to stretch the envelope in order to bring foot traffic to his store. "We ran a poultry show and it brought a surprising number of people into the store, and people heard of the store who never would have heard of it otherwise," he said later.[36] His poultry shows were no different from the store's award-winning flower shows, sales of goldfish, or pet contests, all staged to attract shoppers.

From the start the new store made money and assured its shoppers that the items they purchased there lived up to the claims made for them. False advertising, in Bamberger's opinion, was the quickest way to ruin his customers' trust. As Felix Fuld explained, "We are compelled to sell reliable goods and to be honest with our customers, even if the policy means forfeiting profit at times."[37] Other stores did not observe the same strict truth-in-advertising policy. For example, Chicago's stores were said to run pages of large newspaper advertisements, boldly proclaiming the arrival of new merchandise and often misrepresenting the quality of the goods.[38] The same practice existed in department stores throughout America—but not at Bamberger's.

As Bamberger's grew, its advertising increased. This made sense. The bigger the store, the more shoppers were needed to fill the aisles, and the only way to significantly increase foot traffic was to advertise in newer ways. In 1920 the advertising department pulled another stunt with all the earmarks of Bamberger originality. They inserted a four-page rotogravure section in the *Newark Evening News* featuring sixty-four of the finest gift articles from fifty different departments.[39] This was the first time a colored or rotogravure section appeared as part of a regular edition of the paper.

At the same time, Bamberger's expanded its use of outdoor advertising. Thousands of passengers traveling by train to and from Newark passed by billboards advertising L. Bamberger & Co. Another form of outdoor advertising was the electrical sign. Bamberger's name went up in lights in 1919, in a sign created as a surprise for Bamberger from his electrical department. Attached to the store's roof, it could be seen above Newark's tallest skyscraper and was large enough for pilots to see as their planes approached the busy Broad and Market Streets intersection. No promotion was too outlandish if it drew attention to the Bamberger name.

In 1914 Moler initiated another unique advertising gimmick—a column of public service announcements titled "Between Ourselves." Found on page three of every issue of the *Newark Sunday Call*, this column was small enough to squeeze in between ads for items for sale, so there was no additional charge to print it. Aimed at readers of the ads, it took the form of a conversation in which Moler announced Bamberger's permanent phone number, Market One; gave practical advice; and wrote about what was happening in Newark or in distant countries where wars were being fought (he chose this subject because 80 percent of Newark's population was foreign born or of foreign parentage and kept ties to their native countries).[40] Some saw the column as a waste of valuable advertising space, but Moler defended his decision. By making shopping at Bamberger's a personal experience between the store and the customer, he contributed to the image of L. Bamberger & Co. as a public institution interested in the welfare of all citizens.

Through statements such as "We believe in Newark and its future and we believe Newark believes in us"[41] or "Prosperity here is a matter of course. We have always had it and we are always going to have it,"[42] "Between Ourselves" promoted Newark's progress as a modern, full-service city: "No need to go to New York to make a purchase with Bamberger's so near."[43] Moler also drew attention to "I'm Glad I Live in Newark," a little-known song by local playwright, organist, and composer Philip A. Gifford.[44] The lyrics praised Newark, its men and women, its industries, and its spirit of civic pride.

The column asked customers to purchase only what they planned to keep: "If you spend an hour at the counter making a purchase," Moler wrote, "you should be sure you want it and not return it the next day."[45] He responded to the question "Why does a store as large as Bam's need full page ads to promote all it has to sell?" by explaining, "The store runs like a city with many departments and each needs representation."[46] Readers also learned about the war with Mexico,[47] the advantages of being ambidextrous, the lines at the Paris Galleries Lafayette, where customers were given numbers before making a purchase,[48] and the historic Triple Entente treaty between Italy, Germany, and Austria-Hungary in 1882.[49] Moler advised readers to get in the habit of carrying a small notebook to keep track of important conversations or ideas, encouraged men to read Bamberger's ads, and told women they should thank a man "audibly" when he gave them his seat on the train.[50]

Bamberger himself once gave up his seat on the bus to Anna Heyman,[51] who worked in the store's executive offices alongside him. Her career spanned forty-eight years, another testimony to the loyalty of so many Bamberger employees. It may be surprising that a man as wealthy as Louis Bamberger rode the public bus, but he did. Bamberger was a "hands-on" merchant who liked doing his own research, which included verifying reports he received about how many people took mass transportation to downtown Newark. Since no one knew what Bamberger looked like, he was free to travel around the city unrecognized.

Normally he and Fuld left for work at precisely 8:30 A.M. They took separate cars and instituted a morning ritual of asking their drivers to slow their limousines at the edge of the driveway before driving off. This delay gave the two men time to wave to a group of young boys who routinely waited there for the gates of Bamberger's estate to open just so they could catch a glimpse of the person their parents and neighbors spoke about. One car turned right toward Central Avenue; the other turned left toward South Orange Avenue. Both roads led to Newark. In case of traffic, at least one man would have a chance to be on time to open the store.[52] Then, when they were two blocks from the store, both got out of their cars so they could be seen walking to work. In 1977, Mae Simon of Millburn recalled how Bamberger and Fuld regularly strolled past the front window of her home on Bank Street. They were "distinguished looking gentlemen," always together (as they often were, even walking the aisles of their department store), "well dressed, but not ostentatiously."[53]

Bamberger's former neighbor Ozzie Lax, who was friendly with Bamberger's chauffeur, told a story that one morning, on his way to work, Bamberger tapped his driver on the shoulder and said he wanted to purchase some leg warmers. He asked where he could find them. The driver turned and said with a straight face, "I think that they are sold at Bamberger's."[54] Bamberger had simply lost track of the details of his store's enormous inventory.

In 1915 Moler began still another column, which appeared daily in Newark's papers and consisted of a full page that listed one hundred or more price reductions. The column was variously called "Treats," "Bargains," "Extra," "One Day Specials," and "Pin Points," until one day somebody gave it the title "Important"—and the name never changed.[55] Bamberger's co-workers were instructed to familiarize themselves with the store's own advertisements and "those of our competitors" so they could assist customers with the items they read in this column.[56] Like many major department stores of the era, Bamberger's had its own education department with a full-time director, whose job was to supervise and train staff in all areas of store operations, including keeping tabs on the store's ads.

Still another example of Moler's ingenuity was the Bamberger Golf School, under the direction of William Scott, Mountain Ridge Country Club's golf pro, which gave lessons in the store. It had great appeal for Newark's upper-middle-class residents, who now did not have to travel to the suburbs to polish their games.[57] The idea of a golf school may have come from Felix Fuld, who was an avid golfer. He and Bamberger were founders of Mountain Ridge Country Club, whose members were German Jews like themselves.

It was Moler's job to make sure something was going on in the store all the time. He was a wizard at creating what historian Daniel Boorstin termed "pseudo events," meaning events staged solely for the purpose of publicity. Boorstin's *The Image: A Guide to Pseudo-events in America*, describes the shift in American culture that he claimed was mainly attributable to advertising. If a store generated enough publicity, people would come to see what all the fuss was about.[58] Thus the store's "teen" years were filled with crowd pleasers that included lots of live music in the form of band concerts, store choral groups, string quartets, and recitals that encouraged the sale of pianos, as well as Bamberger's all-important fashion revue. According to Moler, Bamberger's was the first store in Newark to show its fashions on live models. From a simple start in 1906, with one or two young women trying on the new coats and wraps as they stood on a clean strip of muslin stretched across the floor, fashion shows, including Bamberger's, proved so popular that "by 1915, from Baltimore, Maryland, to Waco, Texas, the fashion show, usually free of charge, could be found in nearly every sizeable city in the country."[59]

Department stores were considered arbiters of good taste, or so they claimed. They made it their job to expand a customer's appreciation of good design, particularly in the decorative arts. In 1915 Bamberger teamed up with Newark Museum director John Cotton Dana "to boost the sale of wares of Newark's department stores," including Plaut's and Hahne's.[60] The Newark Museum, then located on the fourth floor of the public library, sponsored a series of exhibitions showing what Dana considered to be good design. He combined art with industry and exhibited both together. Dana suggested that older, well-established museums use department store–type displays to modernize their look. In his opinion, department stores were more influential than all the nation's museums combined, and it would be far better if all museums were like department stores—"honest . . . steel and concrete" structures at the "center" of city life, "filled with objects closely associated with the life of the people."[61] He favored modern industrial design and modern art that fused the past with the present, though critics suggested his exhibits had "a frankly commercial side."[62]

There was a place for well-designed goods, particularly if they were made in Newark, and that place was on the shelves of L. Bamberger & Co. In addition, Bamberger's far-reaching efforts to import products from all over the world permitted customers to purchase items from countries they would never visit, at prices they could afford. Dana taught Bamberger's workers about carpets, silks, and ceramics at the Newark Museum, just as Charles R. Richards, who coined the term "industrial arts," lectured Manhattan department store employees at the Metropolitan Museum of Art. It would be cynical to suggest that the only motivation for Bamberger's or Dana's efforts to promote Newark's economy was that this was good for business. Even if that were the case, there was nothing wrong if all parties profited and prospered from this mutual support. But in fact, Bamberger's broader mission was to educate America's "consumer culture" — a phrase first used by Boston's Edward Filene.[63]

Ward McCallister, arbiter of etiquette to fashionable New York society in the 1920s, noted: "It takes nearly a lifetime to educate a man how to live." In Bamberger's opinion, the products purchased at his department store could also educate a man, or a woman, on how to live. He believed that a well-informed customer became a loyal customer. Promotion of his "Elbeco" brand, ready-made dresses "offering Perfection in Dresses at a Modest Price," included information about these garments.[64] We do not know whether women wanted to know how their dresses were made, but Louis Bamberger wanted them to know. It was not enough just to purchase a dress off the rack; a woman should take pride in the fact that a Newark manufacturer had made the dress and that the fabric had been manufactured in silk mills in nearby Paterson. Such a consumer might also be interested in knowing that "in 1915 the clothing trade was America's third-largest industry, outranked only by steel and oil."[65]

Department stores were beneficiaries of the Industrial Revolution, which had permitted men like Bamberger to take advantage of "more available capital, low taxes and cheap labor to build and staff stores."[66] These factors, together with an improved standard of living and a demand for more and better goods, encouraged Bamberger and other department store owners to expand their operations and create more efficient distribution systems. And because each was adjusting to an expanding economy, it made sense to establish a retail association for store owners to share their mutual concerns.

In 1916, A. L. Filene of Boston invited a group of men in "kindred lines of business" to address the influence of mail-order houses and chain stores, which were making inroads into the retail business.[67] Filene believed that it would be advisable for merchants in the different sections of the country to get together occasionally and see what could be done to combat these businesses. Bamberger concurred. He intended to encourage fellow store owners to share information and to set up a mechanism for noncompetitive buying. It would be a friendly exchange because each store had its own territory and loyal customers. Most people rarely shopped outside their own towns or cities, so what seemed to them like a revolutionary business practice was chalked up to hometown pride. Most shoppers didn't know, or particularly care, that the same business practice was occurring in rival department stores around the country.

Bamberger himself, and his executives, visited every department store of any size in the country. Each year they added a new area. It was common knowledge that "Bamberger's can tell you what almost any store in the country is doing in a particular department at any time."[68]

Bamberger instructed his store managers to share vital statistics, exchange information on new styles and new selling tactics, and practice "group buying," which involved pooling their orders in a single contract while retaining control over the character of the merchandise.[69] In this way he set the stage for what later became the Retail Research Association (RRA), formed to provide a common pool of domestic and foreign merchandising data.[70] Initially, twelve stores were represented. The number grew to nineteen, including one in London.

Faith Chipperfield and her partner, Anne Evans, helped supply this data. Their expertise in French fashion was valued by store owners, who realized as early as 1912 that American fabrics and designs were not ready to compete with those of Europe.[71] These two women, who were stationed in Paris during and after World War I, published their own fashion magazine, *Paris Vogue*, and Bamberger's was a subscriber. They sent information daily to Bamberger's and other RRA members regarding prices, manufacturing processes, the latest styles, and details about orders placed as far as a year ahead by non-RRA members.[72] This was the early twentieth century's version of "fashion espionage," or how to stay ahead of the competition. Wanting an organization for cooperative buying as well as facilities for research, members formed the Associated Merchandising Corporation.[73] Bamberger was active in both.

During what was known as the Progressive Era, roughly from 1900 to World War I, reformers sought to improve the lot of the American worker. Owners of large department stores without employee benefits in place were forced to add them, accepting that they were the cost of doing business. However, Bamberger's had no fear of employee dissatisfaction. Benefits for its employees were in place from the start, and co-workers knew Bamberger valued them, as he never missed an opportunity to credit them for his success.

Bamberger's advertising department worked with its personnel department to create ads to attract applicants for sales positions. They read "Notice! Capable salespeople wanted now. Offer: good salaries, commissions, short hours, not open at night, fine ventilation, educational facilities, Mutual Aid Association, free medical advice, employee restaurant and permanent positions with advancement opportunities."[74] The Mutual Aid Association, welfare programs, paid vacations, emergency relief funds, savings plans, programs to boost morale, and partial tuition for education were all routine benefits paid for in part by a small deduction from the worker's weekly salary. However, these deductions never covered the cost of benefits paid out, and Bamberger's long-standing practice was to instruct his treasurer to make up any shortfalls. When the Mutual Aid Association fell on hard times in 1918, the management provided life insurance for employees (while making sure that the newspapers published stories about its generosity). The idea of publicizing Bamberger's generosity as an employer was Moler's; he "realized that employee relations and public relations might go hand in hand."[75]

In 1916 Bamberger's confidence in the future was vindicated when Newark hosted a six-month-long 250th anniversary celebration. He agreed to join a committee of three hundred citizens assigned to raise a celebration fund of $250,000.[76] Former New Jersey governor Franklin Murphy boasted that not only did the committee succeed in raising $250,000, but also that "no other city in America had provided a larger sum for a similar purpose."[77]

Among four thousand donors, L. Bamberger & Co. gave $2500.[78] Participating merchants received signs to post in their store windows to indicate their support and were promised that the *Official Celebration Guide and Manual* would be circulated from coast to coast and put in the hands of between 200,000 to 350,000 people. "It will be the most attractive and useful guide book published by any American city."[79]

Newark's anniversary celebration became a subject of national interest. Thousands of people from all over the country entered competitions to create the best posters and poems symbolizing Newark's history and progress.[80] New Jersey congressman Townsend boasted on the floor of the US House of Representatives that "there is not in the United States an important manufacturing city which is a better index of industrial and manufacturing business conditions than is the city of Newark, New Jersey, which I've the honor in part to represent."[81] Mayor Price of Wilmington, Delaware, remarked, "I was actually astounded by what I found in your city. I didn't know or realize what a bustling, busy, pretty place Newark is."[82]

The anniversary committee adopted the slogan "Newark Knows How." In fact, it should have read "Bamberger's Knows How." Bamberger saw the occasion as an opportunity to showcase the city's industries. He organized the most important industrial show in Newark's history and opened it in his store. Like President Wilson two years before him, Newark mayor Thomas Raymond flipped the switch that started up all the motors throughout the various exposition floors.[83] Newark's board of trade sponsored a "Shop in Newark" campaign[84] supported vigorously by Bamberger. Thus began a long, successful relationship between Newark's popular mayor and its equally popular merchant. Mayor Raymond looked to Bamberger to help him make decisions about expanding services to Newark residents, and Bamberger looked to Raymond to pass the necessary legislation to keep Newark moving forward. The two men were so close that Bamberger was a pallbearer at Raymond's funeral.[85] Both were pleased with the well-timed announcement in 1915 that the Pennsylvania Railroad planned to build a line through Newark to New York City.[86]

Meanwhile, expansion and enhanced distribution had presented Bamberger with a dilemma. His workers knew how to describe the products being sold, but not how to sell to Newark's upper-middle-class customers, who considered themselves as sophisticated as New York shoppers. As John Wanamaker had said, "We have got to have people that the customers will recognize from their manner that they have an idea of what a refined lady should wear."[87]

During the teens, Bamberger's workforce was recruited primarily from Newark's immigrant neighborhoods. Clearly the process of assimilation could not educate the children of immigrants into the middle class fast enough to supply the necessary number of salespeople. Thus Bamberger's began educating its workers. The first salesmanship classes were held as early as 1914, and they offered women new opportunities.[88]

A 1919 article in the *New York Sunday Times*, "Woman's New Field in Department Stores—The Opportunities Awaiting Girls," which extolled the virtues of a capable saleswoman over those of an equally capable salesman, was reprinted in *Counter Currents*.[89] The article noted that since women were the majority of shoppers, their preferences must be followed. One customer was quoted as saying, "I'd so much rather buy silks from an efficient saleswoman than from an efficient salesman." She had just purchased silk for a new gown, and the salesperson who had helped her make so satisfactory a purchase had been a young woman. On this basis Bamberger's told its female workforce that they could expect to "find both their horizons and salaries expanding." Bamberger invited nearby Rutgers University to operate an extension division in his store because he was convinced that a well-educated workforce would be beneficial on both sides of the counter. The students were primarily women. Like it or not, male managers were forced to overcome their notion that a woman's place was in the home.

Like all department stores, Bamberger's had a dress code. Saleswomen were instructed on how to dress, trained to know their merchandise, required to speak English, and cautioned not to address a customer as "honey" or "dearie" and to avoid such words as "swell" or "nifty" to describe an item. This training helped break down class barriers. It was the beginning of the department store personnel management movement of the 1920s. Bamberger's personnel manager was Michael Schaap, who was married to Bamberger's niece, Stella Frankenheimer. Schaap's experience working for Bamberger paid off; when he left, he became president of Bloomingdale's.

Bamberger's policy of hiring women and encouraging their retail careers was forward looking for its time. However, although female workers were told that that they had a future at Bamberger's, in practice the store's management was dominated by men, who were often related to Fuld or Bamberger. Women were accepted as behind-the-counter help, but not as managers in charge of an entire department. Their jobs lasted until they married, at which time they were expected to become housewives and mothers. A woman's only opportunity for advancement was to become a buyer, whose job was to keep Bamberger's stocked with Europe's latest fashions. Female co-workers might fantasize about what life was like for buyers who traveled on luxury liners to Europe, but these women buyers who went abroad for months forfeited their chance to be wives and mothers. Most female employees remained saleswomen.

The need to train large numbers of saleswomen was filled by a group of organizations that trained both saleswomen and teachers of saleswomen. The prototype was a school founded by Lucinda Wyman Prince at the Women's Educational and Industrial Union in Boston in 1905.[90] In 1912, as the demand for Prince-trained women grew, the school shifted its emphasis to training teachers of teachers of saleswomen. Prince's school became affiliated with Simmons College the next year.[91] Her goal was to make women more efficient so they would be paid more. She capitalized on changes after World War I: not only did the status of the salesclerk rise, but women began attending elite colleges and universities such as Radcliffe, Vassar, Wellesley, and Smith, which offered courses in department store management.[92] Students at Prince's school studied problems of merchandising, the functions of the Retail Research Association (RRA) and the American Merchandising Corporation (AMC), and other topics in courses taught by store executives. Prince's students came from cities across America and did their internships at Bamberger's during Christmas. Prince attended graduation exercises for Bamberger's salesmanship courses, and in 1925 Louis Bamberger presented her with a beautiful diamond bar pin to commemorate her twenty-five-year association with his store.[93]

Bamberger himself had limited contact with the women who worked in his store. They were nodding acquaintances with whom he had brief, pleasant exchanges when he paused in the aisles to inquire about their health or that of their families. He was courteous beyond reproach but was all business. His reserve around women is surprising, since he had grown up and still traveled with his sisters, who must have been interested in family gossip. They were constant visitors to his home. In any case, he thought women had a place in the workforce. For example, he decided to support a newly launched Newark chapter of the Business and Professional Women's Club, whose purpose was to promote the interests of business and professional women. They sought to establish networking and mutual cooperation similar to that of the Retail Research Association. Recruitment for the club was done in the store. Seventy of 843 members were "Bambergerites," not counting Mrs. Felix Fuld and Mrs. Edgar Bamberger.[94]

After women were given the right to vote in 1920, Bamberger's offered three lectures in the store about politics and political power. Bamberger agreed to have the vice president of Newark's League of Women Voters address a group of co-workers in order to explain why it was so important for each one to exercise this right. He introduced the speaker and made sure that five amplifiers were installed on the main floors so she could be heard. Another speaker, Janet Sterling Greve, field director of the Ledger Woman's Political Forum, gave practical instructions on how to mark and fold the ballot.[95] Some might say that Bamberger was motivated at least in part by his desire to increase the number of his shoppers. But another indication that Bamberger supported women's independence was his and Carrie Fuld's friendship with Margaret Sanger, whose campaign for women and birth control was controversial for its time. The three attended a concert in Newark in 1935 and were photographed for the *Star-Ledger*.[96]

A woman whose name *Counter Currents* did not print was hired as Bamberger's first female store detective.[97] Theft in department stores was common, including by women shoppers, so a woman detective would blend in. Another woman, Miss Eyers, became the first traffic manager in an American department store; she was responsible for routing and tracing all shipments.[98] Eyers was a delegate to a conference in Washington, DC, where she made quite a stir when a picture of her holding hands with President Warren G. Harding was printed in the influential *Dry Goods Economist*.[99]

From 1914 until 1917, the year America entered World War I, reports from Europe dominated headlines and dampened much of Newark's municipal enthusiasm. A slow-building antagonism against German-made goods had customers requesting that stores carry only goods made in America. Alert to the possibility that the United States would enter the war, Bamberger sponsored an Army-Navy show honoring America's fighting soldiers.[100] The exhibit was to honor all those who served or were serving in the war. It exhibited World War I cannons, rifles, torpedoes, and armored aircraft in the store auditorium, and the Bamberger store's Cadet Corps, whose members were recruited from various departments and trained in basic marching skills and drills, made its first public appearance.[101] Bamberger invited returning disabled veterans and US Army and National Guard officers to be guests at the opening. Interest in World War I militaria led Bamberger's to display a prototype of a bulletproof armor protector known as the Brewster-Heller Armor Protector, invented by Dr. Guy Otis Brewster, a dentist from Dover, New Jersey, and promoted by Emil Heller, also of Dover. Emil's brother was Max Heller, who like Bamberger and Fuld was a prominent World War I–era New Jersey Jewish philanthropist.[102] The armor was demonstrated to dignitaries from the US Army but was never used in battle.

Newark's wartime industries ran at full capacity through 1917 and 1918. An estimated thirty thousand African American men and women came north from Georgia and Alabama to find jobs in the city's shipbuilding and munitions factories. Some found jobs at Bamberger's. *Counter Currents* later celebrated their years of service with photographs and personal stories, presenting them as part of the greater Bamberger family. Most restroom matrons were black, and so were elevator operators.[103] There was an occasional black deliveryman or stock boy. Records reveal that Bamberger hired black workers in 1909, the year Newark's public schools were desegregated.

For example, Joseph Roebuck came to Bamberger's in 1909 from his job as a Pullman porter on the Pennsylvania Railroad.[104]

He worked as an elevator "starter," who had to know the location of every item in the store so he could tell customers on which floor to get off. He also assisted one day a week in the sample room, checking the work of the store's tailors.[105] According to William Ashby, the first director of the Essex County Urban League, Bamberger's had "enlightened employment policies at a time when not employing blacks was public policy."[106] A series of photographs taken at the co-workers' restaurant and printed in *Counter Currents* shows blacks and whites sitting at the same tables. According to the caption, the photos were taken "for the purpose of coming into closer touch with each other." During the Bamberger era, Newark was home to popular jazz clubs with well-known black musicians, who worked during the day and "jammed" all night. Some of these musicians were in the "Negro" orchestra that played at Bamberger's restaurant throughout the 1920s.[107]

Bamberger and Fuld's policy of hiring blacks made a lasting impression on Fuld's nephew, Bert Berg. After Bamberger sold his store to Macy's, Berg moved to Carmel, California, and opened a successful women's wear boutique in Carmel Valley. According to Bamberger's great-niece, Ellen De Franco, "He followed many of Uncle Louis' (and perhaps Uncle Felix's) merchandise methods and [like Bamberger's] were the first store to use black women as models and sales people."[108]

Under Bamberger, who was chairman of Newark's War Loan Drive, Newark joined with cities across America to encourage citizens to support the war effort. Bamberger worked with banks and other large firms to meet Newark's assigned quotas and put it "over the top." Stores donated window space for campaigns to sell war bonds. These windows were so successful in raising money that display men were exempt from military service.[109] Bamberger headed all five of Newark's loan drives, each of which was oversubscribed. According to one Bamberger advertisement, the unsung heroes of the drives were the letter carriers, "whose task is difficult, but [who] have contributed to the sale of War Bonds with their deliveries and pickups."[110]

The largest single subscriber was awarded an autographed copy of President Wilson's book *In Our First Year of War* as a personal gift from Bamberger, who believed it was everyone's "duty" to buy a Liberty bond.[111] In response to requests, and as a patriotic gesture, Bamberger's provided a list of days on which the American flag should be flown. It also printed the words to the "Star-Spangled Banner" in advertisements, asking readers to cut them out and memorize them.[112] Walter Moler reported brisk sales of bonds at Bamberger's Liberty Loan booth on the first floor—prime selling space. Customers were told, "If you cannot pay cash, Bam's will arrange terms of payment."[113]

Life at Bamberger's slipped into a rhythm shaped by the war. After the opening bell at 8:30 A.M., co-workers listened to the Bamberger Liberty Chorus. Shoppers came in to purchase piano rolls of the "Liberty Loan March" or "Hello Red, White, and Blue (America and All Her Allies Too)" by John Philip Sousa. Lucky shoppers might discover popular composer Irving Berlin autographing copies of his sheet music in Bamberger's music department and selling war bonds in a booth on the first floor.[114] Passersby paused to admire window displays that plastered the store's exterior with the theme "The Road to Victory." War-related windows became one of the most important features of all types of stores. Signs, or "tickets," made for every bond campaign were displayed in Bamberger's windows, and a big electric sign flashing from the building at night read, "Buy Liberty Bonds." The largest window sign, on the side of the building, was "War Savings Stamps." It measured 35 by 11 feet.[115]

Meanwhile, the store was adapting to ever-changing government regulations imposed on businesses. A welcome one was a War Industries Board policy of no store returns after three days, since returned goods resulted in higher prices.[116] In compliance with a ruling by the state fuel administrator, Bamberger's closed on Mondays and made no deliveries; however, workers still received their salaries. In the spring, clocks were adjusted for daylight saving time, so co-workers came to work a half hour later and left a half hour sooner to go home to tend their backyard gardens.[117] As part of an effort to conserve paper, *Counter Currents'* covers were discontinued for the duration of the war.[118]

Co-workers were advised to save sugar, sell their platinum jewelry, and donate walking canes and invalid chairs for returning soldiers.[119] Despite wartime shortages, Bamberger still managed to find new merchandise at "old" prices because his suppliers honored their contracts with the store.

Surprisingly, Bamberger's business did not suffer. Profits at the end of World War I were remarkably strong—just like the store's remarkable owner. You could count on Bamberger to embrace economic downturns and then be ready to capitalize on the upswings. His timing was uncanny. At the end of 1917, L. Bamberger & Co. reported that it had become a $5 million company.[120]

Bamberger had a particular interest in soldiers. When he learned that Newark's relief organizations were not sending packages or necessary supplies to soldiers from the city, he donated Thanksgiving dinners to Camp Dix, paid $1.50 per meal, and had the store's motor delivery service deliver them.[121] Two months later Bamberger and Fuld paid a visit to Camp Dix.[122]

Over 50 percent of all military explosives produced in the United States during World War I were made in New Jersey.[123] Ads warned, "If we can't provide housing, Newark will lose valuable war contracts."[124] Bamberger's advertisements encouraged Newarkers to provide vacant rooms for war workers in Newark's shipyards and munitions factories, and *Counter Currents* urged co-workers to "rent a room" to a war worker.[125]

Bamberger kept in touch with each employee serving overseas, and they kept in touch with him. He was more than a boss to these soldiers; he was someone with whom to share their experiences. One soldier wrote about his escape from a German prison camp, another about fighting in the Argonne Forest. Still another was gassed and in the hospital for some months before he came home. They trusted Bamberger to share their letters to him with fellow workers, and he did. No matter where a "Bamberger boy" was stationed, he was assured of receiving packages for Christmas and copies of *Counter Currents*, which printed the soldiers' letters. Three recipients of Christmas packages in 1919 wrote:

> Dear Mr. Bamberger,
> We the undersigned sincerely thank you for the fine Christmas packages which we had the pleasure of receiving. The store has left nothing unturned in seeking the means to make us feel that it is backing us up — to make us feel that we are still members. It certainly has succeeded in every respect. We have kept in touch with the store through *Counter Currents*, which the firm was so good to send to us, and now, to top it all, we receive these packages. Things like these which you — and by this we include the firm and our store also — have done are greatly appreciated and make us realize so much more why our store stands first among them all — why we feel proud to be a part of it. Wishing success combined with the season's greetings to you and all our co-workers.
> — Richard T. Wigfall, Frank J. Oberlies, and Nathan Lebowitz, Company H, Thirty-Fourth Engineers, A.P.O. 713 American Expeditionary Force, via New York[126]

When possible, employees stationed in France used their leave time to explore stores in Paris and reported their findings to Bamberger. From A. M. Brown in France came the note, "I visited the Bon Marché, with a Mr. Davis of Boston, who, by the way, was formerly on the editorial staff of the *Dry Goods Economist*. The first thing he said to me was that Bamberger's had it all over these stores. In fact, I think that the only one that compares with Bamberger's is Selfridge's in London, and then, the building is only five stories high and hasn't the floor space that we have."[127]

During the war, the personal shopper had become popular. Personal shoppers were another way that stores provided customer service to middle-class shoppers. Women who needed reassurance that their clothes were in style and men who had no time or desire to shop relied on a personal shopper. When Bamberger learned that the paperwork required to send packages to soldiers overseas was complicated and that mail had become slow and unreliable, he found a solution. He sent a personal shopper who spoke French to Paris to buy and ship Christmas gifts from French stores to soldiers in the American Expeditionary Force. Bamberger's offered the same service to the general public. People could place orders and deposit cash at the foreign department on the seventh floor. The store charged 10 percent of the gift price to cover delivery costs in France.[128] A soldier's comfort shop for those wishing to send packages on their own adjoined the men's department.[129] As a constant reminder of their sacrifice, in 1919 Bamberger's started a "service roll" with the names of 167 Bamberger boys who had died while serving in the military.[130] Their names were printed on the back cover of *Counter Currents* continuously for one year.

In 1918 Bamberger and Fuld began to focus on raising funds for Europe's Jewish refugees made homeless by the war. A mass meeting under the auspices of the Jewish Welfare Board with Felix Fuld presiding was held at Temple B'nai Jeshurun to explain the board's welfare activities in France.[131] Both Jewish and non-Jewish store workers were targeted as potential donors. Inherent in the appeal was Bamberger's belief that as a member of a greater store family, each co-worker was obligated to consider the lot of those who were suffering no matter where. A letter from Nathan Straus thanked Bamberger's co-workers for the four thousand dollars they had raised on behalf of the Jewish War Relief and Welfare Fund.[132]

At war's end, soldiers who had served in New Jersey divisions were welcomed home.[133] Bamberger's welcome was in stark contrast to the practice of other businesses in Newark, which paid lip service to supporting the troops but upon their return had no jobs waiting for them. Bamberger's co-worker veterans were reintegrated into store life and advised not to let their war risk insurance lapse—but if it did, they would be shown how to reinstate it.[134] *Counter Currents* also advised workers to continue buying war savings stamps regularly, since this was a way of forcing themselves to save for the future. They were also advised to open vacation accounts, save money, and live within their means. All this advice ultimately came from Bamberger. In 1920 Bamberger's published a booklet for co-workers entitled "How to Save." The us Treasury Department praised the Bamberger store's "real spirit of co-operation and development of mutual interest between the institution and those employed by it."[135]

There were skeptics who accused Bamberger of having an ulterior motive for every move he made; however, the facts do not bear this out. For example, Bamberger was not obligated to make up the shortfalls of the store's mutual aid association, nor to visit or send flowers to employees in the hospital. Certainly he was not forced to hold a job open for an indeterminate time for a soldier who had served abroad.

In 1919, *Counter Currents* returned to featuring store news instead of news from government agencies. The annual election of Bamberger's Mutual Aid Association made headlines again, the number of suggestions from co-workers for the Six-Months' Suggestion contest increased, business picked up noticeably, and crowds of shoppers filled the aisles. The signing of the armistice coincided with a tremendous increase in business—"way ahead of all previous Christmas seasons" —a sure sign that Bamberger's was returning to its prewar status.[136]

Newark honored its war dead with a memorable parade and other patriotic gestures.[137] On Armistice Day several thousand workers assembled on Bamberger's first floor, where a bugler played reveille and the entire gathering sang the "Star-Spangled Banner." Fuld read the names of the Bamberger workers who had died in the war. Then he and Bamberger congratulated their co-workers for their exemplary behavior during the war and their loyalty to Elbeco. A heavy copper plaque bearing the names of the store employees who had served was placed at the store's main entrance (it is now housed in Macy's archives in New York City). At the war's end Louis Bamberger let it be known that he favored President Wilson's idea of world peace and supported the passage of an international disarmament pact.

Under pressure to compete with European styles, Bamberger now needed to resume imports after the war. He sailed to Bordeaux in 1919 aboard the French liner *La France* to investigate the advisability of sending his buyers to scout for new Paris styles.[138] Bamberger's family was accustomed to his frequent trips to Europe, which possibly may have been the only occasions when he allowed himself a sexual life. The sole person who had anything to say about Bamberger's personal life was Sanford Epstein, the longtime superintendent of Newark's Jewish cemeteries, who stated that Bamberger had a female companion who met him in Paris. She was the owner of a fashionable dress shop on Newark's Bergen Street. Their time in Paris was spent purchasing clothing items for his business and dresses for hers, and together they took in the sights.[139] Epstein did not disclose how he knew this, and there is no evidence to either confirm or refute it. When asked about Epstein's assertion, Jeanie Gelbart, daughter of Ellen Bamberger, wrote: "He never married, mysteriously disappeared to Europe on a somewhat regular basis (once a year?), and no one in the family knew what he was up to."[140] Neither she nor her sister or brother ever heard any stories about Bamberger having any kind of sexual or romantic life, whether with women or with men. Gelbart's sister, Cathy Schindel, pointed out that several of Louis's siblings also never married, and there was no speculation about them either. In any case, Bamberger's insistence that his private life remain *private* was consistent throughout his career. He knew that his every move was scrutinized. Therefore, he never told anyone about his plans, whether he was giving Newark a museum or selling his store.

While in France, Bamberger visited battlefield sites at La Ferté-sous-Jouarre, Château-Thierry, and Belleau Wood, where German workers were cleaning and rebuilding highways damaged by heavy shelling.[141] He learned that the French appreciated what American soldiers had done, but complained that the Americans were creating overinflated prices because they had money to spend. On his return, Bamberger told a reporter that the "store's orders will be delayed because of lack of transportation and a shortage of materials in a country (France) too busy with war problems."[142] He advised the woman who dreamed of owning a Paris gown, "You'll pay about $1,000 for one of any pretensions."[143] Instead, Bamberger suggested, she should purchase a good copy of a Paris original at L. Bamberger & Co.

As soon as Bamberger returned from Paris, a new "shop within a shop" selling negligees opened in a little corner on the third floor. It featured large crystal chandeliers, concealed lights over the windows, and glass bars on which the garments were hung when being shown to a customer—all the glamour of shopping in Paris.[144] While salespeople were accustomed to seeing Bamberger checking showcases, fingering the elaborate furnishings in the men's shop, or peering behind counters to see that all was clean, it seems he never visited the store's negligee department.[145] Negligee saleswoman Alida Michelson, who saw Bamberger walk by, laughed when asked if he ever came in. "Oh, no!" she exclaimed.[146]

As Bamberger had anticipated, there was postwar disruption in the delivery of goods from Paris and elsewhere in Europe. Shipments halted during a New York Harbor strike and an embargo on goods coming from New England made his buyers frantic when, at the last moment, advertising copy had to be killed because the merchandise had not been delivered. Forced to find alternative means to move merchandise, Bamberger decided to experiment with airplane flights as a way to expedite deliveries. This idea was conceived a few days after the armistice was signed. His managers concluded that developing the airplane for commercial purposes was "the only use left for it now that the war was over."[147] L. Bamberger & Co. was among the first, if not the first, department store in America to use an airplane to receive and deliver goods.

Airplane deliveries were a publicity director's dream come true. On April 18, 1919, the *Newark Evening News* reported that a planeload of merchandise was leaving Garden City, Long Island, carrying 175 pounds of women's spring suits, cloaks, and blouses.[148] The plane landed in Heller's field near Newark. Newspaper reporters were on hand to watch the merchandise being put on trucks for delivery to the store. The next flight had all the drama of a murder mystery. Engine trouble forced the Bamberger pilot to land on the roof of a long storage building at Port Newark that was approximately forty feet wide by several hundred feet long. The landing and subsequent takeoff after repairs were made was believed to be the first feat of its kind in America.[149]

On August 16, 1919, an airplane carrying a shipment of pajamas flew over Newark. The pilot was told to dip the plane's nose so a *Star-Eagle* photographer could take a shot from inside it. The pilot was also directed to fly above the intersection of Broad and Market Streets, where the Bamberger building was readily identified by the twelve-foot-high letters on the roof that read "L. Bamberger & Co."[150] When the plane landed in Branch Brook Park in Newark, an estimated crowd of five hundred rode bicycles and motorcycles and drove automobiles to see it. In their mad rush they barely noticed the newly painted sign on the delivery trucks that read "Bamberger's Aeroplane Delivery—An Auxiliary Motor Truck Service."[151]

After a test trip, Bamberger's announced the operation of a regular daily delivery service to the Jersey shore for the summer season. Seaplanes carrying merchandise from Bamberger's storage facility in New York landed on the Shark River in Belmar, where an automobile waited to take parcels to customers' homes.[152] One package weighing 102 pounds was dropped by parachute from a plane five hundred feet in the air. The attempt to drop the package from the air straight into a van was not successful, but the story made great copy.

Bamberger's made more history by scheduling the first international commercial flight from Canada to the United States. The cargo consisted of raw fur pelts destined for Bamberger's fur storage vaults. When the pilot landed in Elizabeth, the US government impounded the plane; and Bamberger's was notified that it did not have a proper manifest for each item in the shipment. The store got busy and supplied a bond, and the plane was released.[153]

In an interview in *American Magazine*, Bamberger recalled what he considered the two most influential advertising stunts the store used to keep its name before the public. The first was the load of furs imported by airplane. The second was the installation of the first radio station in an American department store. "These two things did more to make our name known than any business transaction we ever completed," he asserted.[154]

Bamberger never forgot how successful the airplane was in promoting his business. In the early 1930s he formed a model airplane club, whose members were twelve-year-old boys who wore Bamberger Aero Club badges.[155] This idea was copied by Macy's, which gave its youngsters Macy's Aero Club badges. The badges are on now on permanent display at the Smithsonian Air and Space Museum in Chantilly, Virginia.[156]

"At the end of the war," Frank I. Liveright wrote, "L. Bamberger & Co. was successful and secure.... Our building program was well-in-hand, merchandising practices were respected and imitated, and advertising and public relations programs were the wonder of the retail trade."[157] It was time for another expansion. Store records from before and during the war showed that sales continued to climb to the point where, despite the wartime restrictions of 1914 through 1919, "We had outgrown the great white colossus and more space was needed."[158] As Bamberger explained to the *American Magazine* reporter, "We are adding to the building because we have been crowded; our goods could not be well shown, nor could our customers get as good service."[159] He assembled the workers in large groups and explained in person that the proposed expansion "sounds as if it was very easy, but actually it requires a great deal of planning and forethought accompanied by hard work on the part of everybody."[160]

On July 22, 1917, the *Call* reported that Bamberger and Fuld had purchased over two-and-a-quarter acres of ground on the same block where the current store was located for $2.2 million.[161] They now owned an entire block of some of the most valuable property in the center of Newark's downtown shopping district. They had bought the land secretly, since announcing their plans to purchase it would have sent prices soaring. After eighteen months of negotiations, the entire block, bound by Halsey, Market, Bank, and Washington Streets (including the southwest corner of Market and Halsey Streets, which they had to lease for ninety years), became part of a greater plan to "increase the ground area of the present establishment by 33,000 sq. ft. for a total of 80,000 additional sq. ft. of selling space."[162] This purchase meant that the existing Market Street front could be doubled in length anytime the firm desired. When asked by a *Call* reporter why he had made this purchase, Bamberger responded, "We are preparing for the future . . . We have, as you must know, boundless confidence in Newark." Ten years later Sebastian Kresge, owner of Kresge's department store, followed Bamberger's lead and bought his building at 640 Broad Street instead of signing another ten-year lease.[163]

More than ever, Bamberger needed to educate his sales force so they could keep pace with his plans to grow his business. Thus, in 1919 *Counter Currents* reminded the workers that the daily operations of the business occupied more than six nearby buildings. The Van Horn building was used for storage; the Bamberger stables on Plane Street housed one hundred horses and wagons. There were also a furniture warehouse, the old Bamberger building, and the Washington building on the corner of Bank and Washington Streets. Altogether they totaled 475,000 square feet that, added to 500,000 square feet of selling space in the current Bamberger building, came to nearly a million square feet of floor space, or about twenty-three acres.[164]

Did co-workers know, *Counter Currents* asked further, that Bamberger's had in-house laboratories that manufactured Chantrey brand beauty products, a Fruitidor department that sold specialty imported foods (which Bamberger said was his favorite department), and a candy and ice cream factory on the fourth floor?[165] Store manager Abe Schindel expressed his confidence in "knowing that products with Bamberger's store logo, including radios and other electrical appliances manufactured in factories contracted by Bamberger, were as good as can be produced anywhere for the money."[166] At this time Bamberger's held a contest for the design of a new "L. B. Co." logo, won by employee Margaret Hooper because of her beautiful penmanship.[167] Bamberger's business required great command of details. Co-workers were informed about "ticketing"; up to sixteen hundred signs and tickets (that is, price tags) were printed in-house weekly.[168] They were told about the great effort put into conserving three thousand pounds a day of "waste paper," which had to be sorted, pressed, weighed, put into a baling press, and taken to the paper mills to be recycled.[169] Being able to inform a customer that she could order an item as small as a spool of thread by calling a toll-free number and expect delivery the same day was essential, and so was writing legible sales receipts and correctly spelling addresses supplied to the delivery department. Contests were devised to convince employees that these things were important. The Benedikt Spelling Contest, named for a popular store manager whose idea it was, began in 1918 and became an annual event. In one contest cycle 956 co-workers received prizes for meeting spelling standards. A store directory contest rewarded those who could identify the floors where specific items were located. On one occasion Felix Fuld won the contest. Not only did he know the floors, but he also could name which items had multiple locations.[170]

"If this store depended on Mr. Bamberger and me for its ideas it couldn't last," Fuld told the *American Magazine* reporter. "We learn every day from our co-workers."[171] For their part, many co-workers considered it a privilege to be employed by L. Bamberger & Co. This is confirmed by the hundreds of co-workers who were celebrated in *Counter Currents* for their long-term service. The low turnover was an advantage for store managers who did not have to constantly train new employees. A new pin designed by the Bamberger jewelry department featured the insignia "Omnia Labore Florent" ("by work everything flourishes"). In 1920 six hundred workers with five or more years' employment, or one-fifth of the total, were entitled to this service pin and told to wear it proudly.[172] Bamberger's invented other unusual promotions. In 1921 a series of expositions were held in the auditorium: a showcase for Newark's Boys Vocational School, with demonstrations of students assembling automobile engines or operating printing machinery; an electrical household appliance show; and an exhibit of time-saving office devices, all reflecting consumer interest in modern technology.[173] On Armistice Day, a Bamberger advertisement in the local papers and the *New York Times* listed the signatures of US presidents from George Washington all the way up to the newly elected twenty-eighth president, Warren G. Harding.[174] This unusual promotion prompted nationwide comment and earned Bamberger's more goodwill than anyone in the store could have imagined. The district superintendent of the New York City public schools asked if the firm "might be willing to re-issue the complete advertisement in the form of a souvenir to be distributed. . . . If so, I will be glad to have you send me 1,000 copies so that each class in my schools might have a picture of the Capitol, and the autographs of the various Presidents."[175] In August 1921, work began on a new addition costing approximately $1.5 million.[176] "Are you watching the new building?" *Counter Currents* asked co-workers. "It only takes fifteen minutes of your lunch hour to see how newly dug foundations and use of structural steel for walls that [*sic*] are giving way for the new Bamberger addition."[177]

Bamberger hired one of the biggest construction companies in the country, which had built Newark's Robert Treat Hotel, and the Commodore, Biltmore, and Plaza Hotels in New York. Of course, "most of the labor was recruited from local sources."[178] Trusting that Mr. Bamberger would never disappoint them, Newark's residents were prepared to wait and see what he had in mind. One thing was clear. By 1921 L. Bamberger & Co. had reached a point where it could no longer be described merely as Newark's "Great White Store," since there were other stores in America with the same attribute. Instead, Walter Moler suggested that this department store empire built by one of America's great merchant princes adopt the sobriquet "One of America's Great Stores."

4

ONE OF AMERICA'S GREAT STORES, 1922–1929

The Roaring Twenties were particularly hectic years. Business was on the upswing after the war, and to Louis Bamberger the brief deflationary recession known as the Depression of 1920–1921 was just another economic crisis to be overcome. In fact, he decided to increase the store's capital stock from $5 million to $10 million to finance the $1.5 million expansion. The addition was finished in 1922, a banner year in which Bamberger's added fifty new departments,[1] launched the first radio station in an American department store, built the largest privately owned delivery station in the world, opened a basement store, furnished and promoted one of America's original "ideal" model homes, introduced the store directory contest, published one of America's most influential women's magazines, *Charm*, and even advertised a new line of "Bam's" golf balls. A major dry goods merchant who preferred not to be identified told a reporter, "For thirty years that store has been forging ahead at a rate faster than any other department store in the country,"[2] even despite its proximity to New York and the competition from some of the biggest stores in the world. In light of this phenomenal growth, Walter Moler rebranded Bamberger's as "One of America's Great Stores," which it was.

For the third time in its history L. Bamberger & Co. hosted a grand opening. A weeklong celebration featuring in-store promotions and special attractions started on October 30, 1922, with Bamberger and Fuld hosting lunch for six hundred friends and business associates in the store's restaurant. Bamberger reluctantly agreed to make a few introductory remarks in which he credited his three thousand fellow co-workers for the firm's success. He then introduced Fuld, whose reputation as a great storyteller made him an excellent toastmaster.[3]

Present were the owners of New York's leading department stores, including Jesse I. Straus of R. H. Macy & Co., Messrs. Bernard and Louis

Gimbel of Gimbel Brothers, and Samuel Bloomingdale of Blooming-dale Brothers.[4] At the speakers' table were two Newark councilmen; two US congressmen; the presidents of Public Service, Prudential Insurance Company, National Newark and Essex Banking Company, and Fidelity Union Trust Company; and the owners of the *Newark Evening News, Newark Star-Eagle, Newark Ledger,* and *Newark Sunday Call.* In other words, all of Newark's power brokers had come to honor Louis Bamberger and Felix Fuld, who that same year had been chosen by *Sunday Call* readers as two of the "fifty men and women who accomplished the most for Newark."[5]

Louis Wiley, the business manager of the *New York Times,* speaking on behalf of New York's newspapers, congratulated the firm for building what he termed "one of the largest department stores in the East."[6] Keynote speaker James W. Gerard, ambassador to Germany, said that America's department stores were a key to the nation's economic progress: "Department stores did more for democracy than any other agency, because they brought to the people an opportunity to obtain the things that once upon a time were available only to the rich."[7] Newark mayor Thomas Breidenbach told the audience that these two merchants had positioned their store as the nucleus around which a greater Newark of a million people could be built.[8] More important, Breidenbach asserted that the "future development of Newark was not hampered by its proximity to New York."[9]

The festivities did not match the fanfare of the store's 1912 opening, attributable to the dampening effect of what was described as America's worst depression in thirty years.[10] Critics asked: Didn't Mr. Bamberger realize that America was in the midst of this depression caused by post–World War I overproduction and surplus of inventories? Experts argued that business needed to take a breather and wait for a return to "normalcy" and greater growth in the economy. "The store," Bamberger responded, "has felt the depression of course, but what is depression but a forerunner of good times to come?"[11] "Furthermore," he continued, "the store will hardly be ready for good times before they are upon us—and we won't have time to build then."[12] Accordingly, the editors of *Charm,* which started in 1924, avoided the word "depression" and instead referred to a "slump."

The critics did not take into account the "sea of easy credit" made available through Bamberger's use of installment buying and newly established charge accounts. Bamberger was not among the merchants who "hesitated to press desirable customers for prompt payment for fear of driving them to more lenient competitors."[13] Not even the top executive who threatened to close his account because Bamberger's refused to carry his account for a full year could get his way. He reportedly said, "You have more nerve than anyone I've ever known." But he still paid up—and kept the account![14]

The new addition added approximately 118,523 square feet, increasing the store's area to one million square feet, or 22.7 acres. The actual selling space now amounted to over a half million square feet.[15] "The first steel column was set in January 1922 and so rapidly was the work of construction carried on that May 30 saw the second floor opened for selling, fully two months before the building was actually completed," reported the *Newark Evening News*.[16] The Newark papers reported every detail of the eight spacious selling floors, 146 selling departments, the co-worker facilities, the view of the Orange Mountains from the building, the furnishings and wall treatments, the Ivy Tea Room seating 275, and the thirty-five-foot-long soda fountain in black and gold marble, specializing in orange drinks, hot dogs, and a favorite chocolate drink youngsters called "Elsie the Cow"; and the advertising department estimated that the soda fountain would sell one million drinks.[17]

Soon after the opening, Moler presented Bamberger and Fuld with a novel idea for promoting a new line of radio equipment. Moler suggested that creating a radio station would be an indirect but powerful promotional gimmick that could help sell the new wireless sets they stocked. The idea was that customers had no reason to buy a radio receiver if there was nothing to listen to. Fuld, who was easily convinced, turned to Bamberger and said, "Let's try it!" Bamberger nodded yes.[18] Radio was in its infancy when the Bamberger broadcasting station aired its first broadcast on Washington's Birthday 1922. Two days earlier, Bamberger had sent radio engineer Jack Poppele to Washington to personally fetch a radio license from the US Commerce Department. Bamberger wanted his station to be called WLB, but those call letters had just been assigned. Instead, the new station was assigned the call letters WOR and given permission to operate with a transmitter that could broadcast for several hundred miles.[19] WOR was the forty-ninth radio station in America to receive a broadcasting license and the first department store station. Other stores soon followed Bamberger's lead, so that in a few years department stores held 10 percent of all such licenses in the country.[20] According to Newark historian Nat Bodian, "WOR was the only station to broadcast on Christmas Day in 1922 and thus was the first sound heard by those who found a crystal set, or radio, under the tree."[21] Though Bamberger was shown letters expressing how much listeners enjoyed WOR's programs, he remained skeptical about the station's future. No one then making decisions about the station understood radio's potential to entertain and educate or to become a great industry.[22] Rather, Bamberger saw WOR as a "one-year experiment," after which, he told his management team, he would decide whether it should continue. He had to be convinced that his substantial investment of $20,000 was paying off.[23] Bamberger had many things on his mind at the time—overseeing the latest addition, tracking progress on a new delivery station, and opening his basement store. His skepticism about WOR was because of his concern that its added expense would eat into his profits. No day went by that Bamberger did not ask, "What's the bottom line?"

There was nothing glamorous about WOR's first broadcasting studio. Initially it was located in a fifteen-square-foot cubicle in a corner of the radio and sporting goods section on the sixth floor. Rugs borrowed from the carpet department deadened the sound.[24] In 1923 the initial antenna—a piece of wire strung between two poles—was replaced by new two-hundred-foot antennae with a range of one thousand miles. Reception improved and calls came in immediately reporting pickups in Atlantic City, Brooklyn, Staten Island, and as far away as Providence, Rhode Island.[25]

Bamberger tested WOR in January 1923 while on board the SS *Homeric* headed to the Mediterranean. There were other Newarkers on board, and Bamberger thought to entertain them with daily radio concerts and lectures from WOR, since his onboard radio was equipped with an amplifier.[26] To his disappointment, this special wireless apparatus failed to pick up transmissions once the ship was two hundred miles out at sea.[27]

Upon his return, he considered whether to continue WOR. Certainly Bamberger was never afraid to try something new: he was an outspoken enthusiast for scientific advances and modern technology, and the store carried a line of state-of-the-art laborsaving appliances manufactured specially for it. But a radio station was not a product to be sold, and its potential to boost sales was still unknown. Gene Karlin, who worked for the Poppele family in the early 1980s, recalled radio during Bamberger's time "as a medium whose reach and influence on buying habits was still to be determined."[28] WOR's programs were limited to "songs and instrumental selections by local artists, talks for Boy Scouts, weekly tips for motorists, short stories by magazine writers, and bedtime stories for children."[29] Most homes did not yet own radios, and Bamberger gave radio receiver sets to Newark's public schools so schoolchildren could hear some of the cultural programs he funded for their benefit.[30] But so far the radio station had not affected the store's bottom line.

It was Poppele who convinced Bamberger not to "pull the plug" on WOR at a meeting that Poppele and fellow engineer John Gambling (who later became a well-known radio personality himself) never forgot.[31] The two men listened as Bamberger informed them that the store had been in the broadcasting business fourteen months, spent $20,000, and in his opinion had gotten all of the promotion out of WOR that it could.[32] "It has been an interesting experiment," Bamberger said, " but we don't see much of a future for WOR, and we agree that at this point, the best thing to do is to turn back our license to the government. Is there anything that you would like to say?"[33]

Fuld, who was also there, asked how Poppele knew that radio would be commercially successful. Poppele responded that "radio can reach all the people on the air" and that there would come a point when "people wouldn't have to buy records anymore."[34] Harry Hatry, vice president of clothing, also present, sided with Poppele and suggested that WOR stay on the air for at least another two years. When Bamberger asked whether the station was earning any money for the store, Poppele paused, thought for a moment, and proposed an experiment that would determine WOR's fate.

Leaving the meeting, he went directly to Bamberger's housewares department. He introduced himself to the department's china buyer, Pauline Bachmeister, and explained his idea for a radio promotion. The two selected a slow-selling dish, doubled the selling price from seventy-five cents to $1.50, advertised the dish on WOR, and promptly sold two truckloads.[35] "I didn't get in trouble because they sold out," Poppele said.[36] WOR was secure. The next year Poppele married Bachmeister, and WOR got a newly furnished broadcasting station.[37]

No one was happier about Bamberger's new radio station than the sixty-five-year-old, hard-of-hearing gentleman who told a reporter at the New York *Sunday Times* that he had heard a WOR broadcast of a wedding ceremony being conducted in Newark. "Even when I had the best of hearing," he declared, "I never heard a marriage ceremony with such distinctness, including the bridegroom's kiss, as if the whole affair were taking place five feet away in my own home."[38] In October 1923 WOR's listeners were treated to a broadcast by comedian Charlie Chaplin, described as "handsomely garbed in blue and gray."[39] Yet Chaplin drew fewer fans than WOR's broadcasts of morning gym exercises; many listeners wrote to express their appreciation of these shows.[40] It is not known how many listeners tuned in to hear a lecture on the kinds of poisonous serpents found particularly in the Northeast, how to readily distinguish them, and how to treat snakebites with the recent discovery of antitoxin serum. The talk was promoted as featuring a singing snake, and, wrote a *Call* reporter, "Speculation is rife as to what selection will be offered by the singing snake, but odds are on 'How Dry I Am.'"[41] Like the poultry exhibits, the snake was an example of how Bamberger's used the unexpected in its promotions.

In 1923 the store was involved in a test case involving the use of copyrighted music heard over WOR. The American Society of Authors, Composers and Publishers (ASCAP) brought a lawsuit.[42] The issue was whether someone who used copyrighted music for advertising purposes should be required to pay a fee to the copyright owner. The complaint charged that Bamberger's used its broadcasts to advertise itself and stimulate business. Bamberger was not around to respond to the suit—he was on board a ship headed for the Mediterranean. Moler followed his own inclination, which was not to negotiate or settle. In the end Judge Charles Lynch of the New Jersey Federal District Court ruled against Bamberger's, finding that its motives were sufficiently commercial to require that it pay a fee.[43] This victory enabled ASCAP to begin collecting licensing fees from radio stations that played copyrighted music.[44]

The station's value was again clearly evident on January 16, 1924, a stormy Wednesday night when the *Shenandoah*, a big dirigible, wrenched loose from its mast at the naval air base in Lakehurst. Listeners who spotted the dirigible kept the station informed by telephone as to its whereabouts. Their messages were relayed to the *Shenandoah*, helping the ship steer a course to safety.[45] In 1926 WOR got a news scoop, when the steamship SS *President Roosevelt* helped rescue a British cargo ship, the SS *Antinoe*, in the Atlantic. Ten minutes after the *President Roosevelt* was secured at a pier in Hoboken, WOR's crew had pulled microphone and telephone lines aboard and were broadcasting the news of the homecoming heroes to the world. Welcoming the crew and captain of the *President Roosevelt* were Louis Bamberger and Felix Fuld. Seizing this opportunity to promote WOR, Bamberger put the ship's lifeboat at the store's Washington Street entrance.[46]

WOR pioneered a number of technological experiments that proved to be real contributions to broadcasting science and the industry, including the first radio transmission of a photographic image. In 1926 a picture of L. Bamberger & Co.'s buying office in London was sent by radio to the Newark store. It was "the first time in America that a photograph of this kind was used for commercial operation."[47] In 1927 a photograph was sent via radio from Harrods, Ltd., in London to Bamberger's in Newark. It was accompanied by a telephone call from Harrods' owner, Sir Woodman Burbridge, shouting "Hello, Newark!" to Louis Bamberger over a new transoceanic telephone service.[48]

Bamberger believed that transoceanic telephone conversations were the wave of the future and that it would become common practice for companies in Europe and America to order merchandise by telephone. The personal element in a telephone conversation, he told a *Call* reporter, would tend to create a better understanding than was possible in an exchange of cables. However, he warned, "Consideration should be given to the cost for a call lasting five or six minutes—that cost is between $125 and $150."[49] Regardless of cost, "store officials predicted that radio would make it possible to transmit the latest fashions from Europe speedily."[50]

In 1927 Bamberger's management announced that WOR was breaking its tradition of only airing programs with entertainment value and would now add commercials promoting the store's products.[51] The station's new two-hundred-foot broadcast towers were then relocated to a more effective site in Kearny, New Jersey, and WOR was assigned the position 710 on the radio dial, where it has been ever since.[52] Station manager Alfred McCosker believed that WOR would have a greater future if it was tied to New York City, and he transferred its studios and offices to a building near Times Square[53]—though he maintained a recording device that said "WOR, Newark" in order to deceive Newark listeners.[54]

By the late 1920s WOR had become an industry standard. Under Bamberger's ownership, WOR was the first radio station in the East to broadcast opera and air a morning gym class, one of the first to have live audiences (the studio could seat twenty-five) and hold auditions, and the first to be heard across the Atlantic. In 1923 Paul Whiteman and his full orchestra came to Newark to broadcast a "test" program to Japan; and Japan, not used to jazz, nevertheless heard and enjoyed it—seven thousand miles away![55] WOR broadcast Newark's reception for South Pole explorer Admiral Richard Byrd, dedication ceremonies for Beth Israel Hospital, and interviews with sculptor Gutzon Borglum, Charlie Chaplin, Harry Houdini, Thomas A. Edison, Rube Goldberg, and the state's governors and US senators.[56]

Moler's initial idea paid off in a big way. Bamberger's estimated in 1928 that it had received $1 million worth of publicity value from WOR in the previous four years, twice its operating expense.[57]

Starting in 1928, a monthly "Air-Colyum" in *Counter Currents* provided news about WOR. One story reported that M. H. Aylesworth, president of the National Broadcasting Company, asserted at a Washington hearing that it was time for radio authorities to concede that WOR had earned a place among the Big Three privately owned radio broadcasting stations—"not because of its power, nor the amount of money expended, but solely on the basis of the merit of its programs."[58]

In 1929, when Bamberger sold his store to Macy's, WOR was part of the deal. According to Morton Schindel, Louis Bamberger's great-nephew by marriage, Percy Straus called Louis Bamberger to say, "Look, we are getting bills for a radio station. Did we buy that?" Bamberger responded, "I don't have any use for it, just take it." That was how Macy's came to own WOR.[59]

Though he had no interest in running a radio station, Bamberger was a great radio listener. He owned a Capehart radio, the finest of its time, and used it to entertain visitors to his home. His favorite programs were Carnegie Hall Philharmonic concerts featuring Arturo Toscanini.[60] At Fuld's suggestion, they also bought an Estey pipe organ that was kept in the billiards room for guests who wanted to entertain themselves.[61]

On September 13, 1922, Bamberger's introduced yet another innovation when it opened its basement store.[62] There was nothing new about basement stores, which sold discounted items. Marshall Field's called its basement the "Budget Floor," Wanamaker's opened a "Downstairs Store," Stern's in New York had an "Arcade of Inexpensive Shops,"[63] and Filene's "automatic" bargain basement, where the price went down the longer the item stayed on the floor, was perhaps the most famous of all. No matter what they were called, basement stores were responsible for a sizeable share of a store's sales.

In anticipation of the opening, Bamberger instructed his building manager, Abe Schindel, to create a separate entrance at Halsey and Bank Streets leading directly to the basement.[64] The intention was to draw a clear distinction between discounted merchandise and regular priced goods on the upper floors. After all, Bamberger's had spent years cultivating its reputation as a store for middle- and upper-middle-class customers and that image had to be preserved.

For some, basement stores were a way to separate different classes of shoppers. Store owner Louis Stern wrestled with the implications of this practice. "I do not admit there is a necessity for the basement," he said, "since such distinctions [as it fosters] are undemocratic and un-American and alien to the New World ideas of equality."[65] Nevertheless, his store had one. Like Bamberger, he surely realized that the basement store made it possible for less-affluent shoppers to buy products frequently associated with a wealthier middle class. For Stern and other store owners, there was "no reason why Bargain Basements should not be a success."[66]

During the 1920s, the psychology of the modern consumer was taking shape. Shoppers had begun to link their social status to material goods. Their desire to acquire new products and labor-saving appliances to make their homes "modern" was a department store owner's dream that lasted until the 1929 crash pinched most people's pockets.[67]

Bamberger's and other stores added their basement stores in response to this desire among consumers to democratize their shopping experience. Average income earners wanted access to items traditionally associated with upper-class Americans, and the department store was the place to make this happen. The trick for store owners was to capture both markets: those with limited resources and those who were more affluent. Bamberger's was one of the last to take advantage of basement sales to increase its revenue. Bamberger was acutely aware of the growing number of new retailers—variety chain stores

81

such as Kresge, Woolworth, and Penney. Reports of their increased yearly revenue (47 percent versus 38 percent for department stores) had convinced him that it was time to act.[68] Customers had changed, particularly working women who wanted what basement stores and discount chain stores had to offer—cheaper price without sacrificing style. The department store was now "essentially a store of the masses" that catered to a new democracy of consumers as places where "anyone could enter . . . [and] see and handle the most elegant furnishings."[69]

Bamberger's innovation was to break with the pattern of dingy, depressing basements by making its basement store as pleasant as the regular store. It had special ventilation systems, crisply painted white walls, contrasting dark mahogany tables, and generous lighting to make it comfortable to shop in.[70] Basement managers reported that on opening day 21,800 shoppers came to check out the store's newest department.[71] Merchandise sold out fast, prompting Bamberger's to increase the advertising budget in order to create a separate basement advertising department.[72] Joe Farrell, a well-known store detective, was hired to see "that customers didn't have their pockets picked."[73] At night Dobermans checked security on all floors; the kennel was on the roof of the store.[74]

Bamberger's promoted the basement as "a store in itself." Separate pages of advertising were devoted solely to items sold there, including ads promoting a "basement fashion show" of the up-to-date merchandise it carried. Sales personnel were expected to welcome basement shoppers with the same courtesy as those on upper floors. After all, a woman on a tight budget would still want to brag that she shopped at Bamberger's. In one promotion, Mrs. A. Harry Moore, the wife of New Jersey's governor, agreed to judge a junior girls' sewing contest. Forty-three schoolgirls assembled dresses in two-and-a-half hours, sitting at sewing machines lined up in the aisle of the basement store.[75] The basement store supplied the silk for free. The fifty dollars in prizes awarded to the three winners was nothing compared to the priceless citywide publicity the store received.

One contest conducted by the basement store had nothing to do with fashion. In 1925 Bamberger's participated in the thrift essay contest being conducted in stores nationwide to encourage Americans to save. After receiving five hundred essays from youngsters age ten to eighteen, store executives said they were delighted with the response. The contest also reinforced Bamberger's constant reminder to its employees to save for a "rainy day."[76]

With the war over, Bamberger's upper floors were once again stocked with items purchased by its buyers in France, Belgium, Holland, Germany, Czechoslovakia, and Italy.[77] In contrast to the fine china, Venetian glassware, English pottery, mechanical toys, and sturdy Scotch table damask and napkins upstairs, the basement held sales on endless yards of oilcloth.[78] "My first memory of the store," recalled Dorothy Kosec, "was being dragged there by my mother as she shopped in the basement. It seems we never got to shop above it."[79]

At this time of prosperity, a "splendid tall doorman in [Bamberger's] employ watched over infants sleeping in their carriages waiting for their mothers to finish shopping and [would] wheel them inside into the vestibule to get them out of the cold."[80] The doorman also opened cab doors for passengers dropped at the main entrance.[81] Another of his duties was to keep one eye on the nun stationed outside the entrance who sat with a donation basket on her lap and the other eye on a crippled man selling pencils.[82] The rumor was he died a rich man from selling those pencils. George Zeevalk had a pretzel stand in front of Bam's.[83] "I have never had a soft pretzel as good as the ones sold right in front of Bamberger's," remarked pretzel fan Leslie Pumphrey.[84] Her friend Janet B. Davidson washed hers down with an orange drink at the stand adjacent to the escalator on the store's first floor.[85]

Inside the store, some customers, such as Dorothy Strand, checked a small table filled with odd spoons, hoping to find a silver pattern matching the one they had at home.[86] Others descended the "incredible gold swirling stairway" whose marble steps led to the Tea Room, where for many the dessert choice was a "no-brainer": the clown ice cream cone, in which the ice cream (the clown's head) sat on a round cookie (the clown's collar) with raisins for the eyes, nose, and mouth and the cone sitting like a dunce cap on top.[87]

In 1927 Bamberger's adopted the slogan "All Roads Lead to Newark." An advertisement showed a map of New Jersey towns with the number of miles and minutes required to reach the store by automobile from each one. Many residents traveled by bus. But whether you took the bus, the train, or the subway, you were likely to meet someone under the Bamberger clock. "Newark was the greatest city in the state and Bamberger's was the center of our universe," recalled Ruth Dargan, summing up what Bamberger's meant to people.[88]

With the expansion came more benefits for employees. Employee welfare programs sponsored by department stores were not new, though Bamberger's policy of "merit holidays," under which employees got half-days off based on perfect attendance, was perhaps unique. Perfect attendance during the holiday season from Thanksgiving to the end of December was mandatory. In 1897 when the Co-Workers Association had been created, it was viewed as an experiment. By the 1920s it was one of the most important aspects of store life. The association's continued growth was made possible by the firm's generosity, since "the financial statement showed that dues from co-workers did not nearly meet the sick benefits paid back to them."[89] Death benefits, never part of the arrangement with the Co-Worker's Association, were automatically charged to the firm.[90]

By 1922 Bamberger's had expanded its in-house hospital and medical department, which had been created in 1913. There was a dentist's room with up-to-date equipment that provided treatment at small cost to the worker. Co-workers were constantly reminded to make an appointment to have their teeth cleaned, since a sweet smile went a long way in making a sale. There was a medical doctor; a chiropodist, or foot doctor, to provide care for the aching feet that were a hazard of the profession; and nurses who made house calls. Tending to a worker's health was good business. So were the co-workers' cafeteria with inexpensive meals, rest lounges and meeting rooms for employee clubs, an in-house branch of the Newark Public Library, marching bands and choral groups, rooftop dances, and sports teams (golf, baseball, bowling, and rifle competition) that improved morale. The store also provided free legal services to its co-workers. Many, if not most, of America's department stores instituted similar amenities. However, few (if any) were contacted by the government of the Soviet Union, whose authorities "had been informed that, in their opinion, Bamberger's employee cafeteria was one of the best from the standpoint of organization, layout and equipment."[91] Wanting to keep pace with rapid industrialization, including "the trend towards organizing cafeterias in factories, stores, and schools," the Soviets asked Bamberger's to send an "outline" of its cafeteria plan, which would be included in the government's "Russian

Food Industries Bulletin," to explain the organization and management "of a representative cafeteria such as yours."[92]

Communicating with five thousand employees on a regular basis was no small task, and Bamberger used every means at his disposal to earn their loyalty. Since management could not speak directly to co-workers individually, a large assembly hall on the street floor of the Union Club building adjacent to the store's main building was used to host continuously rotating "big group" meetings,[93] which large numbers of employees were required to attend. Not every employee read *Counter Currents*, so this was an opportunity to learn about what was going on in the store, such as a selling department being relocated to a different floor. Bamberger wanted his employees to know that he trusted them to be fair and honest in their jobs, so the routine of punching a time clock was eliminated in favor of an "honor time system" of time sheets on which workers recorded their own hours.[94] In this way co-workers came to realize that Louis Bamberger really did see them as members of his greater Bamberger family.

As every shopper knew, Bamberger's prided itself on its ability to deliver packages to a customer's home quickly. The earliest delivery route went through Verona, Caldwell, Boonton, Parsipanny, West Livingston, and back to Newark for a total round-trip of ninety-six miles.[95] Summer routes were added for Jersey shore residents whose orders were relayed by telephone twice a day to the store and delivered the next day by the Asbury Park service station. As the territory covered by Bamberger's delivery service expanded and orders by telephone increased, it became evident that the delivery department had to be enlarged and streamlined. As Bamberger told the *Call*, "Something had to be done to get the store's delivery trucks and wagons off of Halsey Street to eliminate congestion in the thoroughfare."[96] Bamberger searched Newark for land close to his downtown store suitable for a large delivery station. In May 1924, Bamberger's bought the site of the old city almshouse on Elizabeth Avenue at public auction for $200,000. The estimated cost of erecting the delivery service station and warehouse was $1 million. In 1925, in anticipation of the increased demands on its business, Bamberger's announced the opening of "the largest remote delivery building and service station operated by any retail dry-goods association in the world."[97] Its priority was to consolidate merchandise located in the outer buildings surrounding the main store.

Among the service station's features were a three-minute car wash and a conveyor belt that made it possible to unload fifty furniture trucks simultaneously.[98] Keeping track of each delivery truck as it arrived was the task of a full-time garage attendant who relied on roller skates to get around the thirty-thousand-square-foot space.[99] Records set for volume of packages delivered by the store's drivers were impressive by any modern standard. Tours of the facility were conducted for visitors who came from large department stores around the country, including one foreign delegation.[100] There was one unexpected visit from a "certain gentleman well known to everybody, who when he walked in was almost handed an application form to fill out. It was Mr. Bamberger!"[101] By 1929 Bamberger's trucks were delivering an average of twenty thousand packages every day to customers in 543 towns.[102] One can imagine Bamberger's satisfaction in knowing that his substantial investment had paid off.

Bamberger's policy was to "offer the service of its men and trucks unreservedly in any emergency."[103] It was not unusual for deliverymen to help a distressed housewife find her child's bicycle, rescue a cat from a tree, change the tire of a stranded motorist, or help mothers find missing children. When an explosion at Hercules Powder in Dover captured nationwide attention, two Bamberger deliverymen, Joseph Orsi and Eugene Belanger, who were returning to the store when the explosion occurred, turned their truck around and rushed to carry 270 people to safety zones. Orsi also gave money to a woman he didn't know so she could get herself and her children home.[104]

Driving shiny trucks with Bamberger's green-and-gold logo on the side and dressed in specially designed uniforms, Bamberger's deliverymen represented customer service at its best. Numerous letters praising a driver's good deeds were sent to Bamberger's attention and printed in *Counter Currents* for fellow workers to read. Several examples stand out. One deliveryman climbed to the second story of a customer's home and through an open window because the customer's door had accidentally closed. Another called the customer to say that he was delivering her son's bicycle to the back of the house to avoid being spotted by the boy, who was playing out front. He knew the bicycle was meant to be a surprise.[105]

On December 31, 1922, the headline of an article in the *Newark Sunday Call* reported that L. Bamberger planned "To Erect Model Home in Newark." The store had bought property and intended to construct an eleven-room brick home, the store's "Ideal Home," at 725 Elizabeth Avenue, opposite Weequahic Park. The model home was designed to capitalize on a nationwide program promoting home ownership that was sponsored by the Commerce Department's Division of Building and Housing. Under Commerce Secretary Herbert Hoover's supervision, America was "blanketed with home buying ideas."[106] Department stores and museums cooperated by adding model rooms to their offerings. Hoover, who wanted people to consume all the new goods America's industries were producing, hired a staff to investigate what the nation's consumers wanted. Little wonder that several years later department store owners backed Hoover's presidential campaign; his strategies coincided with their interests.

The model home had proven popular in other cities, but Bamberger's was the first one to be erected in Newark. It functioned as a showcase for items sold at the store. It had three floors with living, eating, and sleeping areas and novel features such as hot water heaters for the baths, burglar alarms, burglar lights, a radio set without an outside aerial, electric range, washing machine, mangle clothes dryer, and an intrahouse telephone system with call bells (doorbells). A two-car garage in the rear had a heating plant, electrical lathes, and a workbench. There was an all-electric laundry room, a garbage incinerator, and other labor-saving devices. The cost of all this luxury was $75,000.[107] As was its custom, Bamberger's listed the names of local firms and individuals involved in the construction. It was expected that the contents of the rooms and the labor-saving devices would tempt even the most resistant buyers to makes changes to their homes. After all, it was the "Ideal Home."

Once the guest registers showed that more than two hundred thousand people, some from foreign countries, had visited the site, it was decided that all who were going to visit had done so. A year after its opening, the home was sold for $80,000 to Harry A. Braelow, who had made his fortune in the newspaper delivery business.[108] A second fully furnished model home, in Teaneck, opened in 1926 and was intended to expand Bamberger's coverage to towns in northern New Jersey. A third home fully furnished by Bamberger's, Nottingham House, was built in Short Hills, to the west.

Bamberger's "Ideal Homes" were promoted in *Charm*, a new upscale women's fashion magazine that debuted on February 1, 1924.[109]

Charm, which consistently focused readers' attention on a New Jersey world with Newark at its core, was in the tradition of earlier upscale department store magazines—Wanamaker's *La Dernière Heure à Paris*, Marshall Field's *Fashions of the Hour*, and Filene's *Clothes*,[110] but its content was more sophisticated. Its only competition among department store publications was the sleek and glossy *Modes and Manners*, produced by Standard Corporation of New York for eight major department stores in Toledo, Cincinnati, Boston, St. Louis, Pittsburgh, San Francisco, Philadelphia, and Los Angeles, with different ads for each store. All these publications were intended to create the desire to acquire goods by associating "feminism" (a word whose meaning has changed since then) with luxury and social status.[111]

The *Call*'s managing editor, William S. Hunt, gave *Charm* a generous review. "It is every inch a peer among its kind generally, and among a select class of the best of its kind and it stands among those at the top."[112] "Its scope as revealed by the contents of the first number, is generously broad, and its readers will find themselves in an atmosphere of aesthetics, information and suggestion much wider and free than any of any business between four walls."[113] He added that it would be no surprise if *Charm* were read with as much interest and profit in Los Angeles as in Newark.

Charm was published in-house by a new company called the L. Bamberger & Co. Publishing Company. The editor was Elizabeth D. Adams. Its editorial staff, composed mainly of women recruited from the best magazines in the country, was housed in separate quarters at 50 Bank Street.[114] *Charm* was the brainchild of Walter Moler. It was, according to authors John E. O'Connor and Charles F. Cummings, "the most ambitious effort of any American retail establishment to identify with its clientele through the publication of a general-interest magazine."[115] Subtitled "The Magazine of New Jersey Home Interests," it was also a running cultural commentary for a new generation of progressive women interested in 1920s modernism.[116] Alongside pieces aiming to inform and entertain these women were extensive fashion features to guide their clothing choices.[117] Readers could expect to find items on sports, drama, fiction, fashion, society, gardens, decoration, and household advice, as well as essays about poetry.[118] It seems that Bamberger, as an enthusiastic patron of the arts and humanities, was responsible for the magazine's focus.

Charm was sent to eighty thousand residents of northern New Jersey who had charge accounts at Bamberger's.[119] *Charm* had snob appeal; it flattered its readers by addressing them as though they were members of the country club set, for example, with articles about European travels, debutante "coming out" parties, dog and horse shows, and how to choose a country club or private school.[120] Judging by letters sent to the Bamberger store, the magazine was well received. One patron wrote, "My first copy of *Charm* reached me this morning, and I wish to thank you for numbering me among the recipients. I am sure that I shall enjoy it as thoroughly as I have enjoyed dealing in your wonderful store. Thank you again and my good wishes for your continued success."[121]

Charm's contents set it apart from other department store house organs. It was not a merchandise catalog or advertising brochure but a magazine showcasing the good life. Each issue opened with a section of real estate advertisements for expensive homes in exclusive neighborhoods; real estate developers assured potential buyers that the communities were "rigidly restricted"—an indication that Jews and other undesirables need not apply. (One might wonder whether this restriction would include Mr. Bamberger; it was not a secret that he was Jewish, and it was known that he preferred not to mix business with religion or politics.) The articles might suggest fairly subtly that, for example, life would be more pleasant if shoppers took advantage of Bamberger's free package delivery. From time to time *Charm* held meetings to inform salespeople about its future plans. There is no record, however, of how a saleswoman working long hours standing on her feet might have felt about New Jersey yachting or sports fashions shown at Giralda Farms, the estate of Geraldine Rockefeller Dodge.[122]

Above all, *Charm* promoted the advantages of living in New Jersey by receiving support from Newark's newspaper editors. Thus *Charm* hailed the opening in 1927 of the Holland Tunnel, which by connecting New Jersey to New York automatically increased the property value in northern New Jersey. Now, the editors pointed out, New Yorkers would have increased opportunities to shop in Newark, the metropolis of New Jersey and the retail center for approximately one million people.[123] At *Charm*'s invitation, Lois Long, a regular writer for the *New Yorker*, authored a piece titled "A New Yorker Shops in Newark," in which she touted that city's shops in general and Bamberger's in particular, and ended up wondering "why the New Jersey population doesn't snub New York entirely."[124]

Articles by John Cotton Dana, director of the Newark Museum, paid homage to the rise of the American department store with its products of "a thousand varied industries that challenged the museum as we know it." In one article published in the *Museum*, the official publication of the Newark Museum, Dana named ten items priced below one dollar and explained how they "may be arranged into an exhibit that combined beauty with simplicity and utility."[125] Dana, probably the first US museum director to dare conduct large expositions of industrially made goods, told *Charm's* readers that the function of museums was to show the meaning of the arts in relation to industrial society to be "filled with objects closely associated with the life of the people."[126] The items he chose for his exhibits were from Bamberger's. Not coincidentally, it was Bamberger who financed the Newark Museum and indirectly Dana's job.

In April 1928, at a time when the art world's favorite word was "modern," *Charm* featured a cover designed and signed by Pablo Picasso. The editors wanted readers to identify Bamberger's with the idea of modernism. In March 1929, six months before the "crash" ushered in the Great Depression, *Charm* ran a cover featuring a prosperous New Jerseyan being handed stock quotations from his butler, as his hunting trophies looked on quizzically. The illustrator was Constantin Alajalov, who also did "modern" covers for the *New Yorker*.

Walter Moler, *Charm's* guiding hand, died in 1928, and in December 1929 *Charm* moved to new offices on the seventh floor of the main Bamberger building. During the Depression, the editorial staff was cut back; and the magazine became strictly a merchandise promotion vehicle, a fate that befell other department store publications as well.[127] *Charm* lasted only two years into the Depression. It had never been meant to pay for itself, and even at a greatly reduced forty-eight pages per issue, the expense of publishing it had to be justified. With Moler gone, no one was left to advocate for continuing it. The February 1932 issue asked readers to send in a ballot indicating whether they were willing to contribute fifty cents toward postage and handling. Too few responded, so that issue was the last. While it was published, *Charm* served its purpose of maintaining a positive public image of Bamberger's exceptionally well. Ultimately, it merged with *Glamour* magazine.[128]

During the 1920s, Bamberger had become concerned by the growth of the city's suburbs. Small-town merchants were eating into his trade. As long as affluent people lived in Newark, there was no question that they would shop at Bamberger's: Bamberger's had built its considerable reputation on servicing their needs. However, once resettled in the suburbs, previously frequent customers might be tempted to buy what they could in their local specialty stores, saving trips to the city for items that could be found only there. Bamberger's tactics for regaining these shoppers were similar to those of Gimbels, Hudson's, Macy's, and Schuster's in Milwaukee. For example, he added a Thanksgiving Day parade to the store's schedule of holiday events.[129] Creating events leading up to the Christmas buying season was the lifeblood of any retail business.

"The first (and original) Thanksgiving Day parades were presented by Bamberger's starting in 1924," asserted a 1984 letter-to-the-editor in the *Star-Ledger*. "Macy's bought Bamberger's in 1929 and 'kidnapped the parade.' How do I know? My father, Abe Schindel, was the Bamberger executive who helped stage the parade."[130] "The Straus brothers at Macy's did not originate the spectacle Thanksgiving Day parade; Gimbels in Philadelphia and Eaton's Department Store in Toronto were moving in this direction for many years,"[131] and Bamberger would have known this. Although Macy's purchased Bamberger's and took the parade to New York, it is still remembered by thousands throughout North Jersey as a tradition that originated in Newark.[132] In 1931 a "new" Thanksgiving Day parade under Macy's control returned to Newark; it remained an annual event through the early 1950s.[133] Newark residents recalled store workers "in white gloves and white face" who were paid to march in the parade and entertain thousands of spectators lining the five-mile parade route, which ended at the store. At that point, Santa stepped off a huge float onto a marquee located on the store's second floor and waved to the cheering crowds before entering the store. Once inside, he was enthroned at a spot of honor among the stacks and racks of toys in Bamberger's Toyland.[134] Thus did Bamberger's Thanksgiving Day parade signal the start of the Christmas shopping season.

For Bamberger's the parade was more than a way to increase sales. The management saw it as a community service and made sure the parade route included stops at the city's orphanages, nursing homes, and poor neighborhoods, so all could share in the Christmas spirit. After the parade, there was a big party for all the employees and their families. Gretchen Fisher, whose father had the job of overseeing the parade, recalled that Mr. Bamberger "gave her a really pretty doll with a little suit case filled with clothes."[135]

There was no Christmas without at least one Santa. Bamberger's had three, stationed on three different floors, so that youngsters could meet Santa and have their picture taken with him. In 1926 a suggestion that children write to Santa and tell him what they wished for netted 55,000 letters.[136] In this season, toys were Bamberger's chief moneymakers, and they took over the store. Parents were told to see Toyland through the eyes of an eight-year-old in order to appreciate the store's efforts to make Christmas special for youngsters of all ages.

Christmas was the only time that department store window displays were exempt from "good taste." It was not unusual to put "live people, animals, and moving objects in holiday windows that were accepted and admired by all."[137] In 1927 Bamberger's featured six live reindeer flown in from Sinrak, Alaska, and accompanied by a family of Eskimos that included Iutuk, his wife, and their three children, who tended the reindeer and sat in the store's toy department. They arrived before Thanksgiving to get the Christmas shopping season started. WOR broadcast a half-hour spot in which Iutuk, with a translator standing by, spoke to listeners in his native tongue.[138] When the Eskimo family came to dinner at Edgar Bamberger's home in West Orange, the Bamberger youngsters at the table kept sniffing the air, wondering where the "unusual" odor was coming from, until they realized that the Eskimos' clothing was saturated with the smell of whale blubber.[139]

An estimated one hundred thousand visitors over ten days made the trip to Newark to gawk at the Eskimos in their native dress and to stare at the reindeer bedded down in the windows. There was a "traffic jam on a scale Newark had never seen before."[140] The idea was that shoppers would get their fill of the novelty and then go inside to make their Christmas purchases. Unfortunately, because this particular November was unseasonably warm, the reindeer began to shed their antlers. This created a major problem, since the highlight of the Thanksgiving Day parade that year was supposed to be the real reindeer pulling Santa's float. A smart employee came up with the solution of wiring the antlers onto the reindeer.[141] After the season, the reindeer were moved to High Point Park as permanent guests, while the Eskimo family returned to Alaska.[142]

In 1925, the year after the International Exposition of Decorative Arts in Paris, so-called "modern windows" or "artistic showcases," critical for establishing a department store's reputation as chic and up-to-date, were introduced. During the 1920s, Bamberger's windows followed Paris's lead by showcasing visions of the good life. Their simplicity, style, and careful placement of mannequins captured Paris elegance, creating an "atmosphere of reality" that complemented the stories in *Charm*.[143] Window displays had themes: sports; vacations (for example, mannequins playing shuffleboard); what to take on an airplane flight; toys galore. Outfits for college, for horseback riding, for the opera, and for the winter social season were accessorized to look real. According to Morton Schindel, the displays were designed by Tony Sarg, the puppeteer who also staged Macy's earliest Thanksgiving Day parades.[144]

Other displays featured promotions for Westinghouse products and a display of antique violins worth $7.5 million.[145] Bamberger's participated in a citywide celebration of Thomas Edison's Golden Light Jubilee. A window displayed a relief of Edison, but no caption identifying him. One young mother threw her arms up and said to her son, "Joey, look, Columbus! Now ain't that nice of Bamberger's to put Columbus in the window on his birthday!"[146] Bamberger's even brought Chopin's piano to Newark.[147]

Bamberger's closed its books in 1925 with the largest gross volume of business in its history.[148] Such success convinced Bamberger it was time to plan another expansion, no matter how messy and disruptive the process was. On June 14, 1925, he announced plans for a fourteen-story addition to the original building. His architect was Jarvis Hunt, who had designed the 1912 store and the Newark Museum. The new building was constructed between 1926 and 1929, with 1927 being described as the "best business year shown in the city's history" by Charles D. Brady, district manager of R. G. Dun & Co.[149] Attributing Newark's prosperity to the large amount of labor it employed directly and indirectly in all kinds of construction, Brady added that "in mercantile lines the outstanding feature is the prosperity enjoyed by the large department stores, an indication of which was the completion of a building erected for one concern at a cost of $12,000,000."[150] He was referring, of course, to Bamberger's newest addition. The final cost was closer to $14 million, because they added such features as a tearoom and pet shop that had not been in the original design.[151]

To fund this ambitious project, in 1926 L. Bamberger & Co. announced an increase in its capital stock from $5 to $10 million. Bamberger, the majority shareholder, held 19,249 shares—one more than Fuld.[152] Typically, Bamberger wanted to share the windfall; and he suggested to Fuld that they reserve a block of shares for the co-workers, who were given a chance to purchase up to ten shares on installment through deductions from their salaries, not to exceed two years. More than seven hundred co-workers had the opportunity to purchase eleven thousand shares of stock.[153] It is not known if Bamberger's employees took him up on his offer.

During 1928 Bamberger's management was totally occupied with the impending opening of the newest and most ambitious addition in the store's history. The building committee tested chairs for the new shoe department, while engineers, electricians, and carpenters pored over blueprints "rolled on desks, standing in corners, on shelves, spread out on long tables." Even as wrecking was under way from the top of the building, the foundations were being put in. The intention was that the work would proceed without discomfort to employees or shoppers during the Christmas rush season, which is what happened.[154]

The last beam was raised on March 1, 1928. Sidewalk spectators watched as workmen climbed out on the overhanging boom, some two hundred feet in the air, to release the guy ropes attached to the derrick. The steel workers paused for a moment and unfurled an American flag, which they placed at the top of the beam. It drew applause as it flew in the breeze.[155] In mid-January 1929, the *Newark News* reported, "All is completed about the conversion of two buildings into one. Unique about the connection is the fact that it not only will tie in the old and new structures, but will be superimposed on the old one so that six stories of the connection will overlap the old eight-story building"— which was done by welding.[156]

On completion the new addition towered sixteen stories above street level and descended four stories below the street. Each of the eight aboveground selling floors comprised approximately eighty thousand square feet. Two of the four basement levels were selling floors for the basement store. Delivery trucks could drive directly into one of the freight elevators and be taken down four levels to the area where the cargo was unloaded — an engineering feat for the time.[157]

The store proper now totaled 1,240,000 square feet and required an "electric generating plant sufficient in size to light a city of 65,000" to run it (which included cooling the fur storage vaults holding $8 million worth of furs).[158] The addition had doubled the store to twenty-six acres of selling space. Every improvement was reported. There were manufacturing facilities on-site as well as a completely furnished three-story model home. Every floor of the old building was completely remodeled. Thirty-two elevators traveled six hundred feet per minute with every rider feeling confident that the elevator operator knew where to let each one off.

Bamberger's dream of his store filling an entire city block had now actually come true.[159] For a small city such as Newark, this modern, larger Bamberger's was akin to the "eighth wonder of the world." Its size and the diversity of its offerings required some adjustment, particularly among longtime shoppers. During construction, Bamberger had fed public curiosity by issuing regular progress reports. Before the official opening, Bamberger's provided an in-store tour guide titled "What to See — and Where to See It in the Greater Bamberger Store," which gave customers a plan of every sales floor and the precise location of each department on that floor. It advised customers to start at the top (or tenth floor), noting that they could reach it in fifty-two seconds on one of the sixteen new elevators,[160] and then work their way down to the basement. "If you were to examine every detail beginning at the street floor we fear you should never get beyond that fascinating section. But if you start at the top you'll at least know that you must reach the bottom by nightfall in order to get home." The printed guides were available at each entrance and could be taken home for study to make return shopping trips easier.[161]

Like other department stores, Bamberger's had special in-store services unknown to shoppers of today. Long gone are places to apply for fishing and hunting licenses, branches of the US Post Office and the public library, custom-embroidered linens, and in-house engraved stationery, jewelry, gold watches, and silver. You could get cutlery, hosiery, umbrellas, eyeglasses, gloves, jewelry, shoes, oriental rugs, furs, and luggage repaired; and if you were willing to wait, you could get your tennis racket restrung. The four Grossman siblings asked their aunt

Bessie Posner to purchase silverware at Bamberger's for their parents' twenty-fifth wedding anniversary. A Bamberger's saleswoman who knew her stock offered Posner an unclaimed order of silver flatware for twelve that had been engraved with the letter *G*, so Posner bought the silver at a significant discount.[162]

If Bamberger had been asked what department he truly cherished, he probably would have said fine groceries. It stocked cheeses from all over; English biscuits; Scotch and Irish jams, preserves, and marmalades; and German and Austrian tins of fancy fish. "If it was rare and exotic, Bam's had it in the grocery department along with home-baked goods," recalled Ben Kanter.[163] Bamberger's had a grocery house label, Fruitidor Brand. Paul Shapiro became a salesman, then a buyer, in the Fruitidor department. In 1941 the army considered this a qualification for making him a cook before shipping him to the front lines as a combat infantryman.[164] Richard Schlenger worked "in the food department which I think was on the seventh floor. I had to remove the labels on nationally known food products and attach new labels on jars/cans with Bamberger's private label 'Fruitidor.'" He thought this switch probably "enabled the store to charge more than the normal manufacturer's price."[165] Fan G. Mulvaney, who sold cosmetics in the basement store, also recalled how Bamberger's put its name on everything it sold — even bottles of Chanel No. 5.[166]

Comptroller Frank Liveright marveled that "as our physical plant grew our sales kept pace!"[167] With a gross profit of $38 million at the close of 1928, Bamberger's ranked fourth in sales nationally behind R. H. Macy, Marshall Field, and J. L. Hudson. According to Newark historian Nat Bodian, Bamberger's was "unquestionably the most diversified of any of the top four."[168] Felix Fuld's New Year's forecast in January 1929 predicted another good year for Bamberger's ahead.[169] Then on January 20 Fuld died of pneumonia. Less than six months later, Bamberger accepted an offer and sold his business. Characteristically, he was careful to secure his employees' future by negotiating the best terms possible.

A collective gasp was heard throughout Newark and Essex County on June 29, 1929, when the *Newark Evening News* announced, "Bamberger & Co. Reported Sold to R. H. Macy of New York."[170] The sale came as a complete surprise. "Mr. Bamberger had taken few persons into his confidence while negotiations with the Macy representatives were taking place," the *News* reported.[171] Frank Liveright recalled receiving a call "one day in June" from a broker who said, "I understand Macy's is going to buy Bamberger's. Macy's stock is going up like crazy."[172] The next morning Bamberger was besieged with requests for interviews by reporters looking to confirm that negotiations were going on and asking whether a deal had been made and what the terms were. "I have no statement to make," Bamberger responded. "If Macy's wants to tell about it that is up to them. If I had anything to say about it at this time I would tell a representative of the *Newark Evening News.*" Macy's executives admitted that there was a deal, but would say nothing further.[173] Bamberger told Liveright that he wouldn't be at the regular 9 A.M. meeting of the store's executives—a surprise in itself, since Bamberger was a creature of habit—but he would be in the office at 4 P.M. and wanted to meet with the executive committee then.[174] Most of the members came on the run, and all were obviously agitated until Jesse Straus and his two brothers, who were present, assured them that L. Bamberger & Co. would retain its characteristics and the policies that made it the remarkable store that it was. Only then did they smile and offer a round of applause. Mrs. Fuld was present and took an active interest in the proceedings, since she and Louis had entire financial control of the business. Still in mourning for the passing of her husband, she exchanged congratulations with the Straus brothers, but was rescued from the photographers by Mr. Bamberger. Instead, Bamberger posed for a picture with the brothers, who arranged themselves behind his chair. He turned to the photographer with a smile and said, "You see, I have plenty of backing now."[175]

It had taken exactly ten days to complete the agreement. The New York banking firm Lehman Brothers had initially approached Bamberger in early June with an offer from the Straus interests, then conducted the negotiations.[176] Lehman, which had negotiated terms for Julius Rosenwald when Sears became a publicly traded corporation, was a natural fit with Bamberger and Straus. All three families were part of the close-knit society of well-to-do New York German Jews who knew each other socially, through business, and as influential philanthropists.

The sale went smoothly because Bamberger and Mrs. Fuld were receptive to the offer. Asked if he had acted too impulsively, Bamberger responded, "If you get a good offer, take it . . . Don't wait and bargain."[177] Bamberger never discussed his decision to sell. He was afraid that someone would spill the beans and complicate the sale. Asked what his family thought about the sale, his great-niece Ellen Bamberger De Franco was still of the opinion that the family thought of them [the Straus brothers] as "evil for taking their store."[178] Bea Epstein of Bayonne, who can be taken as representative of the general public's reaction, also had a hard time accepting the sale. "It was always there," she said. "We always found Bamberger's name wherever we went. We were always aware that there was a man behind the store name."[179]

Initially it was thought that Macy's paid more than $25 million in cash and stock to acquire the outstanding five hundred thousand shares of Bamberger stock. Later the purchase price was revised to upward of $40 million.[180] Based on past performance, Macy's management expected Bamberger's to do an annual business of over $50 million within a short time and to earn a profit of $4 to $5 million annually.

What prompted Louis Bamberger to sell? He gave out that his age (seventy-four) was his number one reason. "I am getting old and want to be relieved of active management of the business which I founded. It is a big business."[181] Those close to him believed that the deciding factor was the deaths of both Fuld and Moler within months of one another.[182] He would have had to rebuild his inner circle of advisors, a task that would take years, and time was not on his side. It was time, he said, for him to devote more attention to the charities he supported.

Bamberger had survived the historic dips and swings of the American economy, and it is also possible that he simply sensed that it was time to sell. A sudden unexplained drop in stock prices on the New York exchange — the stock market crash of March 25, 1929 — was quickly dismissed by investors, but Bamberger may have taken it more seriously. He had sufficient confidence in the economy, however, to open a new Paris bureau, known as Service Aimee, in May 1929.[183] It offered information about shopping, theater tickets, where to dine, what to see, how to go, where to find an American doctor or dentist, a needle and thread, or a glass of ice water (something that was scarce in Paris). These were the same services customers were accustomed to when they shopped in Bamberger's Newark store (plus there was always a glass of ice water nearby).

A case can be made that it was precisely the overhead required to provide such an extraordinary range of services and amenities that led to stores such as Bamberger's becoming too cost-inefficient to survive. When the Great Depression struck, there was no way to keep up with the cost of these services and maintain the excessive numbers of employees needed to provide them. Stores in major cities, whose shoppers had moved to the surrounding suburbs, discovered that the future lay in chain stores.

Fellow department store owners, including the eighteen members of the Retail Research Association (RRA), were incensed by the secrecy of Bamberger's negotiations. Fred Lazarus and Louis Kirstein were engaged in their own secret plan to create Federated Department Stores, and the sale of L. Bamberger occurred just as the merger was completed. Macy's owners were not members of the RRA and had no plans to join Federated.[184] Why didn't Bamberger give the RRA a chance to buy shares or ownership? Fred Lazarus wanted to know. Louis Kirstein was livid when he got news of the sale and insisted that Bamberger should have contributed some of his stock to the creation of Federated Department Stores, one of the biggest merger events of the decade. They accused Bamberger of "going over to the archenemy" — Macy's.[185] But if Bamberger had signaled that he wanted to include RRA members, that would have been the end of the sale.

Another disgruntled person who felt he was entitled to a share of the profits from the sale was Felix Fuld's half-brother, Horace. Right after the sale was announced, he accused Bamberger and his sister-in-law of stealing his inheritance. Horace claimed that $25,000 had been given to Felix by their father to be used to buy in to the start-up of L. Bamberger & Co. department store, or as Horace put it, Bamberger's "Newark proposition."[186] Horace claimed he was told he would have a job when he returned from World War I and threatened Carrie with a lawsuit. He wanted the money returned. There is no information as to whether he ever filed the suit.

In Bamberger's mind, the only group entitled to an explanation of his action was his employees. Standing on the store's balcony, he told the co-workers assembled on the floor below that "ever since Mr. Fuld died, I have spent a great deal of time thinking about the best thing to do with this institution. I decided to sell the store to some concern or to sell it to the co-workers."[187] He explained that after Fuld died, he had met with the store's executives in his home and with a great deal of emotion had told them that "when he no longer felt he could handle the business that they would inherit it."[188]

But for the first time in his career, Bamberger had let his emotions override his common sense. After he thought it over, he realized that the store was too big an operation for his executives to handle. If he died, there would be no one at the top to guide the transition, since his co-workers and managers had become accustomed to him making the decisions. Bamberger continued, "With neither Mrs. Fuld nor I having any children and old age coming on, the thing would run on the rocks. Something had to be done, so when this offer came to me I thought it over. I thought that the Macy concern was one of the best managed concerns in the country and would give less trouble with the store."[189]

In another surprise, Bamberger announced that he would distribute checks to 235 employees with fifteen or more years working at the store in amounts ranging from $1,000 to $20,000 depending on the length of service.[190] "Today is one of the happiest occasions of my life," he said. "I am doing something today I feel I should do. This business has been a great success and you people have helped to make it what it is. I would not be able to do what I am doing today if it had not been for the loyalty, cooperation and industry of my friends assembled here."[191]

He insisted on meeting in private with these veteran employees on the eleventh floor at the close of the business day, to present their checks and shake their hands. One employee reported that Bamberger's voice "broke a little" and that there were tears in his eyes.[192] Recipients included "colored porters, drivers, matrons, saleswomen, buyers, clerks, and department managers"[193] but not store executives. Bamberger told the assembled workers, "It may surprise you to know that when I asked each of you whether you wanted cash or an annuity, you all wanted cash."[194] Bamberger rarely displayed a sense of humor, but this day he did.

Bamberger made it clear that despite the sale, he was not retiring from the business. As newly appointed chairman of the board of L. Bamberger & Co., he said that he intended to be at his desk as usual. And that is what happened. The following Monday, he was there at 8:30 A.M. ready to tackle that day's challenges.[195] However, his salary, which had been $100,000 when he was president of L. Bamberger & Co., was now reduced to $58,333.[196] Clearly Macy's management believed that interest on the income from the sale of the store would more than make up for the salary reduction. Bamberger was also elected a director of R. H. Macy & Co., but received no compensation in that position.[197]

In October the new addition opened, and a week of special events offering something for everyone began on the twenty-eighth. The public was invited to visit from the second basement up to the ninth floor. Two fourteen-piece orchestras played in the upstairs store, and a band performed in the basement store. A small movie machine showed a film, "Rayon in the Making." The store held a ping-pong tournament and opened a new aviation department. Eight models paraded "Fashions of the Thrifty" in the basement. Period costumes and accessories on loan from the Newark Museum showcased former fashions in furniture and in clothes. Other exhibits included four new model rooms, a $100,000 rug, contemporary art, antiques, Lionel trains, and an electrical exhibit in the lamp department. "Culinary art lectures" were offered once or twice a day. An expanded Bunnyland toy department catered to bored youngsters forced to visit the store with their mothers.[198]

Bamberger's contract required that he agree to be honored at a testimonial given by the new owners to mark the dedication of the completed building. The dinner provided an opportunity for seven hundred of Newark's and New Jersey's power brokers to pay tribute to Bamberger's role in the commercial and civic life of the city and state.[199] US Secretary of Agriculture Arthur M. Hyde was the principal speaker. As part of the event, the public was invited to visit the store between eight and ten. Approximately thirty-five thousand persons toured the building, accompanied by live music heard over loudspeakers throughout the store.[200] Percy, Jesse, and Herbert Straus preferred to remain in the background so as "to preserve the tradition that it [L. Bamberger & Co.] was a Newark institution."[201] Herbert, the new president of Bamberger's, claimed that he wanted to be considered as "just another one of Bamberger's co-workers, ready to co-operate in every way for a bigger and better Bamberger's."[202]

For Bamberger the occasion must have been bittersweet. He still felt the loss of Felix Fuld and needed no reminder that he no longer owned the store. When asked to speak, he recalled the store's beginning, when "the outlook was not so good" and money was tight. Typically modest, he attributed his success to Louis Frank and Felix Fuld. Newark's mayor Congelton then noted, "Two men, Mr. Bamberger and Mr. Fuld who believed in their city and loved it; who have done their share toward developing the spiritual and cultural life of the community, have given a great commercial institution which stands as an imposing monument to them."[203]

Two weeks before the 1929 crash, Newark's landmark store seemed poised for continued success. Yet there were signals of problems ahead, in the form of resignations by veteran executives who were loyal to Bamberger and could not see themselves working for Macy's. Director of Personnel Michael Schaap left immediately to become president of Bloomingdale's and invited Harry A. Hatry, the merchandise manager, to join him:[204] they were absent from the testimonial dinner. Macy's had hoped that Bamberger executives would stay on to encourage a smooth transition, but this did not happen. Store superintendent Abraham Schindel, who had a reputation as a successful store manager and community leader, left in 1931 to become executive vice president of Kresge's.[205] The absence of these executives was felt among co-workers who had grown accustomed to working with them.[206] The decision to leave must not have been easy; jobs were not easy to find, particularly with the onset of the Depression.

Macy's and Bamberger's were two distinct cultures, and managers who were transferred from New York to the Bamberger store had no allegiance to Newark and saw their jobs in New Jersey as a demotion. Consequently, store employees and executives had to be convinced that they could work together. As part of this effort a "service to customers" contest was held the year after the sale, using the standard practice of offering cash incentives to employees for ideas on how to improve the business. First prize went to Irving Hoffman in the rug department, who suggested that co-workers be more fully acquainted with the advantages of the Macy-Bamberger combination, and that Macy's executives appear at graduations from the salesmanship courses and department meetings so co-workers could get to know them and understand their policies.[207] *Counter Currents* explained that Hoffman's plan "embodied the suggestion that service to customers meant starting with interested, contented co-workers." Macy's owners invited Bamberger employees to a summer camp in Warwick, New York. The camp was called Camp Isida after Isadore and Ida Straus, who perished on the Titanic. According to Al Marcus, who worked as a stock boy at age fourteen, if you worked for either store you could go there with your family for one week at no cost.[208]

Everything Bamberger did going forward suggested that he intended to make the best of the merger. He continued to make his customary rounds of the store to convince his co-workers that nothing had changed and maintained his long-standing open-door policy of meeting with customers who had complaints.

Bamberger sent postcards and letters to co-workers when he traveled, which *Counter Currents* printed. He wrote heartfelt messages for co-workers at Christmas and the New Year: "It is my wish today—as it has always been in the past—that the New Year will carry to you all a large measure of joy and contentment."[209] The two store names were hyphenated in all printed material to emphasize that theirs was a joint venture: the Macy-Bamberger training squad, Bamberger-Macy offices, as well as a newspaper item titled "Bamberger-Macy's Warehouse Theft."[210]

Bamberger remained chairman through 1939. At the celebration of the store's fiftieth anniversary he stated, "I am happy to see how well the present executive personnel have preserved it."[211] A local magazine reported that he continued to be a familiar figure, walking up and down the aisles, sometimes fingering the merchandise, sometimes content merely to look at the hurried throngs of people who daily crowded the store. He was particularly fond of the basement store "because it was there that he met small buyers with pinched pocketbooks," the type of shopper who had enabled him to make a success of his first small store.[212]

Harold Krauss, a longtime Morristown resident and buyer for the china department, recalled Bamberger "strolling among the aisles, checking to see if the glass window displays were clean, and talking to employees in the Men's Department."[213] It was customary for everyone to stand at attention while waiting for him to pass by and conduct an inspection. On one occasion Connie Warshoff had come to work in a plaid skirt—not the accepted dress code. Her excuse was that there had been a fire in her apartment the night before. Nevertheless, her fellow employees rushed her out of sight before Bamberger saw her.[214]

As the owner of a store with an entire floor devoted to menswear, Louis Bamberger was arguably one of the best-dressed men in Newark. "I remember vividly as a little lad, going shopping on Saturdays with my mother, seeing Louis Bamberger attired in a gray pin-stripe suit, pince-nez glasses perched on his nose, and his semi-bald pate carefully barbered," recalled Ben Kanter. "He would station himself on the main aisle and greet customers that he knew by name, inquire about births, deaths, graduations and weddings. . . . He was really concerned about your family and your welfare."[215]

Bertha Sossin, her brother Sidney Cohen, and her older sister Frances "Fannie" Cohen all worked at the store around the same time (1926–1941). When Fannie had her tonsils removed, she received flowers and a visit in the hospital from Bamberger.[216] Bertha worked at a desk right outside Bamberger's office. "He was very reserved, a down-to-earth individual," she recalled. "He was a man of medium-to-short stature, knowledgeable, but not very talkative . . . the average person would never know he was the TOP EXECUTIVE."[217]

Like many, Laurie Fitzmaurice, whose great-aunt Nina "Jennie" Zerbino started work in Bamberger's bridal salon one year before the store was sold to Macy's, was surprised to learn "that Macy's had bought the store so early in the 20th century"[218] and wanted to know why it had retained the Bamberger name. But Macy's owners never considered changing the name. Bamberger's was a brand, as much as Coca-Cola or Ford. Everybody knew it; in fact, most people didn't realize the store had been sold. In the public's mind it was still Bamberger's. Thus Macy's waited many years to change its name. It was not until 1986 that the Bamberger name came off the building in Newark and the store became Macy's. In 1992, exactly one hundred years after the original L. Bamberger & Co. had opened, Macy's and Bamberger's left Newark for good.

Bamberger's career was filled with well-timed decisions — the decision to open a store in "sleepy" Newark, to defy critics who said Market Street was not the best location, and to remain in Newark and reinvest profits by continuously expanding the store's selling space. If he had reservations about selling his store, he never shared them, not even with those closest to him. He may have been the right man, in the right place, at the right time, but Bamberger never thought his success was a miracle of good timing or good luck. He did what he thought was right and made his own luck.

1. Louis Bamberger's father, Elkan Bamberger, emigrated from Bavaria in 1840. He married Theresa Hutzler, whose family owned Baltimore's largest department store, Hutzler Brothers. Source: Schindel Family Collection.

2. Bamberger's modest brick Georgian-style house, located at 602 Centre Street in South Orange, was set on a thirty-five-acre estate surrounded by lush gardens and a working farm.

3. Sunday dinners at Bamberger's home were a family tradition. Seated (left to right) are Julius Bamberger, Pauline Bamberger, Lavinia Bamberger, Felix Fuld, Carrie Fuld, and Daisy Bamberger. Standing is Edgar Bamberger. Source: *Schindel Family Collection.*

THE ☆ BANKRUPT ☆ STOCK

— OF —

HILL & CRAGG

MUST BE CLOSED OUT REGARDLESS OF COST!

Beginning Tuesday, Dec. 13th

CONSISTING OF

Holiday Goods,
Cloaks,
Trimmings,
Ladies and Gents' Furnishings,
Dry Goods,
Laces and Embroideries,
Jewelry,
Handkerchiefs,
Gloves,
Toilet Goods,
Corsets,
Underwear,
Leather Goods,
Lamps and Clocks,
House Furnishing Goods,
Dolls and Albums,
Japanese Goods,
Dressmaker Supplies.

All Goods Offered at a Great Sacrifice!

L. BAMBERGER, 147-149 MARKET ST.

4. Bamberger placed his first newspaper advertisement in the Newark Sunday Call *on December 13, 1892. In it he promoted the sale of the bankrupt stock he had purchased from Newark's Market Street firm of Hill and Cragg.* Source: *Macy's Archives.*

5. *Shoppers in the late 1890s and early 1920s got used to the Bamberger store's crowded aisles and overwhelming displays of merchandise.* Source: *Macy's Archives.*

6. *A horse named Finnegan pulled Bamberger's first delivery wagon. Bamberger claimed the horse cost him his last dollar.* Source: *Macy's Archives.*

7. By 1910 Bamberger's packages were delivered by a fleet of electric-powered trucks. The trucks were an indication that Bamberger's was keeping pace with technology. Source: *Macy's Archives.*

8. Bamberger's opened a new, modern eight-story department store in 1912. The opening was accompanied by some of the most beautiful advertisements ever seen in a newspaper. They were the work of the prominent artist Arthur Elder.

9. *"The Road to Victory" was the theme of a Bamberger window display for the sale of World War I Liberty Bonds. Under Bamberger's watch, Newark conducted five Liberty Bond drives, and each one "went over the top." Source: Macy's Archives.*

10. *Nothing was more beautiful than Bamberger's 1920s store window displays. The mannequins and the clothes they wore were statements of elegance, balance, and proportion.* Source: *Macy's Archives.*

11. *Starting in 1912, the phrase "I'll meet you under the clock" appeared in all of Bamberger's advertisements. Eventually the idea for shoppers and visitors to meet under the Bamberger clock became routine.* Source: *Reigel Collection, Jewish Historical Society of New Jersey.*

12. *Bamberger's "Ideal Home" opened in 1924. Located at 725 Elizabeth Avenue, across the street from Weequahic Park, it was Newark and New Jersey's first model home.*

13. Charm *magazine's audience was middle- and upper-middle-class women who qualified to hold Bamberger charge accounts. The magazine promoted the advantages of living and shopping in New Jersey.* Source: *Courtesy of the Newark Public Library.*

14. *Felix Fuld was Louis Bamberger's brother-in-law and business partner for thirty-seven years. Fuld was married to Bamberger's sister Caroline "Carrie" Bamberger.* Source: *Jewish Historical Society of New Jersey Archives.*

15. *There was a shortage of parking on the streets surrounding Bamberger's store, so shoppers were encouraged to park their cars at the Washington Street garage. From there Bamberger's provided a customer parking service that let shoppers off at Bamberger's front door. The nickel park was paid for by L. Bamberger & Co.* Source: *Macy's Archives.*

16. *Groundbreaking ceremonies for the Newark Museum were held on March 14, 1924.* Source: *Courtesy of the Newark Public Library.*

5

"A RECORD OF HIS BENEFACTIONS"

BAMBERGER AS A PHILANTHROPIST

"**M**any wished that Louis Bamberger lived to 200 years so that Newark could continue to profit from his activities," wrote the Newark historian Charles F. Cummings in 1997. "Louis Bamberger, Felix Fuld, and Carrie Fuld probably still hold the record for being the greatest philanthropists of all time in New Jersey."[1] Cummings's comment captured the essence of Bamberger's remarkable legacy. Woodrow Wilson, Warren G. Harding, and Herbert Hoover acknowledged his good works. Cummings's job was to preserve and write about Newark's history. His *Star-Ledger* column, "Knowing Newark," frequently describes how Newark prospered during the "Bamberger era" and asserts the importance of keeping Bamberger's legacy alive.

Bamberger's philanthropy ranged from help and support for individuals to support of local institutions to creating entire institutions for Newark. He is best remembered for his gift of a building to house the Newark Museum and for the endowment that founded the world-renowned Institute for Advanced Study. In both instances he was the *sole donor*, making it possible for him to control the outcome.

As Laura Porter Smith notes, "Bamberger was not the wealthiest, most influential, or best known of the early-twentieth century philanthropists."[2] This relative obscurity was the result of his desire to keep a low profile. Organizations wanted Bamberger's name on their letterhead, since his reputation was as good as money in the bank. But he never accepted the presidency of any organization. He insisted on receiving only honorary titles such as "delegate-at-large" and was satisfied to be assigned to fundraising and finance committees. Well aware of the importance of leading by example, he did allow his name to be attached to certain large donations that he made; but when he could, he gave anonymously, with instructions that if his name was revealed he would rescind his support. He rarely granted interviews, but when he did, whatever he said made front-page news.

Bamberger's reasons for his philanthropic activities were not complicated. Jewish department store owners, like other wealthy Americans of the era, felt called upon to use at least some of their profits "toward the solution of social issues of contemporary significance."[3] For example, Bamberger's friend Julius Rosenwald, the owner of Sears, Roebuck, used his wealth to effect social change by advancing the cause of black education in the South; he helped build more than fifty-three hundred public schools for youngsters in need of access to a basic education. On more than one occasion, Bamberger was quoted expressing his belief in causes that promoted social justice, particularly in support of education. Walter H. Farrier, Bamberger's executive secretary and executor, explained, "Mr. Bamberger would never believe that posterity would be concerned with what he thought, felt, wrote, or said but must have known that it would be concerned with what he did!"[4] Bamberger did not act alone, however. "The old story goes that Louis ran the store, Felix kept the business on track, and Carrie gave away the millions."[5] Their gifts (often not publicized) were endless, and as Cummings remarked, "certainly earned them a rocket ship to heaven."[6]

To Bamberger philanthropy was like running a business. It required research to determine the worthiness of each recipient. Research was Bamberger's specialty. He had initiated a citywide survey of all of Newark's social service agencies that was used to determine the distribution of funds from the city's Community Chest. It was the first time in the history of Newark that a study on so large a scale, covering all phases of philanthropy, had been attempted.[7]

As the owner of a large, important department store, Bamberger was expected to give back to his loyal customers. Requests to use the store's tearoom, restaurant, or auditorium to host a fashion show, bridge party, or fundraising event were encouraged. This is what department stores across America did to boost foot traffic, increase sales, and generate favorable public opinion. The facts that America's "merchant princes" stood in the aisles greeting customers, worked long hours, gave jobs to thousands, and contributed to the progress of their respective cities did little to impress cynics and critics. Thus some viewed Bamberger's charitable contributions as self-serving ways to generate publicity. Yet the millions of dollars he gave to charities, Jewish and non-Jewish, far exceeded what he spent on advertising. Bamberger's role in casting Newark as a city that had compassion for the less fortunate began in his private office on the eleventh floor of the store. Here he met with anyone, politician or private citizen, who wanted his advice—usually financial—about issues related to Newark's progress. Bamberger listened patiently, aware that the purpose of such visits was to ask him for money. He rarely rejected these appeals, but emphasized to each organization's leaders the importance of establishing a policy of fiscal responsibility.

Bamberger's earliest known charitable activity apparently occurred in 1903, when the Orange Bureau of Associated Charities learned that he lived in South Orange. A letter from the group dated 1904 invited him to attend the group's monthly charity conferences, and if that was not possible, requested a ten-dollar donation, or the amount that he had "sent the group the year before."[8] By the end of his career, Bamberger was contributing to 308 Newark volunteer organizations whose representatives visited or wrote him asking for donations.[9]

At the turn of the twentieth century, Newark's reputation as a manufacturing center was a magnet for large numbers of Eastern European immigrants who came there looking for jobs. Then during World War I thirty thousand black workers came from Georgia and Alabama to work in the city's factories and "created a multiplicity of problems which were new and with which no cities had the knowledge to deal."[10] It was left to community leaders such as Bamberger to set up social services to care for these workers. He was among the prominent citizens who actively served on the boards of volunteer organizations that created homes for orphans and worked to help the needy find jobs and housing and get access to hospitals. In 1918 Bamberger helped spearhead the formation of Newark's Council of Philanthropies. By 1920 the council was composed of fifty-three volunteer agencies; however, to Bamberger's dismay they were all forced to compete for the same dollars. In his opinion, this was no way to run a city, so he got behind a movement to make Newark a better and happier place.

Reports of successful welfare agency systems in other cities convinced officers of Newark's social agencies to approve a constitution for a new Council of Social Agencies, which would include such institutions as the Home for the Friendless, Home for Respectable Aged

Women, Home for Crippled Children, Colored Home for Aged and Orphans, Health Council, Standard of Living Council, Civic Council, and
Social Service Exchange.[11] In 1922 invitations to attend a meeting to
decide the future of the new council were sent to fifteen select individuals who had "weight and standing" and commanded the confidence
of the community.[12] The meeting's participants agreed to launch a
movement to unite the city's volunteer agencies through a Community
Chest, a citywide system that required individual social service agencies to join together to sponsor one annual fundraising campaign. The
funds collected would be dispersed by Newark's Welfare Federation,
which was formed in 1922 for that purpose. Over two hundred cities
and towns in the United States had adopted this idea; and Bamberger,
who had already studied the success rates of Community Chest programs in other cities, supported the idea for Newark. He took it upon
himself to convince Newark's power brokers and politicians to adopt
such a program.

William H. Ashby, Newark's first black social worker and executive
secretary of the Negro Welfare League of Newark (1917–1927), later the
Urban League of Essex County, recalled "that opinions were adamant
both for and against it."[13] Agencies with wealthy, influential boards of
directors were against it. Agencies that struggled were for it. The final
decision was made at a meeting held at the Female Charities Building
at Halsey and Hill Streets, which was attended by a select group of individuals appointed by the officers of Newark's Council of Social Agencies.[14] Bamberger was among them.

The meeting opened at 10:00 A.M., and as the morning wore on the
discussion grew heated. At around 2:30 P.M. Rudolph Conklin, exasper-
ation in his voice, stood up to go to lunch. But Bamberger jumped to
his feet and exclaimed: "Oh, no. You're not going. I've had no lunch
either. You're going to stay here like the rest of us and see this thing
through one way or the other."[15] Conklin came from a well-connected
Newark family and was probably used to having his way. But realizing
that Bamberger had reached his boiling point, he backed off. At 3 P.M.
the meeting voted in favor of the plan with the understanding that
membership was voluntary.[16]

A majority of Newark's charitable institutions agreed to support
the citywide plan, but its Roman Catholic organizations did not. Their
leaders may have had the same reservations as did representatives

from the Jewish community. Newark's Jewish social service agencies were reluctant to join. Their boards of trustees preferred to remain autonomous. Bamberger, who by then had enormous influence in the Jewish community, stated on October 13, 1922, "I am heartily in favor of the Community Chest and I hope that the Jewish organizations in this city will see their way clear to enter into this movement."[17] He argued that just setting up a joint effort to raise and distribute funding among agencies eliminated duplication of work, reduced overhead, and provided financial accountability. Shortly after Bamberger made his statement, the *Call* reported, "There is increasing evidence that the Hebrew charities are not averse to joining the Community Chest project."[18] Bamberger also got help from Rabbi Foster, who wrote, "The character of the men and women who constitute the provisional committee of the Community Chest—their standing in the city and experience and achievements in the realm of charitable endeavor and big business responsibilities—make it utterly impossible that all charities will not be treated with perfect justice and fairness."[19] In addition, Bamberger sought to apply pressure on all of Newark's business owners, many of whom belonged, like him, to the chamber of commerce. He was convinced that a Community Chest did more than just raise money. In his opinion, "The Community Chest developed mutual understanding and appreciation between Jews and non-Jews which could only lead to a better and happier city in which to work."[20]

Against this background, the Conference of Jewish Charities was formed. Its thirteen Jewish agencies, having agreed to join the Community Chest, were automatically subject to the decisions made by the newly formed Welfare Federation of Newark, whose task was to decide how monies raised during Chest campaigns were distributed. In this way Bamberger accomplished his goal of uniting all Newark's social service agencies under one umbrella. He was not only the founding officer and vice chairman of the Conference of Jewish Charities, but also the leading organizer and (reluctant) trustee of the Newark Community Chest and Welfare Federation. Even if community leaders wanted to oppose the Community Chest plan, they were not prepared to buck Bamberger or his influence.

The first Community Chest campaign was launched in November 1923 with a goal of raising $1.1 million.[21] Felix Fuld served as vice-chairman and Louis Bamberger became honorary president of the

109

Newark Welfare Federation, a position he held into the late 1930s.[22] Newark's Jews went all out to raise money, but still worried that the return in dollars from the campaign would not match the needs of their agencies. Their fears of not receiving the amounts their agencies needed to function were allayed when all the Jewish charities applying for funding from the Welfare Federation received the full amounts they asked for.[23] Later, however, it turned out that the campaigns were not as successful as many had expected. An analysis of this first campaign revealed that "it was hard to raise funds." The campaign had to be extended for several weeks beyond its target closing date. In the end the campaign fell very short; it raised only $782,719 in support of fifty agencies.[24] An anonymous letter in the *Newark Sunday Call* said, "I have never heard of all the Jewish agencies listed as recipients of monies to be raised." The letter appeared to suggest that Newark's Jews had invented agencies in order to receive a disproportionate amount of money from the citywide campaign.[25] Bamberger and Fuld may have anticipated that funding requests from Newark's Jewish agencies would be questioned. Therefore, they consistently gave the largest individual donations ever made to the campaign.[26] L. Bamberger & Co.'s 4,448 employees, most of whom lived in Newark and greater Essex County, read about the formation of the Community Chest in *Counter Currents* and responded with a 100 percent subscription, exceeding their quota.[27] However, there is no way to know whether their donations were heartfelt or the result of peer pressure and a desire to please Bamberger.

Bamberger continued as honorary vice-chairman of the Community Chest drive well into the late 1930s. Meetings were held at the Down Town Club and Essex Club. These "members only" clubs were where wealthy Newarkers were recruited to serve as heads of campaign committees.[28] Bamberger's belief in the work of the Community Chest is evident from the four-year, one hundred thousand dollar bequest he left in his will, intended to give organizers time to find other sources to replace his contributions.[29] He seemed not to be disappointed by the fact that other Newark leaders, who could well afford to match his donations, never contributed equally; in 1928, for example, the *Newark Sunday Call* took Newark's wealthy citizens and church leaders to task for not participating in the annual Community Chest drive and for leaving it to Felix Fuld and Uzal McCarter to make up the $115,000 shortfall for that year's campaign.[30] It was obvious that everyone involved had become accustomed to Bamberger picking up the slack. He never got involved in finger pointing; instead he tried to lead by example, and when that didn't work, he acted unilaterally. He did, however, refuse invitations to join the influential boards of Newark's banks and insurance companies. Historically, the city's wealthy businessmen gave little or no money to charitable causes, so Bamberger stopped asking. Bamberger supported many smaller volunteer organizations. Generally he chose those that provided social services for children, including orphan asylums, neighborhood houses for working women who needed daycare for their children, camps for undernourished children, and Big Sister and Big Brother groups, for which he paid salaries. His interest in children is curious, since he and the Fulds never had children. Bamberger may have felt that children were society's most vulnerable group. Young people needed guidance if they were to grow up and become productive citizens. Two stories illustrate how Bamberger took youngsters under his wing and paid for their college education. Faith Lurie Grossman recalled: "My father's family was not very wealthy, and my uncle needed money to go to medical school. He went to Louis Bamberger and somehow convinced him to give him a loan for tuition."[31] He promised to pay back every penny. Dr. Wolf Lurie became a prominent heart specialist in Kearny, did pay it back, and he and Mr. Bamberger became almost like family. Garrett Den Braven had a job in high school changing lightbulbs at Bamberger's. His weekly salary was twenty dollars. One week, because of an error, his paycheck was short ten dollars. He was still grumbling when he got on the elevator with Bamberger and complained about the shortfall to him. Bamberger took out a twenty-dollar bill, gave it to him, and said, "Now *you* owe me $10."[32] Bamberger took Garrett under his wing and, as with Lurie, paid for his college education. Along with Fuld and three other prominent Newark residents—Franklin Conklin Sr., Wallace M. Scudder, and Dr. Edward Weston—Bamberger donated seventy-seven acres of woodlands and a twenty-two—acre lake, Lake Genevieve, in Blairstown Township to the Girl Scout Council of Newark for Camp Kalmia.[33] The same group also donated 1,735 acres at Catfish Pond overlooking the Delaware Water Gap to the Boy Scouts for a summer camp called Camp Mohican.[34] One day Bamberger surprised the staff there by showing up for lunch in the camp mess hall. Camper Sheldon Denburg described "an elderly guy" sitting next to him wearing khaki scout shorts. He conducted an animated conversation with the camp-ers, who had no idea who this pleasant man was.[35] Years later, Newark residents who were active in the Newark scouting movement recalled their summers at camp. "For a kid from Newark to be able to leave the city for a week, which cost eight dollars, was wonderful," wrote Al Marcus. "My Dad put me on the DL&W train on Broad Street and I got off in Blairstown where I was put on a truck and taken to camp. It was great when I met kids from other sections of Newark who were in other troops of the Robert Treat Boy Scout Council."[36] "I just loved Camp Kalmia, even having to shower in cold water, live without elec-tricity in our cabins and cleaning the outhouse," wrote Fredi Greenfield Miller. "I think these summers prepared me for life without all the luxu-ries."[37] But Arlene Glickenhaus Rubenstein "hated" the camp, since she associated it with the milk of magnesia dispensed by the camp nurse and head counselor. Any mention of Camp Kalmia to Margie Bauman "made her itch" because of yearly bouts with poison ivy.[38]

Carrie Fuld also left a mark on Newark as a philanthropist in her own right. Although Carrie was not involved in running the store, she was a well-known figure to store employees from 1900 to 1930; she had an office on the seventh floor and came there every day.[39] Her office was convenient for public officials and heads of volunteer organizations, who came looking for money. Since she made most of her donations in conjunction with her husband or her brother, it was convenient to have them close at hand. She was an equal partner in all her hus-band's enterprises, but also won sympathy through her own philan-thropies. After Fuld's death, Carrie told the *Newark Sunday Call* "that so far as it is within her power," she planned to carry on her husband's philanthropic work.[40]

In 1917 William Ashby was looking for a way to purchase a home for young black women who had nowhere to live. He told interested par-ties that he had a "very wealthy friend. . . . [I]f we can interest her, it is very possible that a home for these girls can be purchased."[41] He went to see Carrie Fuld and was ushered into her office. They exchanged pleasantries, and he described his project. Carrie asked, "How much do you expect me to give you?" Ashby requested five hundred dollars. She pressed a button and asked a secretary to call Mr. Fuld. Fuld ap-peared, heard the request, and said, "Well, give him the money."[42] This was the beginning of a productive friendship, according to Ashby, who recalled both financial and personal support from Carrie Fuld in the dark days of the civil rights fight between the two world wars.[43] Carrie also agreed to help Ashby raise the full ten thousand dollars he needed for the home. She gave Ashby the names of important people to ask for donations and postponed her summer vacation for two weeks. Together they raised over eight thousand dollars, and Carrie presumably made up the shortfall. A four-story building at 58 West Market Street was purchased. Newark's newly founded Urban League occupied the first floor, and the three floors above were dormitories and reception rooms for the young women. In 1940 Bamberger and Mrs. Fuld each gave checks of one thousand dollars to the New Jersey Urban League, which together with other contributions enabled the organization to pay off its mortgage.[44]

Despite intense public interest, not much was known about Carrie's private life because she, like Louis, preferred it that way. Even an incident as insignificant as her insurance claim for the loss of a valuable pearl ring, reported as stolen during a stay at the Hotel Biltmore in New York, became front-page news.[45] She had grown up in a home where her father was a "stern disciplinarian who believed in a strict regimen for his daughters."[46] No longer willing to tolerate this, she left Baltimore for Philadelphia, where she met her first husband, Louis Frank. Her sister Lavinia called her a "glamour girl," and newspaper photos confirm her good looks and style. When her first husband lost his fortune after his business failed, she pulled herself together and learned to live within her means. "My sister gave up the wealth with the same grace that she showed later when she acquired it again," wrote Lavinia.[47] When she married the wealthy Felix Fuld in 1913, her life changed again.

Like other wealthy individuals, Carrie received random requests for money from organizations around the country. For example, E. M. McDuffie, principal of the Laurinburg Normal and Industrial Institute in North Carolina, wrote asking for money for a new boiler.[48] "The school's treasury is exhausted," McDuffie wrote, "and as you have helped us so often I am unwilling and cannot ask you to do more. I am wondering if it is possible for you to speak with some friend or get your local newspaper to make a short appeal to help me secure the $530."[49] If her past support for the school is any indication, chances are that Carrie sent the money herself.

The family's charity extended as far as East Asia. L. Bamberger & Co.

had buying offices in Japan and China. Carrie's interest in the Chinese people was inspired by her friendship with the Nobel and Pulitzer Prize–winning author Pearl S. Buck, best known for writing about the terrible living conditions in China. Bamberger family papers contain two certificates presented to "Carolina" B. Fuld. One, issued by the China Relief Legion and titled "Fellowship of the Plum Blossom," recognizes special service to the people of China in their time of great need and is signed by Pearl S. Buck and Secretary of State James G. Blaine.[50] The second is an "Award of Recognition" as "a member of the China Relief Legion for whose humanitarian effort on behalf of the People of China I express deep appreciation." It is signed by Mayling Soong Chiang, also known as Madame Chiang Kai-shek.[51] Carrie also donated to a campaign initiated by Newark's Jews in 1941 to support a China Relief Fund Drive.[52]

Her share of company profits funded numerous other causes, including Fuld Neighborhood House, Newark Maternity Hospital, the Jewish Sisterhood Nursery of Temple B'nai Jeshurun, the Fuld lecture series at Newark's "Y," and the Stadium Concerts, where Newark residents heard the likes of George Gershwin "under the stars." She gave ten thousand dollars to purchase works of major twentieth-century American artists, which she and Felix donated to the Newark Museum. In 1930 she used her enormous inheritance from her husband to endow the Institute for Advanced Study. When she was not at the store or raising funds for worthy charities, she could be found at home, where her greatest pleasure was welcoming neighbors who stopped by to admire her prize-winning gardens.

Of all the public gifts associated with the Fuld name, perhaps the one that has meant the most to the greatest number of people is the Japanese cherry tree grove Mrs. Fuld sponsored for the Essex County Park Commission in 1927. Her gift of two thousand cherry trees, at an estimated cost of fifteen thousand dollars, rivaled—and for some surpassed—the cherry blossoms in Washington, DC. The trees were placed in Branch Brook Park under the supervision of the Olmstead brothers, whose designs included New York City's Central Park.[53] They selected a variety of species, paying attention to the type of flower, placement, blooming time, habitat, and use in Japan.[54] Each spring, Newark gears up for an influx of as many as ten thousand visitors who come to see the display.[55]

Bamberger himself was perfectly aware of the publicity value of this piece of philanthropy. "From [*sic*] November 1927, C. Feland Gannon of the L. Bamberger & Co. advertising department pressed Olmstead's landscape design firm for a statement about the design so he could publicize the philanthropy."[56] "How far afield Gannon publicized this donation" is unknown; certainly he got coverage in the Newark newspapers.[57]

In 1928 Bamberger sponsored a competition for local artists to submit designs for a gold medal to be awarded to each of the city's high school valedictorians, "presented to the most competent pupil of each high school graduating class, competent in the sense of academic attainment as well as general helpfulness to the school, himself and his fellows."[58] The winning design was by noted Newark medalist Charles Keck. In Bamberger's mind, the winners represented a new generation who would be his city's future leaders. The first year's awards went to four young women from Barringer, East Side, South Side, and West Side High Schools.[59] The Bamberger medal was awarded each year until the early 1970s. Recipients considered winning it to be among their greatest accomplishments, and the medals became family heirlooms. Superior Court Judge Miriam Span, named 2013 Professional Lawyer of the Year from Union County, still felt that her "proudest award was the Bamberger Medal at my Weequahic High School graduation in 1960."[60] Fanny Mandel, who received the Bamberger medal when she graduated from Central High School in 1941, felt the same; according to her sister, "This award was one of the high points of her life."[61]

Bamberger's philanthropy went beyond helping individuals and organizations. He wanted to build Newark up to take its place among major cities. On January 20, 1923, he created a flurry of interest when he called around to Newark's newspapers to let them know that he had a statement to make to the press. Since he was known to avoid newspaper reporters, this request made news in itself. The next day's headlines read, "Bamberger's $500,000 Gift Assures City New Museum."[62] He surprised everyone—even his closest associates—with this announcement that he would give the City of Newark an art museum to be known as the Newark Museum of Arts and Sciences.[63] The news traveled fast; and soon after the gift was announced, the American Association of Museums in Charleston, South Carolina, adopted a resolution congratulating Newark and expressing appreciation.[64]

The next day Bamberger felt compelled to amplify his original terse, matter-of-fact announcement. "I have felt for a long time that in as much as I had made a success of my business in Newark, I owed the city something. Newark has needed a museum building and I am glad that it is possible for me to help the city have one."[65] This heartfelt statement contrasts sharply with J. P. Morgan's insolent assertion that he "owed the public nothing" and William Vanderbilt's quip "the public be damned."

"Newark has had other millionaires, but none has dispensed his wealth on so large a scale during his lifetime," editorialized the *Call*.[66] In the *Jewish Chronicle*, Rabbi Solomon Foster said that "the absence of any condition in the gift that would attach the name of the donor to the benefaction is the surest way for his name to be immortalized."[67] Charles F. Cummings noted, "This gift brought unprecedented recognition to this city throughout the country."[68]

Bamberger's support for a museum in Newark had actually begun in 1909, when he was chosen as one of fifty charter members of the newly formed Newark Museum Association.[69] Among his first duties was to sign the Museum Association's papers of incorporation on April 29, 1909. At this time a makeshift museum was housed on the library's fourth floor under the supervision of its director, head librarian John Cotton Dana. Dana told the museum's trustees that he and his staff spent too much of their time fending off well-meaning donors who offered items for the collections that were not really worth displaying. In 1913 a conversation regarding attendance, acquisitions, and overcrowding of gallery space in the library began in earnest. Board members voted to investigate the acquisition of a "fire proof building and one which could be extended in proportion with the growth of the city."[70] Bamberger and four others on the committee were assigned to research the feasibility of erecting such a building. Land for a site was a prerequisite; and with Bamberger's encouragement, Newark's elected officials agreed to purchase the Marcus L. Ward estate at 49 Washington Street for $200,000 as a permanent home for the museum.[71] Bamberger went one step further and insisted that the city deed over the entire Ward plot to the Museum Association so that it would be "impossible to divert any of this property to other uses, for it should be kept intact to provide for future development of the museum."[72] He stated:

"The day will come when the building will have to be enlarged and the rest of the ground will be needed."[73]

As a charter member of the museum, Bamberger regularly attended trustee meetings. Typically he sat in silence listening to grievances about lack of space, lack of members, and lack of funding. What impressed him most was Dana's assertion that a museum was a means to promote Newark's image as an up-and-coming city.[74] It was this argument that eventually made him decide to give Newark a museum. Another, lesser-known reason was that Bamberger had a hobby of collecting historical objects.

Bamberger had little faith that a museum could be built through citizen donations and subscriptions. The first subscription campaign netted only fifty-five dollars from two local residents.[75] Bamberger had anticipated this: "I feel that if the city had to wait until the money for a museum was raised by subscription or otherwise, it would be a long time before we would have the building."[76] It was clear that city funds would not be forthcoming either; trustees asked the city to increase the 1923 appropriation for museum activities from $15,000 to $25,000 and were turned down.[77]

In a January 19, 1923, letter to the trustees Bamberger stated, "I do not propose to give to the Museum Association a sum of money. I propose to give to the Association a completed building suitable for its purpose, to be, with the tract of land whereon it stands, irrevocably dedicated to the Museum's use so long as the Association continues to function as contemplated by its charter."[78] To avoid endless debates among the members of the Newark Museum Association, Bamberger insisted that no outside sources could intervene in the building process. "I desire to be in unrestricted control of the building operations until the building is completed and ready for occupancy."[79] He advised the trustees that they had precisely three days to respond to his offer, after which he would be out of the country. They promptly accepted his terms.

Bamberger had never mentioned to anyone his plan to donate a museum. Those close to him heard the news at a store meeting just minutes before he spoke to reporters. Not even Dana knew, even though Bamberger had conferred several times with him about the type of building that ought to be erected.[80] Dana was not present at the announcement because he was home with a cold.[81] Since it was Dana who had originally promoted the need for a museum, Bamberger was in effect stealing his thunder, much to his shock and disappointment.

Bamberger was the first to acknowledge Dana's contributions to Newark's cultural life and said that he never intended to diminish his role as museum director. But his practice was to play his cards close to his vest, and he probably felt it was so big a story that someone was bound to leak it. This would explain why he gave the museum's board of directors only three days to respond to his offer. He also may have suggested that they not speak to reporters until they had made their decision.

Anticipating the notoriety his announcement would produce, he avoided inevitable requests for follow-up interviews by arranging to leave immediately on an extended trip aboard the SS *Homeric*, a luxury ocean liner bound for the Mediterranean, accompanied by his sisters Pauline and Lavinia.[82] He stayed away for two months, although he telexed his store daily asking, "What are today's numbers?"[83] By the time he returned, the story had lost momentum, and he began a series of meetings with Dana and architect Jarvis Hunt about the requirements for the proposed building.

Although everyone had long agreed in principle that Newark was an important city and should have its own cultural showcase, nothing happened until Bamberger stepped up, even though the Museum Association's board of trustees, who were among the city's most affluent businessmen and manufacturers, had the means to fund the project. Rabbi Foster perhaps had this in mind when he wrote, "The example which Mr. Bamberger now sets [for] the wealthy men of the community is one of the most auspicious signs of the greater and better Newark which we are trying to help evolve. Mr. Bamberger throws out a challenge which ought not, really cannot, be unheeded."[84] One donor, Charles J. Sandrue, in the nearby town of Bloomfield, did rise to the challenge. When he heard of Bamberger's gift, he donated a collection of Eskimo artifacts.

On March 14, 1924, a brilliant Friday morning, Louis Bamberger, silver-plated shovel in hand, broke ground for the museum building. Store superintendent Abraham Schindel, whose job was to report progress on the building to Bamberger, was among the onlookers representing L. Bamberger & Co. "It was a proud day for the City of Newark," Schindel boasted in *Counter Currents*, "and we as co-workers can feel an especial pride and part in the event because it was our own 'big boss' Mr. Louis Bamberger, who by his very generous gift has made such a building possible to this city."[85]

Bamberger and Dana's work together to design and build the Newark Museum was part of a twenty-year association ended only by Dana's death in 1929. Dana was already well-known among a group of men termed "museum masters," men "whose vision, commitment, and innovative talents were shaping the future of the modern museum world."[86] Dana studied Bamberger's department store as a model for his museum and described his ideas about attractively designed department stores in his bulletin, *Newark Museum*, asking readers to think about the question "Is the department store a museum?"[87] He asserted that "a great city department store of the first class is perhaps more like a good museum of art than are any of the museums we have yet established. It is centrally located, it is easily reached, and it is open to all."[88] To further his relationship with Bamberger, Dana established a branch of the Newark Public Library at L. Bamberger & Co. for the store's employees. He did the same at Hahne & Co. and the Beehive.[89] A 1921 Bamberger advertisement linked the store and the library as public institutions, claiming, "We know of no other store so closely linked with the public. It is as much a part of Newark as the Free Public Library."[90]

A year passed before Bamberger's gift was mentioned in the Museum Association's minutes. This was not an oversight. The museum's trustees chose not to bruise Dana's ego any more than necessary.[91] They waited to thank Bamberger officially until Dana was on vacation in Europe.[92] Then, in January 1924, trustees Chester H. Hoag and Arthur F. Egner stated for the minutes, "We now enter a new epoch in our history, ushered in by the munificent gift of Mr. Louis Bamberger of a home for the museum."[93] It was not until that March that Dana brought himself to thank Bamberger, and even then he did it indirectly. In a letter from Florence, he wrote to the trustees: "You must send my thanks and congratulations to Mr. Bamberger, and tell him that none of us this generation can even half-way realize how great will be the influence on Newark of what he has done."[94] Dana's letter, which was published in the *Call*, was so heartfelt that it prompted Louise Upton Brumback, one of America's foremost women painters, to give Newark Museum what would become one of its best paintings.[95]

In their earlier meetings Bamberger and Dana had discussed space requirements and agreed that exhibitions should be relevant to the lives of ordinary citizens. This meant devoting space to the industrial arts, especially products manufactured in Newark.[96] It became evident that $500,000 was not sufficient, and Bamberger announced his intention to add an additional $150,000 to his original estimate.

The dedication ceremony was held on May 14, 1925, one day before Louis's seventieth birthday. Jarvis Hunt handed the keys to the building to Bamberger, who gave them to museum president Chester R. Hoag.[97] *Counter Currents* published the details of the ceremony, which included sealing a time capsule in the cornerstone, a tin box containing mementos of the occasion: the museum's annual reports, newspapers, old and new coins, a small American flag, a list of the board of trustees and museum employees, plans of the building, copies of remarks made at the dedication by the speakers, and a picture of Mr. Bamberger, who sat quietly, responded politely to the applause when his name was mentioned, and nodded graciously when he was praised for his generosity.[98] After the speech making was over, Rabbi Foster delivered the benediction.[99]

When the Newark Museum opened to the general public, on March 16, 1926, Mr. Bamberger was not there; he was in Florida, but sent a telegram apologizing for his absence.[100] Typically, he preferred not to be the center of attention. About three thousand people showed up on opening night, an occasion unprecedented in Newark's cultural history, according to newspaper reports.[101] The New York art world, including Mr. and Mrs. John Sloan and Mr. and Mrs. Robert Henri, came to view a collection of twenty-three works by modern American painters, sixteen of which were gifts from Mrs. Felix Fuld. John Flanagan, said to be the foremost medalist in the country, struck a medal to commemorate the museum and its donor. The museum's leather exhibit drew the largest crowds. Newark was home to a prosperous leather manufacturing industry, and the comprehensive exhibit ranged from specimens of leather dating from Egyptian times to leather manufactured in Newark as recently as the day before the opening.[102]

Newark Museum was built to last. It was constructed of steel, concrete, and brick with a façade of Deer Island granite and Indiana limestone. The magnificent sliding bronze doors, Grecian in style, were designed by Jarvis Hunt. Each door weighed more than a ton but moved at the touch of a hand.[103] There was 64,000 square feet of floor space. The first floor featured sample collections of everything to be seen in the museum, including jewelry, Oriental figures, lace, miniatures, fans, silver, china, brass, pottery, porcelain, paintings, a figure of Venus de Milo against a blue drapery, and a central court with three adjoining rooms featuring exhibits from Japan, China, and Tibet.[104]

The second floor displayed lusterware, a type of clay pottery; examples of early American lighting; a replica of a Colonial kitchen; and a remarkable leather exhibit. The third floor, "fascinating to a metallurgist and mineralogist," displayed radioactive minerals and ores, stones, and coral.[105] The basement level included a large auditorium.[106] As the museum could not possibly show all its material at one time, there was natural disappointment at the absence of many valuable collections.[107]

As soon as the museum opened to the public, Bamberger and Dana took up the subject of adding a science wing and a planetarium. Bamberger was so serious about the planetarium that on one of his tours to Europe he went to Switzerland to inquire about purchasing a planetarium from a manufacturer there.[108] According to Newark Museum archivist Jeffrey Moy, in spring 2005 a set of badly degraded architectural prints were discovered in the museum's Ballantine House basement. They had been stored in an acidic cardboard mailing tube and labeled "Blueprint, Bamberger proposed Planetarium, 1927." A set had been mailed to John Cotton Dana's residence in Woodstock, Vermont, sometime during the summer of 1927. However, the science wing was never built, because in 1929 Dana died, L. Bamberger & Co. was sold, the stock market collapsed, and the Great Depression began, all of which derailed momentum. Still Bamberger maintained his interest in the science department through the 1930s and 1940s.

Newark at the time was preeminent among American cities for its jewelry manufacturers and silversmiths, including Tiffany (although its owners, who did not want their silver stamped "Made in Newark," denied having a factory there). Accordingly, Bamberger requested that the museum's curators begin a collection of silver and said they could add to it on his account. His intention was to place before Newark's silver workers designs they could improve upon and utilize. "So, as it is with all of Mr. Bamberger's gifts to the Museum, each had some practical significance," explained a story in the *Star-Ledger*.[109] Years later, longtime Curator of Decorative Arts Ulysses G. Dietz asserted that this collection was of only modest quality and importance, except for four specific pieces: an eighteenth-century silver cann, or mug; a porringer, or community drinking cup, dated 1750 to 1760; and two pieces by renowned Swedish silversmith George Jensen purchased by Bamberger in 1922, a compote and covered sugar bowl—the first works by Jensen to be acquired by any American museum.[110] Bamberger gave many items to the museum over the years, but none was more popular than the "Mechanical Wonderland" acquired in 1930. Created by South Orange resident William M. Clark, it represented the history of mechanical inventions, all of which could be operated with the touch of a hand. The exhibit revealed such mysteries as the inner workings of a clock, a water faucet, a sewing machine, and 197 other mechanical movements. Some considered this an unusual purchase for a museum, but since Newark was the fourth-largest manufacturing center in America, the exhibit fit in perfectly with the city's identity. "Reminiscent of earlier industrial expositions held in the Bamberger store in the mid-teens, it was viewed and studied by thousands of craftsmen, scientists, inventors, teachers, and educational bodies, schools and colleges, together with prominent industries in the metropolitan area."[111] Special evening viewings were held for groups, including educational institutions that used the exhibit for instruction.

Mounted on ten portable panels, the exhibit traveled throughout Newark courtesy of public service; by 1938 it had been seen by 180,903 viewers.[112] Given that it demonstrated how four basic mechanical principles—inclined plane, lever, wedge, and screw—were applied in household devices such as sewing machines, vacuum cleaners, clocks, and radios sold in Bamberger's store, it was in fact another example of Bamberger's policy of educating Newarkers to be knowledgeable consumers. Although the models were last exhibited in 1987, volunteer docents Richard Denby and Ruth Karp—who both remembered it vividly from their own childhoods—were still fielding questions regarding their whereabouts as late as 2011.

Museum officials made every effort to keep Bamberger active on their board of trustees, where he served for thirty-five years (1909–1944). At different times he was treasurer, first and second vice president, and once treasurer and vice president at the same time, and he sat on the executive committee and the committee on purchases and donations.[113] In 1941 the museum board unanimously made him its honorary president. This move allowed the museum to use his name for promotions while also giving the aging Bamberger a way to avoid meetings that taxed his health.

In 1934, in conjunction with its twenty-fifth anniversary, the museum issued a twenty-seven-page pamphlet entitled "Louis Bamberger: His Benefactions to the City of Newark." It listed items he had donated to the museum that revealed his diverse interests: decorative arts, sculpture, armor and weapons, and textiles, as well as Cypriote, Egyptian, and classical antiquities. He gave some 175 of these items anonymously, with his name recorded on "anonymous cards" only accessible to museum staff. Rabbi Foster wondered openly why Bamberger chose "to remain anonymous to the institution whose building he erected!"[114] As the following chapter will show, Foster was a quite different type and couldn't understand a personality like Bamberger's. In 1936 Bamberger was honored at a reception celebrating the building's tenth anniversary. Museum officials were very careful to confirm the date with him to make sure he would show up.[115] President Arthur Egner's affection and admiration for Bamberger were evident in his remarks: "One of the reasons we are here tonight is to honor Mr. Louis Bamberger. He is a person who does not like to have his deeds praised, but we are making this the occasion to demonstrate our great joy that Mr. Bamberger, having made such a great gift to the Museum, has remained with us and has seen how far we have come in these last ten years. . . . It is gratifying that we may make this record at a time when he [Mr. Bamberger] may read it himself."[116] Egner's remarks were printed in the museum's bulletin and distributed to dignitaries attending the celebration. Egner also advised Newark's citizens not to take Bamberger's generosity for granted.

In 1940 museum director Beatrice Winser wrote Bamberger a note: "I find that you, Mr. Bamberger, have been a Member-in-Perpetuity of our museum since 1910."[117] This status signified that the member had made a donation of at least five thousand dollars. "We seem to have no record of the form of announcement or certificate which was used at that time . . . However, the enclosed little booklet, designed by Mr. Dana, is intended to be the equivalent of the certificate mentioned . . . I thought you would like to have a copy."[118] By that time, Bamberger had already donated over one million dollars and was in a special category known as Fellows of the Museum. He paid her the great compliment of adding her name to a short list of people who had been recommended to receive a copy of the Institute for Advanced Study's much-anticipated *Bulletin No. 1*. Memberships-in-perpetuity were transferable, and Louis transferred his to his nephew Edgar, who transferred it to his daughter, Ellen Bamberger De Franco.

Louis's final donation was a bequest in his will of fifty thousand dollars to create an endowment, dividends from which continue to purchase items for the museum's collections. Carrie was also generous; the Museum's signature painting, Joseph Stella's five panels titled "New York Interpreted," was purchased with a bequest from the Fuld family in 1929. Upon her death the paintings and tapestries in her home were given to the museum.

Bamberger's legacy was remembered in 2009 at a gala luncheon commemorating the museum's one hundredth anniversary. History came full circle when the speaker that day told the guests that they were seated in the same room that Louis Bamberger had sat in when he attended the dedication ceremonies for his museum. The Newark Museum is still considered to be the greatest gift ever given to the City of Newark.

Most of the charitable institutions and social service agencies created through Bamberger's generosity still exist, albeit under different names. It is odd that Newark never honored Bamberger with a public monument, although a number of attempts were made to name streets after him, and one World War II Liberty ship — the SS *Louis Bamberger*, launched on November 29, 1944 — was named for him.[119] But this lack of public recognition was in keeping with Bamberger's own rejection of all attempts to honor him.

Though he was quite wealthy, he was not in the same league as the excessively wealthy American businessmen known as the robber barons. Still, he modeled his philanthropy after that of Andrew Carnegie, as well as his friend Julius Rosenwald. In his 1889 article "The Gospel of Wealth," Carnegie said he believed that wealthy people were morally obligated to redistribute their money to others. He told industry titans such as Rockefeller that they should be embarrassed if they died with their wealth intact. This principle was certainly congenial to Bamberger, who had been raised in a family used to helping those in need. In May 1929, a month before Bamberger sold his store to Macy's, Rosenwald published an article titled "The Principles of Public Giving," in which he criticized foundations and boards of trustees that preserved principal rather than investing in new programs that kept pace with the times.

This is perhaps why Bamberger did not establish a foundation to manage his estate, a common practice among wealthy donors who wanted their names and legacies perpetuated. It would have required selecting a board of directors whose job after he died would be to distribute the interest on an estimated $19 million to causes that they, rather than Bamberger, deemed worthy of support. Not only did the idea of perpetuating his name have no appeal, it was impossible to predict what public charities would be needed ten, twenty, or more years in the future. Instead he followed Rosenwald's advice: "When the time comes—as it does come—when a philanthropic enterprise no longer is needed, it should not be kept alive by a perpetual endowment operated by a dead hand."[120] Bamberger gave his fortune away in his will and never looked back.

6

BAMBERGER, THE FACE
OF NEWARK'S JEWS

Louis Bamberger spent his entire career moving successfully between two tracks: his role as a prominent citizen of Newark and his role as a prominent Jewish citizen of Newark. Newark's Jews were happy to claim both him and Fuld as "one of their own." Beyond that, both enjoyed a nationwide reputation as men who "took hold of what, in 1917, was a moribund community, galvanized it into action and made it today the pattern for a number of Jewish communities in the country to follow."[1]

In 1927 the *Jewish Chronicle* noted that Bamberger's "influence and philanthropic assistance to practically every Jewish project in the city are almost unprecedented by any one citizen in the State."[2] This attitude toward Bamberger persisted throughout his career. A resolution passed by Newark's elected officials honoring Bamberger at the time of his death referred to him as Newark's "first citizen," yet stressed that "his philanthropies, welfare institutions, and hospitals, no matter how important to Newark's progress, were institutions sponsored by [and for] his race."[3] In other words, they saw him as a Jewish philanthropist. Yet as we saw in the last chapter, his philanthropy was certainly not restricted to his "race," so it is interesting to consider what made people think so.

This mistaken belief that Bamberger restricted his philanthropy to Jews is in line with the assumption some made at the time that "Jewish customers, at least in some cities such as Baltimore and Philadelphia and probably many others as well, tended to patronize department stores that were Jewish owned although there was evidence that customers neither knew nor cared about the ethnicity of the owners."[4] Neither Bamberger nor other German Jewish department store owners ran their businesses on the assumption that they would be successful solely on the strength of their Jewish customers. Not even the estimated fifty thousand Jews living in Newark in 1912, when Bamberger opened his first multistory building, were enough to support a department store the size of Bamberger's.[5] Rather, men such as Bamberger had interests that far exceeded local politics and profits. Their gifts were nondenominational and not intended to benefit only Jews. Alan V. Lowenstein, founder of the New Jersey Institute for Social Justice, argued that Bamberger had no reason to treat Newark's non-Jews differently from its Jews. After all, Bamberger used his influence to establish Newark's Community Chest, which encompassed residents of all faiths.[6]

"One can clearly discern, in the charitable giving patterns of Louis Bamberger, a propensity to give to both Jewish and non-Jewish causes,"[7] historian William Helreich wrote. Certainly his gifts to the Institute for Advanced Study and the Newark Museum were much larger than his gifts to Jewish groups, but Bamberger understood that expanding educational and cultural opportunities for Americans in general would ultimately benefit Jews.[8] In any case, he never would have put himself in a position where he felt the need to justify his actions. If people saw him as a Jew, so be it.

When Bamberger's great-niece, Ellen Bamberger De Franco, was asked what was Jewish about the Bamberger family, she replied, "Absolutely nothing."[9] She did not recall the family celebrating Jewish holidays. She and her sisters attended Dearborn-Morgan, a private school in Orange, where they were the only Jews. According to Ellen, neighbors walked past the Bamberger house at Christmas to admire a display of lights and festive decorations. However, these decorations were not religious; the display was essentially an extension of those at Bamberger's store. Bamberger had never forgotten his years growing up in Baltimore: the unpleasant treatment he had received as a student at the Knapp Institute and his lack of interest in the rivalries among the city's synagogues, whose problems he was forced to listen to at his parents' home. He simply had no interest in synagogue life or in attending services. He agreed to become a member of Temple B'nai Jeshurun only because Carrie and Felix were members. On his own, he joined the Ethical Culture Society; a religion centered on ethics, not theology, appealed to him. Fuld, in contrast, was so highly regarded by Rabbi Foster that the temple president, Philip Lindeman, presented him with a card stating, "Please permit the holder of this card, Mr. Felix Fuld, to park his car in front of the Temple every Friday night, without extra charge."[10]

Bamberger's charity work in the Jewish community began in 1900, when he became a member of the Hebrew Benevolent Society and Orphan Asylum.[11] Then new in town, he was quickly drawn to activities sponsored by a relatively small but successful group of German Jewish businessmen, who considered it their obligation to care for Jewish orphans while also helping non-Jewish youngsters. He had had experience with a similar group in Baltimore. Former asylum resident Allan C. Kane recalled seeing Louis Bamberger on Sunday afternoons when the board members made their customary visits.[12] About ninety-five children were raised at the asylum, and all went to Newark public schools. Dee Gulkin Sherman recalled her uncle, David Erlbaum, a former asylum resident, who "in retelling tales of his youth often remembered the kindness of the Asylum's board members."[13] Bamberger stood out in his mind because of the kind way he spoke to the youngsters; he even attended their Passover Seders.[14] "Each year on Passover for the holiday children received new shoes and suits and Mr. Bamberger supplied Cub Scout and Boy Scout uniforms to any male who wanted to participate in scouting."[15] Bamberger provided other in-kind donations too: cases of toys, game balls, ice cream and cake, and all the trimmings for a traditional Thanksgiving dinner.[16]

At the golden jubilee celebration of the Hebrew Benevolent Society and Orphan Asylum in 1911, Bamberger, a member of the reception committee, attracted as much attention at the dinner held in Temple B'nai Jeshurun as governor-elect Woodrow Wilson, the keynote speaker.[17] The success of the celebration was an indication that Newark's Jews had established themselves as a contributing force to the city's progress. In 1925 an impressive tribute was paid to Bamberger at the annual meeting of the society, at which he was reelected treasurer. Though Bamberger was unable to be present, "When his name was mentioned those at the meeting stood as one man and cheered."[18]

Bamberger was among the society trustees who agreed that there was a need to change the way social workers viewed orphans and troubled children. The word *asylum* was pejorative, suggesting that the residents were treated harshly, and in 1930 a resolution was passed to change the institution's name to the Jewish Children's Home.[19] The records show that the youngsters played sports and musical instruments, participated in a marching band for which they wore elaborate uniforms, studied for their bar mitzvah, and spent time outdoors raising vegetables and tending fruit trees in the field next door.[20] The new name was chosen in a contest conducted among the home's residents. According to Arthur Kligman, who was living there at the time, one young man submitted the name "Jewish Country Club" but was overruled.[21]

When a group of social workers approached Bamberger in 1928 with a proposal for a Jewish child guidance bureau, he agreed to fund this institution and to serve as its honorary president. Social and psychiatric casework with children and their families was a cutting-edge idea at the time. His willingness to go along with these new theories on how to treat young people diagnosed with physical or behavioral problems, which in the social workers' opinion made them prone to influences that could lead to crime, provided a new model for these and other social workers. Bamberger's earliest appeals for funds for the Hebrew Orphan Asylum were made in conjunction with Temple B'nai Jeshurun's Rabbi Solomon Foster, whose career as Newark's most influential rabbi began in 1902. The two were given the job of personally asking well-to-do businessmen to contribute money or donations-in-kind for homeless orphans and families who had fallen on hard times. The longer they worked together, the more it became evident that Bamberger did not like Foster. Bamberger was a member of his congregation, but despite persistent efforts, Rabbi Foster was never able to interest Bamberger in taking a leadership role. He made several attempts to organize Jewish education in Newark, but Bamberger rejected his requests to contribute to a fund to establish the New Jersey Normal School for Jewish Teachers, whose purpose would be to instruct youngsters to "enlarge and develop their knowledge of Judaism; its religion, morals, language, and history."[22]

In another attempt to get a contribution out of Bamberger, Foster tried to flatter him by reminding readers in an editorial he wrote for the *Jewish Chronicle* that Bamberger's gift of a museum to Newark was "significant and portentous, because it consecrated the spot on which future generations will be reminded that the most magnificent gift which the city has ever received in its 258 years of existence was donated by a Jew whose Jewish heritage prompted him to think of the community and its development in spiritual and aesthetic interests."[23] Foster then suggested that a department to be known as Jewish Antiquities be developed at the museum and asked Newark's Jews to contribute money to purchase items for it.[24] Bamberger saw no reason for it, and neither did Newark Jews, who never sent a penny. Since Bamberger sat on the museum committee that selected items to be added to its collections, it is safe to assume that he stopped any attempt to establish a Judaica collection. Yet he and Fuld donated funds for archeological digs in Israel under the joint direction of the Jewish Palestine Exploration Society and the Hebrew University that became the subject of a series of lectures heard around the country.[25] They also contributed to the American Jewish committee to enable scholars in Russia to make copies of documents in the Russian archives related to Jewish history.[26]

Unaccustomed to his congregants not complying with his requests, Rabbi Foster resented these rejections, as is apparent in a letter he wrote to Bamberger asking for a hundred-dollar contribution to the New Jersey Normal School for Jewish Teachers. "Of course I know that it is not the question of money, for if you wanted to give one hundred dollars or so to the cause, you would not mind it any more than I notice the purchase of a newspaper. . . . However, I shall not hesitate to do exactly as you have done in your fine charitable work as a collector, ask again and again." Foster continued, "It begins to dawn on me (though I hope that I am mistaken), that with two exceptions, every appeal for help in the past 25 years that I have addressed to you has been politely turned down by you. . . . I do not join any committee that visits you as I had the feeling that it would be better for others to see you rather than me without disclosing the reason. . . . I admire your public spirit and generous impulses as much as I deplore your inactivity as regards religious welfare." Portions of this letter were scratched out, and it is not known if Foster actually sent it.[27] Having failed to convince Bamberger to support the normal school, Foster did an end run around him and at a testimonial dinner nominated Fuld as "the leader of Jewry in our city and State for life."[28] However, Fuld stood with Bamberger. He did not donate, and the rabbi was forced to look elsewhere.

Although Bamberger rejected Foster's request for the normal school, several years before he had donated a thousand dollars for Jewish education work by the Jewish Chautauqua Society. The group was raising funds to establish a lectureship in Kansas City, Missouri, whose purpose was to end what the *Chronicle* called "the campaign of lies and slanders so active against the Jews."[29] Bamberger volunteered to start a similar fund in New Jersey. For him there was a significant difference between the religious teachings of a Jewish normal school and an organization that sponsored adult education programs intended to bridge the gap between the Jewish people and other religious groups.

Bamberger's reluctance to support specifically Jewish schools and universities was again evident in 1935, when he rejected appeals on behalf of Yeshiva College in New York City.[30] Bamberger was invited to a benefit dinner arranged by the local "Friends of Yeshiva College," who thought that "since a number of young men from this locality [Newark] were students at Yeshiva College, it was imperative they receive scholarships and moral support."[31] Sixty years later, author Philip Roth sent Lou Levov, the main character in his Pulitzer Prize–winning novel *American Pastoral* (1997) to this same dinner, where in Roth's words, he "went right to the top and brazenly talked his way into an introduction to the legendary L. Bamberger himself, founder of Newark's most prestigious department store."[32] However, Roth was taking liberties with history, since as far as we know Bamberger did not attend the dinner.

As noted previously, Bamberger supported the creation of a Community Chest, and he was instrumental in convincing forty thousand members of thirteen Jewish organizations to join it.[33] For these groups, joining was not an easy decision. Long-tenured trustees were not anxious to give up their control, particularly in volunteer organizations whose board positions were passed from generation to generation within a family, such as the Hebrew Benevolent Society (now the Jewish Family Service of Greater MetroWest New Jersey), founded in 1861. But Newark Jews trusted Bamberger, who assured them that there would always be an exit strategy should revenue not meet requirements. His willingness to risk all he owned to develop Newark as a prosperous, progressive city made them realize that he had their best interests at heart (as well as his own).

After the Chest had been created, hundreds of women who belonged to the local Hadassah chapter grumbled over a denial of their request for permission to raise fifteen thousand dollars.[34] But Bamberger opposed fundraising outside the Chest's annual community-wide campaign, which he considered a dangerous precedent that would defeat the purpose of having a central federation. The first Jewish organization to endorse participation in the Community Chest was the Newark Beth Israel Hospital, but the Ladies Guild of the hospital was also displeased with restrictions on their fundraising and insisted that they be permitted to continue their activities until their pledge to the Beth Israel Hospital Building Fund was paid.[35] Again, Bamberger stated that "much harm was done in permitting such activities to continue."[36]

On November 16, 1923, Louis Bamberger, Felix Fuld, Frank I. Liveright, Nathan Bilder, Martin Goldsmith, and Leo Stein signed the incorporation papers for the Conference of Jewish Charities.[37] Bamberger was a "delegate-at-large" with the Conference from its inception. He attended meetings in that capacity regularly into 1941, when the group was reconstituted as the Essex County Council of Jewish Agencies, at which time Bamberger agreed to accept the title of honorary president.

In 1924 Bamberger declared that he was "very sanguine" about the outcome of the second Community Chest campaign.[38] Still he was concerned that "there were many who did not clearly grasp the aim of the new movement."[39] However, he thought that given time they would. But in 1925 the Conference expected to "be in financial straits at the end of this year to the extent of $80,000 or $100,000."[40] It looked as though Bamberger's idea to merge the city's Jewish charities with the Welfare Federation was in trouble. Yet he rejected suggestions to borrow money from the banks to cover the deficits. If the Welfare Federation failed, he asked, would the Conference borrow another one hundred thousand dollars next year and establish another precedent?[41] He advised them to clear up the deficits first and start with a clean slate, adding, "There might be extravagances in the maintenance of the various institutions" that required looking into.[42]

What was more, board of delegates trustee Leonard Dreyfuss stated, "There seemed to be an erroneous opinion among our Jewish people that 50 percent of the moneys collected by the Community Chest were contributed by them, and that only 25 percent was received in return."[43] Bamberger believed that the Jewish community should know the actual figures. He emphasized the necessity that the Conference continue and that the spokesman to the Community Chest for the Jews should be the Conference of Jewish Charities. He wanted to prevent it from pulling out of the Welfare Federation before its board members could convince the greater Newark community that centralized fundraising was good for all concerned. He and Conference president Abe Dimond reassured the heads of Newark's Jewish agencies that "if injustice be done to the Jews, we step out and still have our Conference."[44]

In 1926 it was agreed that the conference would conduct a joint drive for the United Palestine Appeal and the United Jewish Campaign, as well as cover the deficit of the Conference.[45] The *Chronicle* reported that the largest donors at a fundraising dinner for this drive, which sought to raise six hundred thousand dollars, were Bamberger and Fuld, "each of whom pledged $30,000 or jointly 10 percent of the entire amount sought."[46] Bamberger was vice-chairman of the drive; Fuld sat on the advisory board.

Despite their prominence, Bamberger and Fuld made every effort to stay out of New Jersey politics unless absolutely necessary. On one such occasion, Fuld responded to an announcement of the formation of the "Hebrew American League of New Jersey."[47] The League, claiming to represent thousands of Jews in New Jersey, advocated voting for Democrat John W. Davis in the 1924 presidential election instead of Republican Calvin Coolidge. The group's leaders maintained that the Republican Party supported the activities of the Ku Klux Klan and restricted Jewish immigration to the United States through the Republican-sponsored Johnson Immigration Bill. Fuld responded vigorously to a letter of October 28, 1924, sent to him and to "many other Jewish citizens as an appeal for the Democratic candidates because of the Klan issue [which] purported to speak in the name of some important Jewish organizations."[48] He held a press conference at which he stated: "I have never heard of the Hebrew American League of New Jersey, and as I am familiar with all institutions which are representative of the Jewish community of the State, I am sure that if it exists at all it is of no importance, and certainly not qualified to speak for the Jews of New Jersey."[49]

Fuld claimed that the four individuals who had signed the letter "only spoke for themselves and not for any Jewish organizations in political matters."[50] "How do you think the Jewish population is going to vote in this election?" Fuld was asked. "Jews will vote as they always do, as good American citizens, and according to what they as individuals think the best interests of the country demand."[51] Fuld himself was an immigrant who had come to America from Germany at the age of twelve. Despite his family's considerable wealth, he had needed to adapt to life in America. When he later spearheaded the movement to build a "Y" for Newark Jews, it was because he believed it was important to have an institution where all Jews, particularly new immigrants, could meet to socialize and become Americanized.

Fuld, who took his rights as an American citizen seriously, also voiced opposition to New Jersey Assembly Bill 118, introduced by Assemblyman Basil Bruno of Long Branch in 1925. The Bruno Bill, also called the "Bible Bill," mandated that the New Testament be taught in all public schools. Seeing an inherent danger in this, Fuld spoke out in opposition. He sent a letter to Bruno saying, "Jews cannot conscientiously consent to have the New Testament taught to their children. . . . Many of these would be compelled to withdraw their children from the public schools and certainly the effect would be to give the schools a sectarian character, contrary to the principles of the Constitution upon which our government is founded."[52] The Bruno Bill "can accomplish nothing toward improving the morals or the religion of our young men and women, either Jewish or Christian, . . . its only result can be to stir up most unfortunate religious strife."[53] Fuld expressed the hope that Bruno would decide not to proceed with the bill, and that is what happened. Bruno's career in politics ended the following year when he was defeated for the office of sheriff of Monmouth County.[54]

Bamberger did serve as a Republican elector for the state of New Jersey, but didn't take it seriously, knowing he had been offered the position as a way to get him to contribute to political campaigns. Otherwise, he was apolitical, keeping his support for the Republican Party and Herbert Hoover to himself. He even avoided active identification with local banks and financial institutions, many of whose trustees invited him to serve on their boards. He rejected their offers because choosing one bank over another was not good business. Nor did he want his name on their letterheads in the event that a bank had problems meeting its obligations, which would leave him to defend that bank's policies. In general, the less anybody knew about his business, the better he liked it, which is why he made his donations anonymously.

On October 2, 1936, a small item in the New York *Herald Tribune* titled "Republican Merchants Meet" reported that Louis's nephew Edgar Bamberger and W. J. Wells, president of L. Bamberger & Co., had sent letters to forty Newark merchants who were Republicans, asking them to attend a luncheon at the Downtown Club in order to "consider ways and means of developing interest in the Republican campaign and to discuss vote getting methods for President Hoover."[55] On November 1, the owners of Bamberger's stated that it was the policy of L. Bamberger & Co. "to maintain an attitude of strict non-partisanship in politics."[56]

Nor, more important, was the public to think that Bamberger himself was involved in the endorsement of Hoover.

Yet the previous day, a front-page headline in the *Jewish Chronicle* had reported that Bamberger was endorsing the Roosevelt administration in the upcoming presidential election.[57] This was big news because Bamberger had been a lifelong Republican — presumably because the Republican Party was favorable to business — and had supported Herbert Hoover as recently as 1932. By 1936 most Americans were blaming the Republican Party for the Depression. Its policies offered no solutions for the country's economic crisis and for what some Jews felt was a resurgence of antisemitism. Therefore, Bamberger was willing to switch parties.

Bamberger and Fuld apparently discussed how to share the competing demands for their time and money. They developed a division of labor such that Fuld was the one who granted interviews and had his picture in the papers. He was a born public speaker, even with his heavy German accent. Those close to both men knew that Bamberger was perfectly satisfied to have Fuld receive the praise as long as he himself could maintain his privacy.[58] Both men masterminded fundraising campaigns for Newark's Jewish institutions. Bamberger's reputation for being detail oriented — it was he, not Fuld, who managed the store's bottom line — made him the logical choice for treasurer and financial advisor. His advice was always the same: pay down debt and run your volunteer organization as if it were a business. However, no one could raise money like Fuld. His infectious humor and "take charge" attitude made him a natural for fundraising. In addition to founding the Conference of Jewish Charities in 1923, their major fundraising campaigns included the nationwide Jewish war relief appeals pre- and post–World War I, and campaigns for Newark's YM-YWHA in 1921 and Newark Beth Israel Hospital in 1924.

Of all the Jewish institutions established in Newark during the Bamberger era, none exceeded the popularity of the much beloved "Y" on High Street, Jewish Newark's center for social and cultural life from 1924 through 1954. The "Y" was part of a movement that had gained momentum in cities with significant Jewish populations. Since Bamberger's hometown of Baltimore was the first city in America to establish a YM-YWHA in 1854, he needed no convincing to back a campaign to raise funds to give Newark its own center for Jewish life.

The Newark "Y" was built by German Jews, most notably Bamberger, Fuld, Abraham Dimond, and Milton Adler, to serve a largely Eastern European population.[59] In 1920 Newark's "men of influence" started a campaign to raise $250,000 for land and a building. Newark at the time was home to sixty thousand Jews, the ninth-largest Jewish community in the country.[60] As one newspaper reporter asked, "How is it Trenton, Jersey City, North Brunswick, Passaic, Camden, Plainfield and Paterson had Y's for their youngsters, and not Newark?"[61] Bamberger responded by contributing $25,000 to purchase land at the southeast corner of High and Kinney Streets for the proposed building.[62] Once board members saw what other "Y's" around the state had built, the original estimate of $250,000 was revised to $500,000 and later to $700,000.[63] The architect for the project was Frank Grad, Newark's only Jewish architect at that time.

The "Y" campaign began in earnest when US Secretary of Commerce Herbert Hoover announced $200,000 of "initial gifts" at a dinner held at the Robert Treat Hotel. One gift stood out: Bamberger's $25,000.[64] Three days later, at another public gathering, Felix Fuld was cheered when he matched Bamberger's contribution.[65] Bamberger and then Fuld were accordingly asked to be the first to sign the "Y's" incorporation papers, dated August 2, 1921.[66] Much of the credit for convincing Newark's Jews that there was a vital need for a "Y" belongs to Michael A. Stavitsky. In 1919 Stavitsky was assigned to be the Newark field secretary for the Jewish Welfare Board (JWB), which had been founded immediately after World War I to support Jewish soldiers. His job was to show city leaders how to establish a Jewish community center. Stavitsky convinced two conflicting groups to merge into one association and work toward the goal of creating a center for the whole community.[67] He saw that the logical men to approach for financial support were Louis Bamberger and Felix Fuld.[68] Once Fuld became interested in "Y" work, it wasn't difficult to get other influential community leaders to agree to organize a drive to raise $500,000 for a building—the largest goal for such a purpose ever attempted up to that time. Bamberger recalled later that the "Y's" trustees "left to my judgment the investment of certain funds."[69]

At the time it was customary for trustees to sign bank notes and personally guarantee loans in the name of a volunteer organization. The "Y's" first president, A. J. Dimond, told fellow board members that

"this obligation should extend to men who until now have not shoul-
dered any communal responsibility."[70] A number of trustees objected
to being required to sign a bond for the "Y's" mortgage until Bamberger
and Fuld volunteered to sign bonds of $50,000 each. This meant that
each trustee would only be obligated for one-thirteenth of the outstanding mortgage.[71]

Fundraising for the "Y" was a sophisticated, well-orchestrated campaign that included asking Bamberger's store employees to do their
share. The store's accounting department was the clearinghouse for
campaign contributions, and Bamberger kept a close eye on what
came in.[72] "Help the Y.M.H.A. and Y.W.H.A. Realize These Dreams,"
read an appeal published in *Counter Currents*, explaining the benefits
that would come from employees' support of the "Y."[73] While a large
number of employees were Jewish, not all were; however, Bamberger
didn't think of the "Y" as a place for only Jews. Membership was open
to all, as were its programs and facilities. "Millions of all faiths came
through its doors to hear famous speakers, to engage in sports, attend
plays, and to further their educations or to hold social functions."[74] The
campaign slogan was, "The next best place to home for your son and
daughter."[75] Apparently, it struck the right note because the campaign,
carried out in only one week, was remarkably successful.

In May 1925, a dinner described as a "debt cancellation party" was
held at the new "Y." The announcement that their donors were canceling the bonds purchased during the building campaign was greeted
with thunderous applause. The dinner's honoree, Felix Fuld, flanked
by Bamberger, thanked the audience for honoring him in this fashion
and then promptly switched gears by challenging everyone in the room
to join him in pledging one hundred dollars to send a needy youngster
to a summer camp.[76] This was the start of what became known as the
New Jersey YM-YWHA Felix Fuld Camps. Fuld had been elected president of the New Jersey Federation of YM-YWHAs for five consecutive
terms and was poised to assume a sixth term when he died. Two sleep-
away camps, Cedar Lake for boys and Nah-Jee-Wah for girls, were dedicated to his memory on June 24, 1934.[77] These camps remained, into
the twenty-first century, a staple in the Jewish community. After Fuld
died, Bamberger served as honorary president of the state "Y" federation from 1930 through 1939.[78] Despite his habit of keeping in the background, Bamberger did not escape the attention of a group of young

teenage boys who belonged to the "Y." They decided to start a Louis Bamberger club and wrote to tell him so, explaining that they admired his good deeds. A few weeks later a box arrived addressed to the author of the letter. In it were sweaters inscribed "LB Club," with Bamberger's compliments. Harry Lebau, director of the Elizabeth, New Jersey, "Y" and head of that city's UJA, told another story of Bamberger's generosity. Lebau had been of some "slight service to the late merchant prince, Louis Bamberger," who in response sent Lebau a subscription to the just-published *Universal Jewish Encyclopaedia*, in which Lebau discovered that his roots were in Riga, Latvia. Riga was also the hometown of Elizabeth's renowned Orthodox rabbi, Pinchas Teitz. These two men constantly disagreed over the distribution of funds until they discovered that they were both connected to the great composer Solomon Rozoski, who was also from Riga. After that, Lebau wrote, "There was peace between the Rabbi and me."[79] Bamberger also gave a "splendid gift of 13 volumes of the *Oxford Modern History* to the 'Y' library."[80]

In 1977 producer and playwright Dore Schary hosted the "Y's" one hundredth anniversary celebration. He said he remembered vividly a banquet that his mother catered at Schary Manor, his parents' catering hall, at which funds were raised to build the "Y." Schary reported that at this event Bamberger and Fuld "electrified the crowd with the announcement that they would match, dollar for dollar, all funds raised from other sources if those other sources could amass one million dollars."[81] "It was done," he said, "as a tribute to the generosity of Jewish leaders." In his autobiography, *Heyday*, Schary writes about other fundraising dinners at Schary Manor, where donors of a few hundred dollars made longer speeches and demanded more attention than Louis Bamberger and Felix Fuld, who donated millions.[82]

How successful was the "Y" at uniting Newark's Jews? Members of the Progress Club, a social club of successful German Jewish businessmen and industrialists, viewed their contributions to the "Y" as a worthwhile obligation. Their willingness to support a "Y" was attributable to the influence of Rabbi Solomon Foster (the only rabbi in Newark who belonged to the club), who advised them "that it was time to end any patronizing attitude toward the city's less affluent Jewish immigrants."[83] Foster described the new center as a much-needed "communal school house, patriotic clearing house, civic home" and way to Americanize the immigrants.[84] Just before it opened, Foster wrote in the *Jewish Chronicle* that he expected people to understand that "no class of Jews is to be honored as superior because of wealth or position or despised because of poverty or obscurity."[85] His role as a rabbi was to say the right thing. However, there was little socializing between the Progress Club's German Jews and the newly arrived Eastern European immigrants, particularly since the Progress Club had the same facilities as the "Y." The "Y" was designed to present all modes of learning and culture "within a Jewish framework."[86] It offered glee clubs, drama and dance clubs, the Hazomir Choir, a young people's orchestra, lectures by well-known personalities, literary and debating clubs, arts and crafts, a swimming pool, a theater and auditorium, educational programs, and musical comedies and revues (known as "Bits of Hits"), whose director, George Kahn, used local talent that became nationally known, including playwrights Moss Hart and Dore Schary, and screenwriter Marion Parsonnet. Hart himself participated in the annual Moss Hart dramatic tournament, in which various theater groups throughout the state competed in staging one-act plays, with Hart donating and presenting the trophy.

The mostly good news about activities at the "Y" made Bamberger curious. He wanted to see what went on there, but chose to show up unannounced and enter the building without disturbing anyone. Fritzi Satz, head of the women's physical education department, recalled, "I caught him sneaking in the back door one day and he confessed to me that he often did so he could browse around unnoticed like anyone else." When he was finished, he saw himself out by the same route.[87]

The highlight of the "Y's" tenth anniversary celebration was the announcement that Louis Bamberger "has paid $5,000 for his ticket," which covered the cost of the ten-dollar-a-plate dinner and left something over for the "Y's" treasury.[88] When A. J. Dimond, the long-tenured president of the "Y," announced he was resigning and moving to Florida, Bamberger asked to resign as treasurer and board member. But no one wanted him off the board, so he continued in these positions on an honorary basis.[89]

Bamberger remained a steadfast supporter of the "Y"; the greatest good he did it was paying its mortgage and daily operating expenses, which he did until the day he died. He left a bequest of $100,000 with instructions that the money be used to reduce the "Y's" mortgage. This amount, together with $75,000 from Carrie Fuld and $100,000 from

Felix Fuld, whose wills contained similar instructions, made it possible to retire the "Y's" mortgage in 1944.[90]

Bamberger and Fuld were also primary benefactors of Newark Beth Israel Hospital. In 1924 Fuld challenged Newark's Jewish community to raise the necessary funds to build a new, modern 350-bed hospital to replace the existing aging, undersized and overutilized one. Fuld appealed to key businessmen to match 60 percent of the contribution he had pledged for the hospital construction.[91] The final cost was $3.3 million.[92] Farmland on Lyons and Schuyler Avenues was purchased in 1926, and a sign reading "New Newark Beth Israel Hospital" was placed in an open field. At the groundbreaking on August 17, 1926, 150 of Newark's most prominent citizens stood in the rain and looked on as Louis Bamberger, described by the *Chronicle* as "New Jersey's merchant-prince," raised the American flag. He did it three times to accommodate each newspaper's cameraman.[93]

Members of the Bamberger family pledged an initial total of $317,000, with Fuld's donation of $250,000 being the single largest contribution by an individual.[94] This amount was 25 percent of the initial estimated cost for construction, or $1.5 million, and made on the condition that 60 percent of the beds would be free to all Newark residents.[95] Bamberger pledged $100,000 and Michael Hollander, chairman of the campaign, pledged $60,000. But Bamberger's generosity also included many forms of in-kind donations: office furniture, furniture for the hospital lobby, and interior design services.[96] Current hospital employees who lived far from the new hospital and were unwilling to make the commute had to be replaced, and the personnel department at L. Bamberger & Co. conducted the interviews and background checks for the new hires. I. E. Behrman, who was on executive loan from the store, stayed on as the hospital's new superintendent.[97]

In 1928 thirty-five thousand residents living in the vicinity of the hospital accepted a weeklong invitation to tour the new buildings. There was such a crush of visitors that hours had to be limited and traffic flow monitored. As a result of the commotion, a woman fell on the front steps and broke her collarbone, and the hospital got its first patient.[98] Despite extremely cold weather, hundreds turned out for the dedication ceremonies on February 18, 1928, to listen to speeches from Governor A. Harry Moore, Newark mayor Thomas L. Raymond, and Prudential Insurance Company president Edward D. Duffield.[99] The entire ceremony, including speeches and music selections, was broadcast throughout New Jersey and metropolitan New York over WOR.[100] A dedication banquet, honoring those who participated in the completion of Newark Beth Israel Hospital, was held that evening at the Robert Treat Hotel.

Bamberger and the Fulds also supported three other hospitals: St. Michael's received $10,000,[101] and Presbyterian Hospital and Orange Memorial Hospital received $25,000 each.[102]

The collapse of the stock market in October 1929 caught the "Beth's" board of directors off guard. Suddenly all pledges were put on hold. To operate Beth Israel through the years of the Great Depression required real grit and determination. The day-to-day business of admitting patients went on. From its inception Beth Israel had provided free medical care on the understanding that shortfalls would be made up by charitable donations. Now there were no donations. Instead, banks were calling in their loans, and frantic hospital board members were confronted with talk of receivership.

Business failures resulting in unredeemed pledges made it impossible to pay the hospital's mortgage. Bamberger met with the banks and insurance companies to assure them they would get their money. He politely suggested to several bankers that it would be better for the banks that were questioning the hospital's management to mind their own business and not try to intervene in how it operated. In turn, the hospital's trustees would mind theirs. He considered it "an outrage for the banks to intervene" in the hospital's business.[103] After this, all threats of placing the "Beth" in receivership ended.

Bernard Miller, one of the guarantors who had received threats from the banks, expressed concern about internal dissention among board members who were also friends.[104] He was disturbed by the lack of cooperation with and respect given to the hospital's president, Frank Liveright. Miller reminded the board that Liveright had been president of the first "Beth" and was an executive of L. Bamberger & Co., saying he was "sure that [Liveright] was largely responsible for the large contributions made by the Fulds and Mr. Bamberger." "Can you picture the thousands of dollars they have saved us by furnishing the institution?" he said, adding,[105] "Surely Mr. Bamberger himself is silently observing the present situation of the hospital and not interfering due to the fact that he is too big a man to do so."[106]

Nonpayment of pledges was compounded by greatly reduced revenue. Newark's Welfare Federation reneged on its payments, leaving the "Beth's" directors feeling betrayed. Many pointed out that Beth Israel had been the first of Newark's Jewish charities to agree to join the Community Chest, but was now being forced to be the first to leave. When they learned that Bamberger had assured the banks that the board management was sound and that they would get payment on their loans, they calmed down and the dissention stopped. They had faith in Bamberger's ability to get the hospital out of trouble. Meanwhile, hospital treasurer Abraham Lichtman put the "Beth's" finances in order.[107] By January 1936, as a result of new contributions (including $30,000 from Bamberger), a new mortgage, and a sale of building and loan stock, Beth Israel was up to date with its vendors, and all bills were fully liquidated with no thanks to the Welfare Federation.[108] Bamberger was satisfied to have Lichtman receive the credit for saving the hospital.

In his will Bamberger reserved his largest single bequest for the "Beth" — an unrestricted $200,000;[109] Caroline Fuld's bequest to the hospital was $100,000;[110] and at the time of Felix Fuld's death, his donations to the hospital were thought to have topped $500,000.[111] After years of ongoing fundraising for what was believed to be the greatest communal undertaking ever engaged in by Newark Jewry and the biggest local fundraising appeal ever undertaken in New Jersey, it was Louis and Carrie who finally paid off Beth Israel's mortgage.[112]

Fuld didn't live to see the effect of the October 1929 stock market crash on the "Beth." He had died of pneumonia the previous January at sixty-one. A service was held at his home in South Orange. A small gathering outside watched the mourners enter and then leave the house to join a slow-moving procession of cars carrying his body to Temple B'nai Jeshurun's cemetery in Hillside. Six days later the Co-Workers' Association Memorial Committee of L. Bamberger & Co. met and adopted a resolution honoring Fuld. Through a voluntary subscription, they endowed an oxygen room at Beth Israel Hospital to treat "the malady which took him from us."[113]

News of his passing was reported in newspapers in Germany, where he still had family, as well as around the United States. For the first time in Newark's history, the flags on all municipal buildings were flown at half-mast for an unprecedented thirty days.[114] Even though Fuld's funeral was held on a weekday, L. Bamberger & Co. closed for business, foot traffic on Market Street was reduced to a trickle, and WOR observed a silent hour. Then instead of scheduled programming, it played somber music. That evening four thousand spectators at the Max Schmeling–Pietro Corri boxing match stood for a moment of silence to pay tribute to Fuld.[115]

Still more remarkable was the community-wide nonsectarian memorial service held at the Old Newark Presbyterian Church. Its pastor, the Reverend Dr. William Hiram Foulkes, asked Fuld's widow for permission to have this service in his church, where services had been held for General George Washington. Fuld was the first Jew honored in this fashion. About twenty-five hundred persons attended the service, but Louis Bamberger was not among them.[116] There is nothing to tell us why Bamberger chose not to attend. Certainly he was not a sentimentalist and would have had nothing to say to well-wishers, least of all at a public gathering. And what could anyone say to Bamberger, who had just lost his best friend and business partner? Perhaps Bamberger felt that the best way to honor Fuld's memory was to remain engaged in raising funds for Jewish causes in Newark and the nation.

As Newark's Jews grew more prosperous, they had become more willing to support Jewish causes that went beyond the city's borders. On January 24, 1915, a mass meeting, headlined "An Appeal to the Jews of Newark,"[117] had been held at the Odeon Theater under the auspices of the American Jewish Relief Committee for the purpose of rescuing Jews in the war-stricken countries of Europe and Palestine. Bamberger was among the sponsors. In 1917 Jacob Schiff addressed a gathering at Temple B'nai Jeshurun at which more than $40,000 was pledged to the Jewish War Relief Fund. Schiff declared that the "present crisis was the first time American Jews had an opportunity to take part in the struggle for democracy" and that it was time for Newark's Jews to do their part for Jews in Europe "without the asking."[118] Bamberger and Fuld had taken his speech to heart and thenceforth made it a priority to actively raise funds for Jewish causes.

In 1919 the *Newark Star Eagle* described Bamberger and Fuld as among New Jersey's leading Jewish philanthropists on the basis of their support for a campaign to send aid to starving war sufferers.[119] They played a big part in a nationwide drive to raise an estimated $14 million for Europe's war-stricken Jews in 1922.[120] Newark's quota was $500,000

—an amount that was not met—but despite this shortfall, the city "established a standard of giving for all time,"[121] as the *Chronicle* put it.

Bamberger belonged to Jewish relief organizations as diverse as the Joint Distribution Committee; the American Jewish Agricultural Corporation, which supported agriculture colonies in Russia; and the American Jewish Committee (AJC). Founded in 1906 by German Jewish philanthropists, the AJC included financiers Jacob H. Schiff and Felix Warburg, Zionist advocate Louis Marshall, Adolph S. Ochs, owner of the *New York Times,* and the Straus family of Macy's, all of whom knew Bamberger. After Fuld died, he became their "go-to guy" for raising money from Newark Jews. This core group of German Jews met at the Jewish Theological Seminary in New York City, where they discussed how to organize and conduct nationwide campaigns for Jewish causes.

In 1925 board members of the Conference of Jewish Charities reported to the member agencies that $15 million was being pledged "for the rehabilitation of Jews in Europe and Palestine" and that the quota for New Jersey was $750,000. Newark's Jews contributed $60,000.[122] The following year the amount to be raised was $600,000.[123] Bamberger and Fuld pledged to bear between them 10 percent of the city's burden. Bamberger pledged $30,000 and so did the Fulds, making them among the largest donors.[124]

In 1926 Newark Jews were asked to "Help the Jew to get back to the soil."[125] This amazing undertaking sought to raise $20 million to develop Jewish farm settlements in Russia. The American Jewish Joint Agricultural Corporation (Agro-Joint) agreed to contribute $10 million. Felix Warburg donated $1 million and Julius Rosenwald offered $5 million, to be matched by fellow American Jews.[126] In response Fuld and Bamberger each donated $100,000.

Bamberger was also receptive to the idea of local Jews earning their living as farmers. The idea that Jews had a future as farmers came from his years in Baltimore, which was home to a group of young Russian Jewish idealists "who had come to America in the late 1800s hoping to establish agricultural settlements on free land."[127] They were hopelessly unprepared, and in some cases starved to death in their attempts to become farmers. Even though their experiment failed, Bamberger still favored the idea.

Thus, when he was asked to represent Newark at a conference of the National Farm School, he agreed.[128] This school in Doylestown, Pennsylvania, had been founded in 1897 to train Jewish boys from cities in practical and scientific agriculture. Bamberger's presence at the conference was a sure sign that some kind of fundraising was going on. Indeed, the delegates voted to raise $15 million to expand the scope of the school to establish Jewish immigrants in agricultural communities throughout the country.[129] Graduates were sent to South America, the Philippines, and Palestine. Bamberger favored giving young boys an opportunity to use farming as an escape from the city. He considered it a productive way to earn a living and to make a vital contribution to America. He himself had a large farm on his thirty-five-acre estate in South Orange that was maintained year-round by workers who planted and harvested the produce. A thank-you letter from Abraham Flexner, director of the Institute for Advanced Study, to Carrie Fuld in 1934 mentioned the garden-fresh spinach served to him and his wife during one of their visits to Bamberger's home.

Newark was always on the list of places where supporters of Zionism came to speak about creating a homeland for Jews in Palestine.[130] Bamberger was not a Zionist. His attitude was shaped by his time in Baltimore, whose new immigrant Jews were careful not to show support for Jewish causes for fear that their loyalty to America would be questioned. Although Bamberger had not previously shown support for Zionism, in 1928 he agreed to serve on a committee welcoming Chaim Weizmann, president of the World Zionist Organization, and Zionist and constitutional lawyer Louis Marshall to Newark. They had come to launch the campaign for Newark's United Palestine Appeal. Jews came from all over the country for what was billed as a non-Zionist gathering.[131] Governor A. Harry Moore chaired the reception committee for Weizmann, and Bamberger and Fuld were honorary vice-chairmen.[132] Louis Marshall died shortly after his appearance in Newark, and Bamberger, who knew and admired him, was among the honorary pallbearers at his funeral.[133]

In 1929 riots broke out in Jerusalem between Arabs and Jews over access to the Western Wall. Newark resident Barney Heyman was quoted in the *Chronicle* saying that he wanted Bamberger to give him money to send "250,000 Hebrews from the United States, Canada, and England to the Holy Land to train under the British army to defend the Zionist settlements."[134] But Bamberger, like his future friend Albert Einstein, was a pacifist at heart and would never have supported violence. He

145

did give five thousand dollars to the Emergency Relief Fund for Jewish Sufferers in Palestine.[135]

In 1932 and 1933 the focus of relief efforts shifted to Europe, with appeals to the citizens of Essex County for funds to aid the Jews of Germany, "now reduced to a state of starvation and subject to a cruel and ruthless dictator."[136] A series of fundraising events were held. At one dinner at the Progress Club, Jacob L. Newman, a vice-chairman of the drive, announced that it was his privilege to reveal that Bamberger would contribute $25,000, since with characteristic modesty he refused to announce it himself.[137] Storms of applause were followed by contributions from seventy-odd guests, bringing the total to nearly $50,000.[138] The *Chronicle* reported that "the gift made by Mr. Bamberger represented the largest individual contribution yet to be reported in the United States."[139] New York Rabbi Stephen Wise said that Bamberger had given the movement a stimulus that helped more than any individual gift in America and had even "worked wonders for Jews in Germany where people are beginning to hear about it."[140]

During Bamberger's honorary presidency, the "Y" federation endorsed a petition opposing participation by American athletes in the 1936 Olympics if the games were held in Berlin, because of the Nazis' treatment of Jews.[141] Newark Jews were asked to support a nationwide boycott of German-made goods, and Bamberger's firm was criticized for selling German-produced goods.[142] Community leader Michael Stavitsky cautioned that "any public accusations against the Bamberger store would inevitably involve Bamberger himself and no one wanted to offend Bamberger."[143] Bamberger was still associated with the store and was there every day watching over the operation.[144] But not even a press release from Macy's owners in March 1934 agreeing to close the store's buying office in Berlin and to cease the purchase of German-made goods stopped rumors that the store still sold German products.[145] In 1938 a group called the "Committee of 100 for the Defense of Human Rights" was formed.[146] Its principal aims were "to alleviate the condition of persecuted minorities in Germany, to prevent the infiltration of Nazi ideology into America, and [to] combat Nazism."[147] Bamberger agreed to serve as honorary chairman of the committee. There is no evidence that he ever discussed his attitude regarding the German goods issue, but he never wavered in his commitment to defend and save Germany's Jews, and this was one way of showing it.[148]

During the 1920s, Bamberger had developed quite a different charitable interest. He began purchasing rare books and manuscripts for the library at the Jewish Theological Seminary in New York City. Louis Marshall had convinced him to serve as a seminary trustee and to join with Marshall himself, Jacob H. Schiff, and Sol M. Stroock to support the seminary. Why Bamberger chose to support the seminary and not Rabbi Foster's request for a Jewish normal school in Newark may be simply because the right person made the appeal. Bamberger knew these men from his participation in war relief drives and giving to Zionist causes. He cemented his relationship with them by heading a drive in Newark to raise $50,000 for a seminary fund.[149]

It was the scholar Alexander Marx, the head librarian, who got Bamberger interested in the seminary library. Through Marx, Bamberger was invited to join the library board. According to Marx, Bamberger gave him carte blanche to look for manuscripts with religious content—even though Bamberger himself had little interest in this area of scholarship—and if they met Marx's criteria for inclusion in the library, he was automatically authorized to purchase them.[150] With Bamberger's help, Marx amassed the largest collection of Jewish manuscripts and rare books in existence. Bamberger had built up his own personal collection of books on Jewish life from the thirteenth to the eighteenth century, as well as books documenting the history of Newark and of Revolutionary-era America. In 1927 he gave his collection of Jewish books to the seminary library.[151] According to Marx, the most important book was *Pinkas of the Community of Finale*, which provided information about economic and social conditions for the years 1660–1693, including relations between Jews and Christians. Since Bamberger's interest in rare books was not restricted to Jewish content, one might conclude that he was interested in history for history's sake.

Bamberger's reputation for philanthropy was such that even Abner "Longie" Zwillman, an infamous Newark bootlegger and gangster, took him as a role model. According to one story, when Zwillman was approached with a fundraising appeal, he responded, "What did Mr. Bamberger give?" "Whatever the amount," Zwillman said, "I will match it."[152]

From early on Newark Jews had been well aware of discrimination against them. They had created Newark Beth Israel Hospital in 1901 because of complaints that Jewish doctors, mainly their own sons, could not get staff positions in the city hospitals. It was also well known that Jews interested in politics were rarely appointed to serve on Newark's policy-making committees. Despite their numbers and their affluence, there was only one Jewish mayor, Meyer Ellenstein (1933–1941), in Newark's entire history. Bamberger was quite aware of antisemitism and discrimination, but was not willing to fight it in ways that would draw attention to himself.

Instead he was instrumental in creating two organizations that were the German Jews' answer to the genteel antisemitism prevalent at the time. The first grew out of a game of golf. One day in 1911, Louis Bamberger and Abraham Dimond decided to play golf at the Essex County Country Club, a restricted club in suburban West Orange. They sought out the manager, stated their names, and asked to play a round. The manager responded that golf privileges were for members only and that Jews were not permitted to play.[153] Of course, Bamberger knew that Jews were not welcome at Gentile country clubs. But this club's members were longtime Newark residents, business owners, and manufacturers who relied on the business they got from him, and it never occurred to him that he would be turned away. Another man might have asked to see someone higher up, possibly another member about to tee off, who might vouch for him. But Bamberger avoided becoming a public spectacle and left.

There is nothing to suggest that Bamberger was angry over this rejection. Instead, his response was to set plans in motion to establish New Jersey's first German Jewish country club. Letters of invitation went out on L. Bamberger & Co. letterhead on November 9, 1911.[154] He held a meeting at the law office of Eisele and King to discuss the formation of the club. Rabbi Foster was asked to attend, since his congregants were primarily wealthy, influential German Jews who were likely to join. The invitation to Foster illustrates Bamberger's ability to disregard his personal feelings toward the rabbi for the greater good of the group. Mountain Ridge Country Club was founded on April 17, 1912. Fuld became the first president and held that post for fourteen years. Mountain Ridge's first clubhouse and golf course, covering about 168 acres, were located across the street from the Essex County Golf Club, the same one that had rejected Bamberger a few years before. During the summer Mountain Ridge was the setting for several golf tournaments, all hotly contested by Progress Club members who, if they were not already golfers, now took up the game.[155] They went to Bamberger's department store for lessons from Mountain Ridge's golf pro, Harry Avery, who would suggest buying a set of Bamberger-brand golf clubs and balls.[156]

In 1926 and again in 1929 Bamberger was nominated to a three-year term on the Mountain Ridge's board of governors, but the minutes reveal he rarely attended meetings; however, Fuld attended regularly. When a motion was made to the board to purchase land for a new golf course and clubhouse in 1927, Bamberger was there and voted in favor.[157] He was also on hand to celebrate Mountain Ridge's twenty-fifth anniversary. Club president Abe Dimond suggested that the Twenty-Fifth Anniversary committee consist of charter members of the club and that Bamberger be appointed chairman.[158] His committee produced such a large volume of business for the club that profits "exceeded any month since the formation of the Club."[159] Here it is worth noting, first, that Bamberger did not like golf—he much preferred fishing—and second, that his agreeing to chair the committee demonstrates his loyalty to Fuld. He knew that if Fuld had been alive, he would have made the club's anniversary an occasion to remember. Chances are that before this occasion, the last time Bamberger had actually been at the club was in 1931, when he and Carrie attended the formal dedication of the clubhouse, made memorable by the unveiling of a sundial erected as a tribute to Felix.[160]

Bamberger joined Newark's Progress Club in response to a second incident of antisemitism. Louis Plaut, owner of Plaut's department store, was rejected as a member of the Essex Club, a social group of influential, well-to-do Newark merchants and bankers, whose president was John R. Hardin, Bamberger's friend and attorney for thirty years.[161] What bothered the Jews was less the exclusion itself than being placed at a "business disadvantage as big deals were consummated at selected restricted social clubs."[162] They may have held leadership roles in the business world, but this did not mean that social clubs whose members were gentiles were open to them.

Social clubs for German Jews had existed since before Bamberger's arrival in Newark. In 1872 a group of ten young men established an organization called the "No Name Club," whose members were unmarried men under the age of thirty.[163] This was the foundation for what became known as the Progress Club. There were Progress Clubs in cities around the country with large Jewish populations. The Newark Progress Club had "the distinction of being the oldest of the outstanding Jewish social organizations in the State."[164] Among its members were successful business and professional men, most of whom belonged to a synagogue and the "Y." Its publicity in the *Jewish Chronicle* featured photos and testimonies to Bamberger and Fuld, who were admired by club members for their leadership in charity and social welfare. However, they were rarely seen socializing at the club.

Committee heads and boards of directors met at the Progress Club to discuss and make recommendations for Newark's Jewish institutions. This was where the decision was made to establish the Conference of Jewish Charities and agreement was reached on campaigns to build a "Y" and a new building for Beth Israel Hospital, and later, on how to save the hospital. When dignitaries came to town to raise money for Jewish causes—everything from the Anti-Tuberculosis League to Palestine Emergency Relief—the Progress Club hosted the event. The only times the Progress Club was not used were when Newark's Jews went "downtown" to settle their differences privately in Mr. Bamberger's office. In the late 1920s and 1930s, the members decided to allow women to use the facilities on Sunday afternoons.[165] Weddings were also conducted there.

The Progress Club was different from the popular Down Town Club. The Down Town Club was located on the tenth floor of Bamberger's store. Its members had a separate entrance and elevator. They conducted business over lunches and dinners, but shared the space for events hosted by the store. The Progress Club met at locations on Washington Street and Market Street, and then leased space at 882 Broad Street before opening an elaborate clubhouse on Fulton Street in 1929. This posh building, designed in Georgian style with a façade of white Vermont marble and red Harvard brick, was a source of civic pride. Every amenity imaginable, including lavish restaurants, meeting rooms, and athletic facilities, represented an "achievement of local Jewry."[166] A group of influential gentiles, including the presidents of Prudential Insurance, National Newark and Essex Banking Public Service Corporation of New Jersey, and Mutual Benefit Life Insurance (the last being John R. Hardin, Bamberger's lawyer), who belonged to the Newark Athletic Club and Essex Club, sent a congratulatory letter: "When we view the beautiful new building erected by the Progress

Club of our city, we realize the tremendous efforts put forth in benevolent and fraternal organizations by the Jews, and it is almost impossible to speak of any such progress without thinking of Mr. Fuld and Mr. Bamberger."[167] Many of these men did business with Bamberger, but few, if any, socialized with him—although this may have been more Bamberger's choice than theirs. He was simply not a schmoozer. To be comfortable he needed a desk between him and his visitors.

Progress Club members conducted business over lunch and dinner, a sure way to put everyone in good spirits. The club's purpose was to cultivate friendship and cooperation among civic leaders and to support Newark's charities, Jewish and non-Jewish, which it did through various social activities, or "amusements."[168] Louis V. Aronson, a world-famous inventor and owner of Art Metal Works, who is best remembered for the Ronson lighter, surprised the club's members at an annual meeting by giving out souvenir cigar lighters.[169] The club's annual Hebrew Charity Ball was described by the *Call* as "the biggest and finest public social event of the winter in Newark."[170] The ball also introduced the season's debutantes, daughters of prominent German Jewish families.[171] As Aronson told the *Jewish Chronicle*, "There is something about the good old Progress Club that breeds an atmosphere of friendliness and contentment. We feel at home here. We are one family. There is no other place like it."[172]

In 1929 Uzal McCarter, president of the Fidelity Union Trust Company, made a speech at the cornerstone dedication of the new Progress Club building, describing himself as a self-constituted envoy from the other clubs of Newark, bringing greetings to Progress Club members. "You people have had the good sense to come into this section, just on the outskirts of the business district, for recreation, instead of building on property needed for business," he remarked, and continued, "I offer one caution from my own experience. . . . It is quality, not quantity that you want. Maintain high standards."[173] However, the Progress Club members needed no advice from Uzal McCarter. Its members had made fortunes as owners of leather tanneries, as jewelry manufacturers, real estate developers, and furriers. They were the who's who of New Jersey Jewry, its "old boy" network and social elite.[174]

Although Bamberger belonged to the club, he was not in the habit of stopping in for a sociable lunch. Except for attending a few select fundraising events, once he sold his store to Macy's and turned his attention to establishing the Institute for Advanced Study, he was rarely seen in the building. During the Depression, the club could not pay its mortgage and turned the building over to Newark University.[175]

Bamberger remained active in charity work for his entire life. He was a delegate-at-large to the Conference of Jewish Charities from 1923 until his death in 1944 and attended meetings regularly. Until 1943 meetings of the board of trustees of the Essex County Council of Jewish Agencies (the new name of the Conference) were still being held at L. Bamberger & Co. to make it convenient for Bamberger to attend. That year the meetings were moved to a different day of the week, which did not fit the store's schedule, signaling an end to the Bamberger era.[176] Still, a new generation of community leaders visited Bamberger at home to keep him abreast of events and, of course, to solicit a UJA pledge from someone who was preeminently "one of their own."

7
"MAECENAS OF ALL THE ARTS"

n 1927 *Jewish Chronicle* editor Anton Kaufman dubbed Louis Bamberger the "Maecenas of all the arts of the city of Newark."[1] Maecenas, a wealthy statesman of the Roman Empire, has come to personify an enlightened patron of the arts who uses his wealth for the greater public good. The phrase was indeed an apt description of Bamberger's importance to culture and the arts in Newark. His interests ranged from history to music to painting to collecting rare books, and he supported a variety of cultural institutions in Newark, Baltimore, and New York City.

Bamberger believed that Newark would not gain national recognition on the strength of its industries. It needed museums, concert halls, choral societies, libraries, universities, and theater to provide cultural resources for its citizens. His friend and attorney John Hardin wrote: "It should not be assumed that these busy merchants [Bamberger and Fuld] were too much engrossed with business to ignore the higher appeals of literature and art. Bamberger's home in South Orange was not elaborate but its inmates enjoyed music and paintings and the atmosphere of a cultured home. They were city dwellers in winter for the enjoyment of the opera and the theater and traveled widely. The rare treasures which they had accumulated were left to the Newark Museum and the New Jersey Historical Society for the benefit of the citizenry of their beloved Newark."[2]

Newark Jews read in the *Chronicle* that Bamberger had decided to serve as treasurer of the Jefferson Centennial Committee, whose mission was to raise money to preserve Thomas Jefferson's Virginia home, Monticello.[3] Jews statewide protested when Bamberger was left off a state committee honoring George Washington's bicentennial, demanding that Governor Larson include members "of the Jewish race" on the committee. Bamberger accepted the governor's apologies for the oversight and agreed to be among four Jews representing Newark on the committee.[4] Italian, Polish, and African American groups that were offended by being excluded from the bicentennial celebration also were represented.[5]

By World War I Bamberger was already a legend in Newark, according to an article in *New Jersey Monthly*.[6] Still, it was not until 1927 that all three of Newark's institutions of higher learning gave Bamberger honorary degrees in appreciation of his importance to the city. Newark Technical School awarded him a doctor of science degree in recognition that managing a large department store was a science in itself.[7] He was "the only living citizen honored in this fashion by the school."[8] Rutgers University made Bamberger a master of arts, with President John M. Thomas reminding the audience at the ceremony that Bamberger's vision of a greater Newark had been a vital factor in the city's progress in business and culture.[9] The University of Newark awarded him a doctor of laws degree. No one mentioned the fact that Louis Bamberger never graduated from high school.

As early as 1902, John Cotton Dana and his second in command, Beatrice Winser, had criticized Newark's leaders because the city had no college-level institutions; they claimed that every self-respecting twentieth-century American city had a university.[10] In response, five such institutions were established between 1908 and 1930: Dana College, the New Jersey Law School, the Newark Institute of Arts and Sciences, the Mercer Beasley School of Law, and the Seth Boyden School of Business.[11] In 1934 all five were incorporated into the University of Newark. Bamberger supported the idea of a university in Newark and agreed to serve on its board of trustees. Moreover, his store paid tuition for its workers to take salesmanship courses to improve customer service skills and to study graphic design, art, business, accounting, or any subject that would advance their careers. Of course, grades had to be high to qualify to take additional courses.

By 1938 the new university was in financial difficulties, unable to make payments on a mortgage on its building, originally a brewery. President Frank Kingdon and the trustees embarked on a million-dollar endowment campaign.[12] Perceiving a genuine need, Bamberger asked his nephew Edgar to serve on a development fund campaign committee. Despite Bamberger's support and efforts by him and a variety of civic groups, the drive never raised enough money to create an endowment. In his will, Bamberger left the University of Newark $50,000, affirming that education "for all the arts" was a priority.[13] The University of Newark merged with Rutgers in 1946; its campus is located a few blocks from the former Bamberger's department store.

Despite his lack of formal education, Bamberger was intellectually curious. Hardin noted that he "was interested in increasing the sum of human knowledge."[14] Unlike other wealthy men of his era, who restricted their cultural activity to amassing collections of great works of European art and eventually donating them to public institutions, Bamberger established a reputation as a collector of rare books and manuscripts and became a familiar figure at auctions. He worked with antique book dealers, as well as private buyers, who tracked rumors regarding new offerings coming to market and negotiated with him directly.[15] On one occasion Bamberger was contacted by a prominent New York City lawyer, Joseph Stroock, who asked him to purchase a valuable collection of books from the widow of Richard Gottheil, a great expert on the Near East who had taught at Columbia University. Bamberger was not interested in the collection, but he was willing to contribute to a fund for the widow—with the provision that if anybody mentioned his $5,000 donation he would rescind his offer.[16] Bamberger did purchase numerous paintings, but according to museum curator Ulysses Dietz, these were only good copies intended for his own pleasure.[17] He donated most of his book and manuscript collections to institutions with which he had a personal connection —the Newark Public Library (which still displays its single page from the Gutenberg Bible),[18] the American Jewish Historical Society in New York City, the New Jersey Historical Society (of which Bamberger was a trustee), the Jewish Theological Seminary Library, and the library at the Institute for Advanced Study.

What is striking is that Bamberger bought these works not for his personal use or pleasure of ownership, but solely to make them available to researchers. He believed that there were lessons to be learned from studying history. His outstanding acquisition was a complete collection of autographs by all fifty-six signers of the Declaration of Independence, one of only twenty such sets in existence. He considered this a coup, since two of the signatures had eluded him for some time.[19] His interest in acquiring this collection and other historic documents speaks to his belief in the power of the written word to protect the rights of all.

Bamberger's interest in American history, particularly the study of the American Revolution, was reflected in the books and manuscripts he collected. After his death, the library committee of the New Jersey Historical Society reported that he had bequeathed "an important collection of autograph letters of notable historians, men of letters, and Revolutionary worthies."[20] He hoped that through the study of history humanity would see the error of its ways. Bamberger had lived through the Civil War and World War I and was alive at the start of World War II. In 1942, at a celebration of the store's fiftieth anniversary, one reporter asked him to comment on the future course of the world. He responded that "his most ardent hope is that restoration of world peace will be everlasting and a better understanding and a higher degree of tolerance among men of all races, creeds and colors will result."[21]

Many of the documents he collected had Newark and New Jersey provenance, and he became a member of the New Jersey Historical Society in 1901 and a trustee in 1918. The next year he made a large donation that qualified him to be a life member. In 1923 the society elevated him to "patron" for having donated the most valuable collections of old manuscripts it had received for many years. One document he had purchased from the Library of Congress at an auction in Philadelphia was titled "Some Early New Jersey Patentees Paying Quit-Rents."[22] Its names and accounts were indispensable source documents for the city's history.[23] It included a mention of "Elizabeth Ogden, daughter of Samuel Swayne, whose town lot was located where now the Bamberger store stands," thus connecting his name to Newark's early history. An editorial in the *Call* maintained that Bamberger's motivation for finding and acquiring such documents was to give his beloved city the documentary evidence it needed to secure a place in American history.[24] Bamberger also gave the society $10,000 in 1929 to support a statewide campaign to raise $350,000 to purchase land to erect a new fireproof building.[25] In 1931 he donated a building at 230 Broadway to the New Jersey Historical Society, enabling it to expand from a smaller downtown Newark location.[26]

Bamberger was so serious about preserving Newark and New Jersey history that in 1938 he hosted a gathering of delegates from more than thirty of the state's historical and patriotic societies at his store to discuss the need to establish statewide cooperation between local societies and the state society.[27] After the meeting, the group was treated to lunch at the store's restaurant. Bamberger also chaired the thirty-fifth annual meeting of the American Jewish Historical Society, which crossed the Hudson River to celebrate at the High Street "Y" with a lecture on Sephardic Jews by Cecil Roth, editor of the *Encyclopaedia Judaica*, and a presidential address by a celebrated bibliophile, Dr. A. S. W. Rosenbach of Philadelphia.[28]

Above all the arts, Louis Bamberger loved music. Like other German Jews, he took great pride in his cultural heritage. In 1875 Rabbi Isaac Mayer Wise had claimed to the German Pioneer Association that "The Germans brought music and song to America."[29] And indeed, Baltimore in Bamberger's time had a professional orchestra, traveling opera companies performing works such as *Norma* and *Faust*, and German-inspired choral associations.[30] Baltimore's German immigrants were said to have founded all of these institutions. Music was played in Bamberger's home in Baltimore and in his home in New Jersey. Visitors to South Orange were expected to spend time listening to concerts over his state-of-the art Capehart radio, and they were invited to play billiards accompanied by music from an Estey organ built in 1917 specifically for his household.[31]

He and the Fulds kept a suite at the Hotel Madison in New York City during the "winter season" to attend performances of the Metropolitan Opera and New York Philharmonic. Their suite was large enough to accommodate and entertain guests. During the day, Bamberger kept busy inspecting New York City's department stores to see what the competition was up to. He traveled a great deal for both business and pleasure, and no trip was complete without attending the opera or visiting Europe's great concert halls.[32]

In 1936, for example, Bamberger, Carrie, and Edgar boarded a steamship for Europe in early February and did not return until late June. Probably for the first time in his life, Bamberger decided to see Europe as a tourist. According to Edgar's diary, they saw all the sights one saw on a grand tour of Europe; and Edgar got to see another side of his famous uncle.

The highlights of their first stop, in Paris, were a performance of Wagner's *Tannhäuser* and an obligatory visit to the Bon Marché department store. Louis and Carrie politely refused Edgar's invitation to join him for a can-can performance at the Folies Bergère. Carrie, who spent her days having fittings at the dressmaker and being treated by a doctor for a stomach ailment, was cheered by a lovely bouquet of white lilacs and roses sent to her room by Louis. She was his favorite sister, and he watched over her "like a hawk." In Monte Carlo, Bamberger told Edgar to put five francs on the roulette table and to put it on even. To Edgar's surprise, he won! They saw Puccini's *Tosca* in Naples, where the Italian audience "expressed their likes and dislikes in a very decided manner,"[33] and Wagner's *Lohengrin* in Vienna. Music kept them company throughout their trip.

In Bamberger's case, I wouldn't read too much into his attending two Wagner operas. He was sensitive to the plight of Jews all over the world, but he was not a zealot. He was the chairman of Newark's Committee of 100, whose members energetically raised their concerns about the rise of Hitler. Their solution was to launch a nationwide boycott of German-made goods, which is discussed in this book. However, no one on that committee would have asked him to get behind such a boycott. By this time he had already sold his store to Macy's, and it was their job to monitor the store's purchase of German goods. Newark's Jews had a hands-off policy when it came to Bamberger. Holocaust studies as we know it today was not something Newark's Jews knew about in Bamberger's time. This had to wait for the opening of the concentration camps by General Eisenhower, who, fortuitously, insisted that photographs be taken of the piles of bodies of Europe's six million Jews. Wagner's music was symbolic of the Nazi movement, but not when Bamberger saw those operas; however, modern-day Israel continues to ban the playing of Wagner's operas in its concert venues. Any attempt to play Wagner is usually accompanied by protests from Holocaust survivors. Can we blame them?

Back in 1892, when Bamberger opened his store, Newark had a reputation as a destination for concertgoers. This changed after the outbreak of World War I, when citizens stopped attending concerts. In 1916 Bamberger joined with other influential citizens to revive Newark as a music center, agreeing to serve as second vice president and board member of the Newark Music Festival Association. However, when plans for a festival were discussed at a public meeting, participants could not agree about what type of music to present. At length C. Mortimer Wiske, a noted conductor with experience in organizing musical festivals, was brought to Newark by a group of music lovers to present a chorus of mixed voices. They believed that Wiske's reputation would attract world-class soloists.

The first concert, featuring a chorus of more than a thousand singers in 1916,[34] was so successful that the following year the organizers agreed to incorporate the Newark Music Festival as an annual event. Box holders and subscribers included the local social elite, among them brewer Christian Feigenspan; Frederick Frelinghuysen, president of Mutual Benefit Life Insurance; Wallace M. Scudder, owner and editor of the *Newark Evening News*; New Jersey governor Walter E. Edge; and Louis Bamberger.[35] Bamberger's meteoric rise as a successful businessman and major employer, who provided thousands of jobs to Newark residents, opened doors normally closed to Jews. He could mingle with these people, but they still did not accept him enough to let him join their country club.

In 1919 a successful performance by Enrico Caruso convinced the Music Festival Association's board of trustees that their time and influence would be well spent in promoting a music revival in their city.[36] A new board was elected with Scudder as president and Feigenspan and Bamberger as vice presidents.[37] Bamberger's efforts to establish the association, and his patronage of the concerts during his entire career in Newark, helped his city reclaim its reputation as a center for music. Festival Association–sponsored performances were intended for local concertgoers, who were also entertained after the show by observing the elegant attire of Newark's fashionable women, getting into their private automobiles outside the concert hall and being whisked away.[38]

As in many American cities, Newark's large community of German immigrants supported its music industry. German Americans were known for developing public festivals in cities where they settled.[39] They created a flourishing piano industry—Newark alone had four piano manufacturers—and established great symphony orchestras. This was Bamberger's own tradition, and his interest ranged from the great concert halls of Europe to benefit performances for the Newark Orphan Asylum. On one such occasion, he and Louis Aronson sat through a musical performance called *Shavings* at the Broad Street Theater.[40]

Bamberger arranged to have the chorus of the Newark Musical Festival Association heard over WOR.[41] Several years later, the station perfected a remote control system, making it possible to broadcast from various parts of the city. In 1924 it aired a concert in Branch Brook Park by the seventy-piece Newark Philharmonic Concert Band.[42]

In 1926 the Festival Association board decided to create a Newark Music Foundation to "develop a greater love of good music and to encourage local talent and musical education among Newark's citizens."[43] Newark had become a musical city, but it did not have "an outstanding position in the musical world." It needed an organization to systematically coordinate and promote its musical activities. The board agreed on a fundraising campaign, with C. Mortimer Wiske as one of the organizers. Rabbi Solomon Foster, whose influence with wealthy Newark Jews was considered essential to the foundation's success, headed the campaign. However, Bamberger's name was not on the letterhead. He was perfectly satisfied to have Foster take the credit, knowing that in the end he would be asked to contribute his fair share to the campaign.[44] After all, it was Bamberger who had revived music in Newark. The goal was to establish a $100,000 endowment to ensure that music performances would continue in Newark.[45] The Newark Music Foundation was incorporated in 1927.[46]

Bamberger was among the first to support the foundation, along with Edgar S. Bamberger, Felix Fuld, and Frank I. Liveright.[47] An impressive list of 224 "politicians, current and former mayors, bankers, judges, insurance moguls, manufacturers, Community Chest activists, doctors, and lawyers" signed on as well.[48] The foundation sponsored a citywide music festival known as Music Week.[49] Not only did Bamberger attend and sponsor the foundation's music programs, he also guaranteed any deficits incurred by citywide performances until 1939, the year he officially retired from business.[50]

In 1927 he arranged to have WOR broadcast Carnegie Hall Philharmonic concerts, which he listened to at home. The Carnegie Hall concerts were not only an attraction for the musical world, but a standard of culture likely to attract the attention of the entire metropolitan audience.[51] Having the concerts heard over WOR was another way for Bamberger to promote Newark's image. He also requested that WOR develop programs featuring local content and talent. WOR began holding auditions to promote and encourage a new generation of Newark musicians. The auditions were held in WOR's studio, which in Bamberger's time was located in the east building of the Bamberger store.[52] In 1929 WOR's fall radio programs included concerts from the Philharmonic Symphony Orchestra, Metropolitan Opera House, Carnegie Hall, and the Brooklyn Academy of Music, as well as the Tuskegee Institute Singers' Aunt Mandy's Chillun singing such songs as "Go Down Moses," "Nobody Knows the Trouble I've Seen," and "Swing Low Sweet Chariot."[53]

Bamberger and Carrie Fuld were also members of the Griffith Music Foundation headed by Lena (Mrs. Parker O.) Griffith, who took upon herself the direction, support, and programming of the Newark Symphony Orchestra. Mrs. Griffith, who took over running Newark's Symphony Hall (formerly the Mosque Theater) in 1938, was also instrumental in instituting Newark's much-beloved Stadium Concerts, for which Bamberger provided generous support.[54] It was natural too that Bamberger be asked to serve on the board of trustees of the Bach Foundation, since he encouraged making the city's Bach Festivals a permanent offering.[55]

Bamberger also found a way to encourage aspiring, talented musicians. In 1926 L. Bamberger & Co. announced the creation of the Bamberger Music Scholarships, the first of their kind to be sponsored by an American department store.[56] "It was intimated that the tender of scholarships were to be an experiment and that the Bamberger firm planned an extension of the idea in the years to come."[57] It was Bamberger's hope that the scholarships would lead to the establishment of a musical foundation of wider scope.[58] He also saw them as another way to encourage youngsters to become useful citizens.

The firm established two types of scholarships: four-year scholarships for advanced piano and violin students at the Institute of Musical Art in New York City and junior scholarships for a similar term with instruction at a New Jersey institute or by a carefully chosen private teacher.[59] Scholarships were open to students of both sexes between ten and twenty-five years of age who lived in Essex, Morris, Passaic, Bergen, Hudson, Union, Somerset, Middlesex, or Monmouth counties —the area covered by Bamberger's delivery service. Applications were available in the store's music salon.

An article in the *Evening News* explained, "In founding these scholarships, Mr. Bamberger believes the time has arrived for commerce and industry in this country to foster the fine arts as much as possible."[60] Bamberger believed that as the years passed, "The winners would form a nucleus of musical thought and action of inestimable value to Newark's civic life."[61] And indeed, to take just one example, Isadore Jennett, who won a violin scholarship in 1930, became concertmaster of the Newark "Y" symphony orchestra in 1933.[62]

In 1927 a ten-year-old boy and a fourteen-year-old girl won Bamberger piano scholarships and got their pictures in the *Call*.[63] Newspapers loved stories such as the one about a young pianist who competed even though her legs had been paralyzed by polio. Bamberger's advertising department publicized these newspaper reports.[64] In 1928 a vocal competition was added, and the scholarships were changed to provide eight study courses of two years each instead of four courses of four years. The scholarship committee explained that after two years of advanced study, students who had advanced sufficiently should be able to win further assistance.[65] Over time the number of contestants increased. By 1930 as many as two hundred pianists and violinists competed for the awards.[66]

In 1926 Governor A. Harry Moore was on hand to award prizes and certificates to the scholarship winners.[67] Three years later Governor Larson praised "the altruism and public- spiritedness of the Bamberger Company" and noted that the scholarship contest "had now become a fixture in the cultural development of this community."[68]

During the Bamberger era, a dazzling array of musicians and soloists appeared in Newark; they came because they saw the city as a place to further their reputations. One prominent venue for performing artists was the "Y's" Fuld Hall, named in memory of Felix Fuld. The quality of the "Y's" program drew Alfred Wallenstein, first cellist of the New York Philharmonic, a protégé of Toscanini, who had played for the great Pavlova, with the San Francisco Symphony, and with the Chicago Symphony. Other performers who appeared at the "Y" included violinists Jascha Heifetz, Mischa Elman, and Yehudi Menuhin; pianists Ignace Jan Paderewski, Sergei Rachmaninoff, and Myra Hess; the Boston and Cleveland Symphony Orchestras; Aaron Copland, Woody Guthrie, and conductor Fritz Kreisler. Announcements in the *"Y" Bulletin* reminded members that tickets for all of these events could be purchased at L. Bamberger & Co.[69]

On Bamberger's eightieth birthday, he and Mrs. Fuld agreed to be among four sponsors of Newark's Stadium Concerts. This idea originated with Lena Griffith and was modeled on outdoor concerts held at New York City's Lewisohn Stadium. Bamberger and Carrie Fuld attended the first Newark Stadium Concert at Schools Stadium in 1933. Mrs. Fuld and Mrs. Wallace Scudder together took on the task of promoting attendance at the concerts and jointly hosted a luncheon and garden party at Fuld's estate in South Orange.[70] This event combined Carrie's interest in music with an opportunity to show off her gardens.[71]

Newark's Stadium Concerts, a special chapter in the city's music history, were a major civic endeavor requiring cooperation from the board of education, the musicians' union, the police department, the Shade Tree Commission, a number of community organizations, and many hundreds of citizens who volunteered their services.[72] This collaboration demonstrated that Newark had serious music lovers willing to support efforts to bring music to their city. Performers included George Gershwin, opera singer Lily Pons, Sir Thomas Beecham with Percy Grainger as soloist, Marian Anderson, and Paul Robeson. Records indicate that in 1936 close to twenty thousand people attended one or more Stadium Concerts. Newark resident Burt Ironson recalled: "I saw Paul Robeson sing at Newark Schools Stadium in the 1940s. The Stadium was packed for Robeson with approximately 25,000 in attendance. The concrete stands were full, but many thousands sat in wooden stands set up on the field. It was a Gershwin program and also featured the patriotic 'Ballad for Americans' for which Robeson was famous. Mosquitoes were a nuisance at that time and prior to the concert's beginning, large spraying machines spread a fine mist over the crowd in an effort to keep the crowd comfortable."[73]

In 1930 the *Sunday Call* featured a column titled "In the Realm of Music," accompanied by a photograph of a very stylish Carrie Fuld, who was sponsoring four children's concerts by the New York Philharmonic.[74] This was the third successive season that she had sponsored the orchestra, and thousands of youngsters were expected to attend. The idea was to imbue "the younger generation with appreciation for the beauty of classical music."[75] The concerts were so popular that they were incorporated into Newark's public school curriculum. An article in the *Call* explained that "Warner Brothers have contributed the use of the Mosque Theater for the series—in spite of the fact that they will have to rearrange the hours of their performances on the concert dates."[76] Warner Brothers were "exerting every effort in the interests of Mrs. Fuld and the children for whom the concerts are intended."[77] In other words, Mrs. Fuld had used her considerable clout to get the use of the theater.

These concerts presented Bach's Brandenburg Concerto no. 3, Beethoven's Symphony no. 3 "Eroica," and selections from Schubert,

Brahms, Hayden, Strauss, and Wagner. Proceeds were donated to the Hospital and Home for Crippled Children and to the Julliard School for the establishment of two music scholarships for New Jersey residents. The neighboring town of East Orange also sponsored a Young People's Philharmonic program for which Louis Bamberger was a guarantor.

After Felix's death, Carrie Fuld was determined to continue in her role as a devoted wife and "champion of his ideals," which included his devotion to classical music. She repeated to a *Call* reporter her husband's opinion that "more good can be accomplished by educating the public up to fine music than writing music down to the public taste."[78] Carrie supported the Newark Symphony Orchestra and continued Fuld's practice of distributing discount tickets for New York Philharmonic concerts, making up the difference herself, for a select group of Bamberger employees who also loved classical music.

In 1933 she and Mrs. Scudder agreed to head a committee of influential citizens to raise funds to sponsor a stadium performance by the Hall Johnson Negro Choir, a leading ensemble of spiritual singers. The singers were said to include descendants of Southern slaves, whose cradlesongs were spirituals. They sang "Carry Me Back to Old Virginny," "Old Black Joe," and a half-dozen others, accompanied by the Newark Symphony Orchestra in its debut performance. The *"Y" Bulletin* printed a favorable review and advised members to get tickets in advance "because of the unusually large response to date."[79] The tickets were available at Bamberger's store.

Louis and Carrie were always ready to take up the cause of an aspiring musician. In 1925 Bamberger received a letter about Abraham Haitowitsch, a blind violinist of exceptional talent who performed in other American cities.[80] Bamberger agreed to serve on a committee to sponsor a concert for Haitowitsch, which convinced others to get involved. Similarly, Carrie agreed to serve as the honorary chair of an auxiliary committee of women interested in sponsoring the debut recital of ten-year-old pianist Julius Katchen. An enthusiastic audience of thirteen hundred people attended the recital, held in Fuld Hall under the auspices of the YM-YWHA,[81] and they demanded two encores.[82] Katchen later moved to Europe, where he became an acclaimed pianist. At the end of his career, the Rolling Stones invited him to play at a two-day show in London that they hosted—a particularly striking example of how the Bamberger influence in Newark bore fruit in unexpected places.[83]

The tradition of a "Y" orchestra featuring local talent got started in the early 1930s. It began as a small group of youthful musicians, mostly cellists and violinists, but by 1932 there were thirty pieces and a noticeable improvement in the players' skills. With funds from Carrie Fuld, the group became a full symphony orchestra under the guidance of director Philip Gordon; and as the *Call* put it, the "Y" "attained a conspicuous place in Newark musical circles."[84] Decades later, the musical tradition begun in the 1930s by Louis Bamberger and Carrie Fuld was being carried on by a community-wide orchestra still performing in Essex County.[85]

In 1934 the New York Metropolitan Opera Company crossed the Hudson River for the first time ever to bring opera to the Mosque Theater. The first performance, of Puccini's *La Bohème*, had been arranged by L. Bamberger & Co. as a benefit for the Hospital and Home for Crippled Children.[86] No expense was spared; the performance included the complete company, orchestra, and chorus, and the same costumes and scenery used in New York.[87] L. Bamberger's management bore the expense—another example of the store's strategy of winning the loyalty of its shoppers by appearing as a public-spirited institution interested in their welfare.

George Bijur, then director of L. Bamberger & Co. publicity and sales, told the *Evening News* that he had attended operas in New York, London, Paris, and Vienna, but had "never seen a more brilliant audience than the one that turned out to welcome the Metropolitan to New Jersey."[88] Despite icy, snow-covered roads, an estimated three thousand patrons attended. "It was an audience that ranked far above the average in its intelligent understanding of music." Unlike most audiences, it did not fall into the frequent pitfalls of applauding at the wrong moments or during unfinished arias. Clearly, "New Jersey need bow to no state in its taste for finer things," commented the *Evening News* proudly.[89]

La Bohème was followed two years later by an equally successful performance of *Madame Butterfly*, also sponsored by L. Bamberger & Co. For lead soloist Susanne Fisher, crossing the Hudson was like visiting a foreign country. She traveled from Greenwich Village by private car and requested a police escort through New Jersey to the theater.[90] The cream of Newark society entertained before, during intermission, and after the performance. Opera dinners were held in private homes and at hotels.[91] Women in elegant gowns, in popular colors of red, black, and white, gathered in the lobby between acts. Bamberger and Mrs. Fuld were invited to a pre-opera party sponsored by socially prominent people from the Oranges, but it is not known whether they attended.[92] Although the opera performances required much rerouting of traffic and parking restrictions, no one ever complained. Ticket prices were high at $2 to $3.50 (available at Bamberger's main floor information desk), but no one complained about that either.[93]

Throughout his life, Bamberger also bought paintings, sculpture, silver, and other objects that he donated to Newark Museum. In 1940 he agreed to fund New Jersey's greatest art show — "Masterpieces of Art," an exhibit of European masterpieces at the Newark Museum. WOR aired a radio preview of the exhibition that discussed the paintings on exhibit. Among the forty-four painters represented were Constable, Degas, Van Eyck, Rembrandt, Turner, and Vermeer.[94]

Indeed, Bamberger's gifts seemed endless. The Newark Music Festival, the Newark Music Foundation, the Bamberger Music Scholarship, and the Bach Society of New Jersey, as well as many other organizations, were all richer as a result of his often unpublicized generosity.[95] He was truly, as Anton Kaufman claimed, Newark's Maecenas.

17. *In 1925 dedication ceremonies for the Newark Museum were held in the museum's Engelhard Court. The museum director, John Cotton Dana, used the opportunity to praise Bamberger's generosity.* Source: *Schindel Family Collection.*

18. *Bamberger's family posed for a picture in front of the Newark Museum in 1926. They are (left to right) Lavinia Bamberger, Louis Bamberger, Pauline Bamberger, Edgar Bamberger, Carrie Fuld, Felix Fuld, Abe Schindel, Ruth Schindel, and Daisy Bamberger. Source: Schindel Family Collection.*

19. Bamberger relied on newspaper stories and photographs to document each step in the construction of his store's final addition in 1929. Passersby were encouraged to check out the excavation site. Source: *Macy's Archives.*

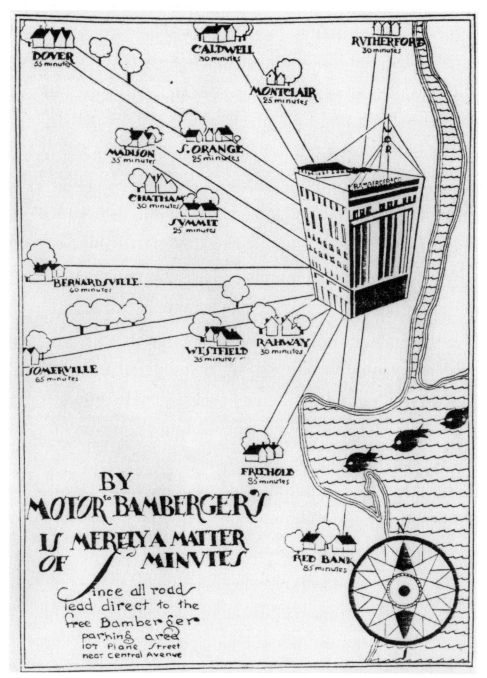

DOVER
55 minutes

CALDWELL
30 minutes

RVTHERFORE
30 minutes

MONTCLAIR
25 minutes

MADISON
35 minutes

S. ORANGE
25 minutes

CHATHAM
30 minutes

SVMMIT
25 minutes

BERNARDSVILLE
60 minutes

BAMBERGER & CO

THE MALL

WESTFIELD
35 minutes

RAHWAY
30 minutes

SOMERVILLE
65 minutes

FREEHOLD
35 minutes

BY
MOTOR to BAMBERGER'S
IS MERELY A MATTER
OF MINVTES

Since all roads
lead direct to the
free Bamberger
parking area
107 Plane Street
near Central Avenue

RED BANK
85 minutes

N

20. *In 1927 Bamberger's encouraged shoppers who drove cars to realize that Bamberger's was "minutes away." The towns he concentrated on were also within the range of his store's delivery service.* Source: *Newark Public Library.*

The New Store of L. Bamberger & Co., Newark, N. J.

21. In 1929 L. Bamberger & Co. was dubbed "One of America's Great Stores." There were sixteen floors above street level and four floors below for deliveries, making L. Bamberger & Co. the sixth-largest department store in America. Source: *Macy's Archives.*

22. *In 1927 Carrie Fuld donated $15,000 to purchase and plant twenty-five hundred cherry blossom trees in Newark's Branch Brook Park. The display of the park's blossoming cherry trees rivals those in Washington, DC.* Source: *Courtesy of the Newark Public Library.*

23. Caroline "Carrie" Bamberger Frank Fuld was a philanthropist in her own right. She was president of the Newark section of the National Council of Jewish Women, funded Young People's Concerts, and enjoyed a reputation as an award-winning gardener. Source: *Jewish Historical Society of New Jersey Archives.*

24. From 1928 to 1974, valedictorians of Newark's public high schools were recipients of this medal, the Bamberger Award for Scholarship. Bamberger believed that Newark's future lay with its youngsters and that excellence should be rewarded. Source: *Courtesy of the Newark Public Library.*

25. *Affectionately known as the Bamberger-Fuld clan, (left to right) Felix, Carrie, and Louis, the threesome spent winters at the Biltmore Hotel in Phoenix, Arizona.* Source: *Schindel Family Collection.*

26. On June 7, 1930, the front page of the Newark Evening News announced that Louis Bamberger and Carrie Fuld were establishing an educational institution called the Institute of Advanced Learning (later the Institute for Advanced Study). Source: *Institute for Advanced Study Archives.*

The Institute for Advanced Study's first board of trustees met on October 10, 1930. Front row (left to right) ~anson Houghton, Caroline Fuld, Louis Bamberger, Florence Sabin, and Abraham Flexner. Back row (left ~ right) Edgar Bamberger, Herbert Maass, Samuel Leidesdorf, Lewis Weed, John Hardin, Percy Straus, ~lius Friedenwald, Frank Aydelotte, and Alexis Carrel. Source: *Institute for Advanced Study Archives.*

29. *On March 25, 1934, Albert Einstein was honored at a gala held at Newark's Mosque Theater. New Jersey governor A. Harry Moore asked Louis V. Aronson, inventor of Ronson Lighters, to serve as chairman. Einstein is seen in the lower right-hand corner of this photograph.* Source: *Jewish Historical Society of New Jersey Archives.*

(opposite) 28. *Albert Einstein was a familiar figure on the campus of the Institute for Advanced Study. In the background is Fuld Hall. Fuld Hall was the institute's first building to house offices and classrooms for its staff and teachers.* Source: *Institute for Advanced Study Archives.*

30. *A solitary bench and a large rock with the inscription "Dedicated to Louis Bamberger and his sister Carrie B. Fuld whose vision and generosity made this Institute for Advanced Study possible" were unveiled on the occasion of the institute's fiftieth anniversary in 1950.* Source: *Institute for Advanced Study Archives.*

8

BAMBERGER, EINSTEIN, AND THE INSTITUTE FOR ADVANCED STUDY, 1930-1944

Accounts of the founding of the Institute for Advanced Study (IAS) give the lion's share of the credit to Abraham Flexner, the education expert who became its first director. Historians have generally thought of Louis Bamberger merely as the philanthropist who threw his considerable fortune behind Flexner's utopian idea, but kept his distance while the decisions were made that shaped what became one of the great American think tanks of the twentieth century. This was far from the truth. Once Bamberger made up his mind to endow the Institute for Advanced Study, he made it clear to Flexner that he expected to be consulted on all matters, particularly the way money was spent. He was aware that Flexner was tempted to spend down his initial endowment on the assumption that Bamberger, once having made his commitment to the success of the institute, would be forced to give additional funds. In fact, Bamberger did so, but not before Flexner demonstrated that he had made significant progress in getting the school up and running.

Why did Bamberger decide to endow the Institute for Advanced Study? Jumping into a new venture that he surely knew would require his ongoing attention, after having said he was retiring from business because he felt he was getting too old to have so many demands made upon his health, made no sense—unless he saw the institute as his chance to be at the forefront of a movement in which a future generation of businessmen pledged to achieve social goals as well as business ones.

Bamberger admittedly was not an expert in education, but he knew something about people. He had built his business by earning the loyalty of his employees and customers and probably thought this new venture would be no different. But it was. It required that in this late stage of his life he establish a new network of personal relationships, this time with the institute's board of trustees, whose careers in academia had accustomed them to catering to men with money. What the trustees thought of Bamberger is hinted at in a letter IAS trustee Frank Aydelotte sent to Flexner a year after the institute opened and Einstein had arrived on campus. "I can't tell you how much they enjoyed the dinner in Princeton," Aydelotte wrote. Mrs. Fuld said that "she felt as if she had known Einstein all her life and that Mr. Bamberger was bubbling over with enthusiasm for the 'highbrow' society in which he has recently been moving."[1] This description of Bamberger being impressed by the guests at the dinner reveals a complete lack of knowledge of who he was. However, once Aydelotte came to know Bamberger, he respected him more. To fellow Newarkers, Bamberger was a legend in his own time, and he moved in a social circle that included America's most successful entrepreneurs and philanthropists. It was his shyness and quiet demeanor that usually led to his being underestimated by more than one casual observer.

On June 30, 1929, the day after the sale of Bamberger's department store was announced, Louis Bamberger told a reporter from the *New York Times* that he "wished to devote more time to his personal interests and to the philanthropic work that he had planned."[2] A year later, the *Newark Evening News* headlined "Louis Bamberger and Mrs. Fuld Give $5,000,000 to Establish Institute of Advanced Learning." The new college, if built as its donors intended, would be located on Bamberger's estate in South Orange and was expected to "make the Newark vicinity one of the intellectual centers of the nation and the world as well."[3] When would it be completed? That question could not be answered.[4]

After the initial flurry of praise had died down, the public was advised that the "opening of the school is some time off."[5] The site and faculty still needed to be selected, and the preliminary steps would take an estimated year or more.[6]

Initially, Bamberger had his heart set on establishing a medical college in Newark. Together he and Felix Fuld had given a third of the funds to build and furnish Beth Israel Hospital in 1924. A medical school in Newark that would provide a continuing source of doctors for the "Beth" made sense; the idea had previously been considered back in 1915 by Princeton University.[7]

Bamberger began by asking two trusted advisors, attorney Samuel Leidesdorf and accountant Herbert Maass, to find the best man to advise him on creating the school. They came up with Dr. Abraham Flexner, whose famous *Flexner Report*, a book-length study of medical education published in 1910, had had a profound effect on the profession. Flexner's reputation convinced Bamberger that he was the right person. He was also partly influenced by his friend Julius Rosenwald, who had used Flexner as his advisor when he endowed a medical school at the University of Chicago and now recommended him.[8] Bamberger invited Flexner to meet with him and his sister in their suite at the Hotel Madison in New York.[9]

Louis and Carrie assumed they would be discussing a plan for a medical school in Newark, but Flexner argued that such a school would not be successful. Newark lacked an important university with a large library, had no teaching hospital to support medical research, and could not compete with New York's medical schools. Instead, he asked if he could describe an idea of his own for an educational Utopia, an institute for advanced study—one of the boldest initiatives ever proposed for the advancement of postdoctoral education in America.

Bamberger was immediately taken by Flexner's concept and appears to have grasped the implications of Flexner's plan, which offered PhD degrees, an opportunity for scientists and scholars to work independently without distractions, and stipends to eliminate a researcher's need to teach. It was Flexner's description of the proposed institute that Bamberger used in the history-making letter he sent in June 1930 inviting select individuals to serve on the IAS board of trustees.

He and Carrie were about to leave for Phoenix, where they spent winters at the Biltmore Hotel. Bamberger was now seventy-five, and both he and his sister were in poor health. "I should like to add a codicil to my will," he told Flexner, "which will secure the use of our money for this purpose, should anything befall us."[10] Flexner then created a draft embodying the purpose of the institute for Bamberger and Fuld to include in their will that read, "We are presently of the opinion that the best service we can render mankind is to establish and endow a graduate college which shall be . . . free from all the impediments which now surround graduate schools because of the undergraduate activities connected therewith."[11] Bamberger also insisted that Flexner accept an appointment as director as soon as the institute was established. He was willing to invest in the idea, but not without the best candidate to implement it. On May 5, 1930, Flexner accepted the job at a salary of $20,000.[12]

From the beginning, the Institute for Advanced Study was a marriage between academia and a no-nonsense businessman. Bamberger instructed his attorney, John R. Hardin, to draft a series of bylaws stating that Louis and Carrie were the sole founders of this educational institution, for which "no gifts, bequests, or devices of real and/or personal property could be accepted from sources other than from Louis Bamberger and Mrs. Felix Fuld."[13]

Correspondence between Bamberger and Flexner indicates that no decision was made without consulting Bamberger. This also may have been a move on Flexner's part to ingratiate himself with Bamberger. In any case, Bamberger defined the mission of the institute, recommended and selected trustees, and accepted and rejected selections of professors. As Flexner wrote in a 1933 letter, he could not take action without Bamberger's knowledge. "Indeed," he wrote during the process of hiring mathematician Hermann Weyl, "I have no legal authority to do so."[14] Bamberger also fostered a congenial relationship with neighboring Princeton University by offering to pay for the use of its classrooms by the institute's mathematicians. It appears that working conditions at the IAS were so agreeable that after Princeton's leading mathematician, Oswald Veblen, joined the IAS faculty, Bamberger had to assure the university authorities that the institute would not in future offer positions to Princeton professors.[15] He even gave thought to Flexner's eventual retirement and early on told Flexner that he should have an "understudy" and groom that person to replace him.[16]

Flexner learned quickly that Bamberger was a stickler for details, particularly when it came to spending money. Thus, in one letter he told Bamberger that he went to Macy's to look at office furniture. Discovering that they no longer handled desks and chairs, he found two other firms that manufactured office furniture at reasonable prices.[17]

Bamberger viewed the institute as a start-up venture just like any other business; and much as with his own business, he insisted on fiscal responsibility. "The Institute," he wrote, should not "under take anything we are not able to comfortably finance."[18] He was willing to invest but would withhold any additional funds until he saw results. Not surprisingly, he agreed to serve on the institute's finance committee. Flexner too recognized that if the institute were to have any chance of success, he had to think like a businessman. In his first "Report of the Director," dated October 13, 1931, he wrote, "Business men know better; they are constant first-hand students of their competitors; on this point an institute for advanced study can certainly learn something important from industry."[19]

Selecting Flexner as director was a calculated move on Bamberger's part. Flexner clearly had the credentials for the job, but that alone would not have been sufficient for a savvy businessman such as Bamberger. Since the institute was planning to hire only top scientists and scholars, Flexner's long-standing connections to American and European universities would be useful. In addition, Flexner had spent fifteen years working for the Rockefeller Foundation's general education board before coming to the IAS, and in that time had given away some $600 million.[20] Flexner had probably anticipated that as time passed there would be a need for additional funding. Therefore, it was to the institute's advantage that he knew which men on that board would be likely to fund future IAS projects.

Progress was quick. On May 20, 1930, the State Board of Education approved a certificate of incorporation in the name of the "Institute for Advanced Study: Louis Bamberger and Mrs. Felix Fuld Foundation." It was signed by Louis Bamberger, Mrs. Felix Fuld, John R. Hardin, Samuel D. Leisdesdorf, and Herbert H. Maas.[21] The original plan was to have it ready for Bamberger's birthday on May 15, but there was a delay in the paperwork.

On June 4, 1930, Bamberger wrote to a select group of individuals asking them to serve on the institute's first board of trustees. "So far as we are aware," his letter explained, "there is no institution in the United States where scientists and scholars devote themselves at the same time to serious research and to the training of competent postgraduate students entirely separate from undergraduate studies." It is essential to note that Bamberger had no intention of establishing yet another elitist university. He had spent a lifetime supporting causes for the less fortunate, who would not have had access to higher education if not for men like him. A man of high moral and ethical principles, he was an active supporter of Newark's Urban League, believed women should have the right to vote, and argued for a world where all people could get along. Flexner may have used Bamberger to realize his dream, but Bamberger used Flexner's "educational Utopia" as a vehicle to realize his own mission, including the desire to create a haven for education free from pressures, social biases, race conflict, and religious and gender discrimination. He wasn't interested in size or numbers, but in quality. "If," he told the trustees, "we hold fast to this standard, the influence of the Institute in the country may be out of all proportion to its relative size."[22]

Thus his June 4 letter emphasizes that acceptance to influential colleges and universities should not, and would not if he had his way, be influenced by "accidents of race, creed, or sex."[23] The wording is similar to that used in 1903 when Congress chartered the Rockefeller Foundation's general education board for "the promotion of education within the United States of America, also without distinction of race, sex or creed."[24] In that instance, Congress had focused on high school education in the American South. Bamberger's adoption of Congress's wording suggests that he may have gotten it from Flexner before he composed his letter.

The trustees met for the first time on September 30, 1930, over lunch at the Uptown Club in New York City. Included were Edgar S. Bamberger, Herbert Maass, Samuel Leidesdorf, Dr. Julius Friedenwald, whose Baltimore family was related through marriage to Bamberger, Bamberger's cousin Dr. Florence Sabin of the Rockefeller Institute, and John R. Hardin. Other influential board members were Percy S. Straus of Macy's and Herbert H. Lehman, lieutenant governor of New York. Four other members had been recommended by Flexner: Alanson B. Houghton, former ambassador to the Court of St. James; Dr. Frank Aydelotte, president of Swarthmore College; Dr. Lewis H. Weed, dean of the medical school at Johns Hopkins University; and Dr. Alexis Carrel of the Rockefeller Institute.

The group met again on October 10 and adopted bylaws locating the proposed institute "in the vicinity of Newark." Louis Bamberger was named president of the board and Mrs. Fuld vice president. This was the first time in Bamberger's career that he agreed to be named the president of any organization. He obviously felt that the institute's unprecedented mission merited a break with his standard practice. Overall, they were a congenial group who sensed they were being given an opportunity to make a genuine contribution to American education.

Though Bamberger's relationship with the trustees was one of mutual respect, it was clear that he had stacked the board with people he expected to be loyal to him. No changes were made to the board until he was certain that the new personalities were a match for the institute's mission.[25] He consistently relied on family to fill openings, and the nominating committee felt it had no choice but to conform to his requests.[26] Edgar Bamberger's presence on the board enabled its members to maintain a direct connection to Bamberger, on whose ongoing financial contributions the institute depended. In fact, everyone associated with running the institute deferred to Bamberger. He was respectful of their time, however, and never asked them to change their schedules to accommodate his.[27]

The only time Bamberger felt it necessary to remove a trustee from the board was when Felix Frankfurter, then an associate justice of the United States Supreme Court, was accused of breaking the board's code of confidentiality by openly discussing a prospective appointment to the board. Frankfurter vigorously denied that he had done this, and then exacerbated the problem by trying to convince another board member to support his claim.[28] This was unfortunate, since Bamberger had greeted Frankfurter's appointment to the board in 1933 with unusual enthusiasm. Frankfurter had then used his influence to arrange for Einstein's visa. But now Bamberger suggested that Frankfurter not be renominated on the basis "of what was described as his cantankerousness at a board meeting." There was no place on the institute's board for a member who had no hesitation in stirring up dissention.[29] Therefore, Frankfurter was advised that to avoid any embarrassment or blot on his reputation it would be best if he resigned, and he did.

During this period, Bamberger's reputation as a philanthropist became not just national but international, as the story of his endowment of the IAS spread on both sides of the Atlantic. On December 1, 1930, Flexner sent a pamphlet titled *Organization and Purpose: Bulletin No. 1*, containing Bamberger's original letter to the trustees and a few other documents, to top scholars, scientists, and heads of universities acquainted with university conditions in America and in Europe, seeking their advice. Flexner was hoping this publication would lead to letters of praise, which he could share with Bamberger. And indeed it did. In no time he received a "flood of communications from all over America," an "outpouring of enthusiasm for the fresh approach to postdoctoral studies," Flexner wrote.[30] Bamberger had the bulletin sent to his associates and friends, including Beatrice Winser, director of the

Newark Museum, and planned parenthood advocate Margaret Sanger. It was rare that Bamberger tooted his own horn in this way, but he was rightfully proud of his role as the institute's founder.[31]

Officials at the Carnegie and Rockefeller Foundations, long in the business of education, confessed they had been caught off guard by the institute's vast potential.[32] "It must be highly gratifying to you, as it is to me, to know how your work at the Institute is being praised on the outside," Bamberger wrote to Flexner.[33] For Harvard's president, James B. Conant, "The establishment of the Institute [was] the most important event in higher education that has happened in America since the founding of the Johns Hopkins University in 1876."[34]

Flexner considered it necessary to do a thorough face-to-face survey of Europe's scholars, mathematicians, and scientists; and during the first six months of 1931, he made the rounds of European universities compiling responses to the formation of the IAS and reported his findings to the trustees in October. Bamberger paid for these jaunts.

Characteristically, Bamberger deliberately made Flexner the official spokesperson for the institute. Thus, in 1931 he arranged for Flexner to speak at the Newark "Y" Lyceum series on "The Status of Higher Education in America." The speech was well attended, but it is not known whether people came because the institute was big news or because the *"Y" Bulletin* had announced: "Louis Bamberger to preside." Bamberger was a draw in his own right.[35]

Historians of the institute's early years frequently omit the importance of personal relationships in creating the IAS, and particularly Bamberger's shaping of his own connections with Flexner and later on with Albert Einstein. Flexner had Baltimore connections; he had spent two years at Johns Hopkins University, a school that stressed postgraduate education. He was also a German Jew, whose reputation as a prominent figure in American education reform, particularly medical education, made him welcome in Bamberger's social circles.

Brisk correspondence between Flexner and Mrs. Fuld, who was the family's letter writer, covered how each was feeling, doctor recommendations, sociable bridge games, vacations, birthday gifts, and personal favors. Flexner used his influence to help Bamberger's greatniece, Jane Bamberger, gain admission to Wheaton College. Flexner forwarded correspondence praising institute accomplishments that he felt Bamberger would enjoy reading, and he issued invitations for

Louis and Carrie to "motor" to Princeton to have tea and to mingle with the institute's faculty. These invitations were rarely accepted, because of Bamberger's and Mrs. Fuld's ill health and not feeling up to the car ride, travel and vacation plans, and other commitments. On occasion, however, Mrs. Fuld escorted to Princeton a "few ladies" who wanted to visit the institute.

Bamberger and Fuld became accustomed to Flexner visiting them in Arizona during the winter to discuss the institute. In one letter Bamberger wrote that he and Carrie had missed Flexner after he left and "consoled one another with the fact that we had some delightful talks with you, where it was felt that we learned to know each other better."[36] Just as with his store, Bamberger made people connected to the institute feel they were part of a family business. Mrs. Fuld established a custom of afternoon tea in the common room of Fuld Hall, after the building opened in 1939 on the Princeton campus. Happily for succeeding generations, this tradition continues.[37] Carrie also may have had a hand in decisions made by the committee on buildings and grounds to make the area surrounding Fuld Hall more attractive. After all, the building was named for her husband, and she was a notable gardener.

While Louis and Carrie responded favorably to Flexner, there were some dubious aspects to his character. For example, it turns out that the idea of a university for postgraduate studies was not original with him. Flexner presented it as his idea, when in fact his vision for the IAS had been inspired by Daniel Coit Gilman's original 1876 plan for Johns Hopkins University. Gilman conceived of a graduate-only university built around superior faculty devoted to research, but outside pressures forced him to revise his program to include undergraduates. In a letter to his wife on June 23, 1931, Flexner wrote, "Can it be that I am starting something as important as Gilman's work in '76?"[38] In his autobiography, *I Remember*, he wrote, "Gilman's ideal had become his dream; over half a century later, Mr. Bamberger and Mrs. Fuld made its realization possible."[39]

Furthermore, in 1918 Princeton's master physicist and mathematician, Oswald Veblen, had done a study of his own that produced a plan similar to the one Flexner presented to Bamberger.[40] Like Flexner, Veblen went to Europe to observe the state of mathematics in universities in Germany, Paris, and Cambridge. His plan was to gather together "a community of Princeton mathematicians whose mission was to re-define American mathematics" and to find the funds to set up an en-dowment for what he called a "Mathematical Institute."[41] He contacted Abraham Flexner's brother Simon, director of the Rockefeller Institute for Medical Research, asking him to "urge the Institute to extend its existing National Research fellowships to include mathematical re-search" and suggested that the research be conducted at Princeton.[42] Veblen's proposal was adopted, and four months later he returned to Simon Flexner with a more ambitious request—one that was remark-ably similar to the proposal made to Bamberger.[43]

Veblen's plan included "sponsoring postdoctoral fellowships for promising young mathematicians, freeing existing professors from crushing teaching loads, and promoting cross-fertilization between mathematics and other fields."[44] Simon Flexner told Veblen, "I wish that sometime you might speak with my brother, Mr. Abraham Flex-ner, of the General Education Board."[45] Veblen never knew that when Abraham Flexner decided that the IAS would begin with mathematics, he had been primed with Veblen's own ideas by his brother. In fact, Flexner incorporated much of Veblen's plan in his own proposal.[46]

Klari von Neumann, wife of the mathematician John von Neumann, who joined the IAS faculty at the same time as Einstein, described Flexner as "a small hawk-like wiry man with a wonderful twinkle in his eye and a front of obviously false modesty that made you suspect the strength and power, the cunning and cleverness that were hidden be-hind a delightful sense of humor."[47] These traits were evident during Flexner's three-year campaign to hire Albert Einstein, and he used them just as effectively in his dealings with Bamberger.

For example, in 1925 Bamberger had allowed his name to appear on the letterhead of a group raising funds for the Hebrew University in Je-rusalem, but in 1935 he refused to support Yeshiva College. Why was Bamberger willing to support the one but not the other? Since Flex-ner was the foremost expert in America on university education and opposed contributing to Yeshiva, Bamberger was prepared to listen to him. Flexner explained that in his experience Jewish students were admitted to universities on an equal basis with non-Jews, solely on the basis of merit.[48] He said he believed that an institution of this kind for Jewish students alone was unwise. Yet Flexner knew that, in fact, major American universities had quotas for Jewish students. Flexner's real agenda may have been to prevent funds from going to Yeshiva or any other university for fear that they would come out of the money Bamberger intended for the IAS. At the same time, Bamberger himself never intended to donate to Yeshiva. He made this evident when he refused to attend a dinner in Newark in 1935 in support of Yeshiva. Flexner's argument gave him the out he was looking for.[49]

One question Flexner faced was what subject the institute should begin with. He considered a school of economics to accommodate Bamberger's personal interest in the subject, but decided instead to start with mathematics, which he explained as "singularly well suited to our beginning."[50] Its theories stimulated all areas of thought. It had practical advantages, since it "required only a few rooms, books, blackboards, chalk, paper, and pencils."[51] As Klari von Neumann put it, Flexner was not a scholar and knew nothing about mathematics, but he "had a very practical mind which conceived the idea that there should be a place where men whose only tools of work were their brains could spend time entirely on their own," or could talk to one another if they felt like it.[52]

Flexner sought advice from Johns Hopkins's president Daniel Coit Gilman, who told him that "there are in America at this time few mathematicians of international repute" and that he should look to Europe for the ablest available scholars.[53] Accordingly, Flexner started his search in Germany. In July 1932, Flexner informed Bamberger that Aydelotte had arranged to have dinner with Veblen, Weyl, and the Einsteins (all three men were in Berlin at the time) and that Aydelotte "was much impressed with the enthusiasm which Einstein and indeed all three expressed for the new Institute."[54] In October two faculty nominations were announced, that of Veblen, already effective as of October 1, and that of Einstein, effective October 1, 1933. Weyl was unable to make a decision. Though it was Veblen who had recommended Einstein in the first place, Flexner took the credit for hiring him.[55]

Of the two, it was Einstein's appointment that captured the public's imagination. Einstein was no stranger to Princeton. In 1921, the year he was awarded the Nobel Prize in Physics, he had visited the campus for three days to accept an honorary degree and deliver five Stafford Little lectures on the theory of relativity.[56] Princeton mathematicians were among the first to accept his relativity theory, which may have played a part in his decision to settle there years later.[57]

At the time of his visit, Einstein was on a US tour with Zionist leader Chaim Weizmann to raise money for the Jewish National Fund. Einstein drew the crowd, and Weizmann made the speeches. Among the organizers of this tour was Louis Bamberger. Einstein's private secretary said later that she thought Princeton had offered Einstein a faculty position at this time, but that he declined.[58]

In April 1930, Oswald Veblen wrote to Einstein requesting permission to inscribe a remark he had made in Princeton in 1921—"God is clever, but not dishonest"—above the fireplace in the professors' lounge in Princeton's Fine Hall. Einstein gave his approval.[59] Between 1930 and 1933 Einstein made four trips to do research at the California Institute of Technology's Mount Wilson Observatory. These visits initiated what Einstein's biographer Walter Isaacson describes as "the inevitability of his emigration" to America.[60]

In 1931 Flexner visited Caltech's president, Robert A. Millikan, seeking recommendations for scholars to appoint as the head of mathematics for the institute.[61] Millikan insisted that Flexner talk to Einstein, who coincidentally was living and working on Caltech's campus at the time—something Millikan later regretted, since he had no idea that Flexner would use this casual meeting to initiate a campaign to lure Einstein to the IAS.[62] During the conversation, Flexner described the IAS and referred to "Mr. Bamberger who wished that his gift be used to create a 'paradise' for scholars and scientists."[63] Flexner refrained from making an outright offer to Einstein at this time, but felt at their parting that Einstein had taken the bait. In 1932 Flexner and Einstein met again. Flexner had arranged to be in Oxford just when Einstein was spending some time at Christ Church College. "I saw him again and we had a pleasant visit together, strolling in the Fellows' Garden," Flexner wrote. They agreed to meet again in Caputh outside Potsdam, where Einstein had a vacation home. It was there that Flexner carefully explained the opportunities a professorship at the IAS offered Einstein: financial security and the promise of a pension; an appointment for Einstein's research associate, Dr. Walther Mayer; a quiet community of scholars, who would have every resource for research available to them; and freedom from the political turmoil engulfing Germany and Europe. When Flexner was finished, Einstein uttered a sentence that Flexner noted verbatim: "*Ich bin Feuer und Flamme dafür*": "I am fire and flame for that."[64]

They then discussed Einstein's salary, and here Flexner tried to take advantage of the less worldly Einstein, who apologized for requesting the trifling sum of $3,000 per year; to him that was almost too much.[65] He asked whether that was enough to support his family in America. At this point Einstein's wife took over, and they settled on $10,000 per year. Oswald Veblen's salary was $15,000, and it is not clear why Flexner offered to pay Einstein so much less. Surely he must have known that the difference would come out once the two men started working together.

In any event, Bamberger insisted that Einstein's salary match Veblen's. He instructed Flexner to tell Einstein that he could either take a salary of $15,000, or allow the institute to set aside for his benefit the $5,000 difference between that and the $10,000 agreed upon, which "would be available to him at any time for any purpose."[66] Eventually, Einstein accepted the same amount paid to other faculty, explaining that he was obliged to take into account the "severe economic conditions which may involve him in obligations to children, relatives and friends and events which he cannot foresee."[67] The *New York Times* reported, "Just what the scale of salaries will be has not been made public; but it is understood that the institute's solution of the salary problem together with its efforts to keep its faculty free from distracting influences so favorably impressed Professor Einstein that he remarked 'This is Heaven!'"[68]

An initial task was finding a location for the institute. Bamberger wanted it to be in Newark, but Flexner asserted that Newark was not an ideal place. Scholars and students were better off in a place with a large university and a multidisciplinary library large enough to cater to serious researchers. For Flexner, a better location would have been Washington, DC, with access to the Library of Congress. If Flexner thought he could change Bamberger's mind, he was mistaken. Bamberger then insisted that the IAS be located in New Jersey; the citizens of Newark and New Jersey had made his business a success, and it was only right that they be rewarded with the economic boost that came with locating the institute in their state. Bamberger never appeared to have had concerns about his decision to locate his institute in New Jersey. He may have felt about the institute's location just like those who questioned his opening his store on a less-desirable street in downtown Newark — that if the institute had something to offer, you could be assured that researchers would come.

Bamberger appointed a committee of four to investigate possible permanent sites. One of these was the town of Princeton. Time spent exploring the countryside around it convinced Flexner that the town and university were ideal. The committee, which included Veblen, agreed but would "do nothing at all without Bamberger's knowledge and concurrence."[69] As usual, though, Bamberger had gotten there first. Weeks before the committee surveyed Princeton locations, he had already been in touch with local real estate agents.[70] IAS trustee Herbert Maass shed some light on Bamberger's way of doing business when he described Bamberger as a man who "never bought anything he didn't want."[71] Thus it was he, not Veblen or Flexner, who made the decision for Princeton.

Flexner rejected outright Percy Straus's suggestion that the IAS be part of Princeton University. "If a formal, definite, legal organic association is contemplated, I should think the Institute would be absolutely destroyed," Flexner argued. "It would inevitably sink both in personnel and in spirit to the level of the graduate school of the larger institution which would really absorb it. We want and need neighbors, but we want absolutely to preserve our identity, and this is not only my view but the view of both President Hibben and Dr. Trowbridge, Dean of the Princeton graduate school, with whom I have had a confidential talk."[72] The *New York Times* reported that "while the Institute will occupy temporary space in a Princeton building, it will not be part of Princeton University."[73]

Former Newark resident Ed Brody recalled rumors that circulated among Newark Jews: first, that the university's trustees did not want to take Bamberger's money because he was a Jew; and second, that they considered his money tainted because he was a merchant, who made his fortune selling goods from behind a store counter.[74] Brody was an active member of Newark's Springfield Avenue Merchants Association, and as such he would have heard stories about Bamberger that were told long after Bamberger had passed. Of course, Bamberger would have known that these rumors were untrue, but whether or not he ever heard them, he would never have dignified them with a response.

In preparing for the institute's launch, Abraham Flexner had called on Princeton president Emil Hibben, who not only welcomed the institute, but when he learned that it would begin with mathematics, offered temporary space in Fine Hall, which housed the university's mathematics department. Welcoming the IAS to its campus enabled Princeton to bask in Einstein's limelight. In Hibben's mind, "The question was not whether we should prefer to have Professor Einstein on our faculty or on Dr. Flexner's, but whether we should prefer to have him at Princeton or Berlin."[75]

Einstein verbally accepted a faculty position with the Institute for Advanced Study on June 4, 1932. A letter Einstein dictated to his private secretary, Helen Dukas, sent four days later, stated, "I am really overjoyed to be united with you in such a wonderful cause and I am convinced that we will have joy in working together." It was such good news that Flexner sent his secretary, Mrs. Bailey, to Newark to tell Bamberger in person.[76]

Despite this commitment, it was not easy to get Einstein and his wife, Elsa, to leave Europe. He had a history of breaking commitments without concern for the consequences, and moving to the United States to spend the rest of his life working exclusively at an institution that had as yet not created a scientific community was a lot to ask of him.[77] He had many other tempting offers and had accepted others in addition to the one from the IAS.

Flexner wrote to Elsa Einstein to complain, "Only a few days ago the *New York Times* printed that 'Professor Einstein has accepted professorships in Madrid, Paris, Brussels, Leyden, and Oxford.'"[78] The only professorship not actually mentioned was the one at the IAS. In turn, Carrie, who had seen the article, sent Flexner a letter saying that she and Louis were unsure whether Einstein was in fact committed to them.[79] In response, Flexner explained that he had more than once asked Einstein to refrain from associating himself "even in an honorary capacity with institutions in different countries."[80] He assured her that there would be no difficulty once Einstein reached Princeton, where he could keep an eye on him.[81] Nevertheless, Flexner decided to withhold any announcement about Einstein's appointment.[82]

However, this news was too big to keep under wraps, and there were constant leaks to the press. Einstein himself revealed the secret in a 1932 letter to Hermann Weyl, telling him that he had taken a position at the IAS.[83] Another leak was traced to a conversation between Einstein and the president of the Berlin Academy, who then revealed that Einstein had accepted a post in America.[84] The Associated Press cabled a report from Berlin that was picked up by the Jewish Telegraphic

Agency and the *Herald Tribune*. Bamberger's office received many inquiries, which were referred to Flexner.[85] On October 10, 1932, the IAS trustees formally approved both Einstein's and Veblen's appointments as the first professors of mathematics and the decision to locate the institute in Princeton. A statement released to the press the following day drew more interest than usually accorded an educational institution, primarily because of Einstein's name.

Among the accolades for hiring Einstein, Flexner got the most gratification from a call from Dr. John C. Merriam, director of the Carnegie Institution, who said, "It would be a privilege if they could cooperate with us in developing the work of Professor Einstein and Professor Veblen in any way possible." "I imagine," Flexner wrote Bamberger, "this is just about the first time in the history of the Carnegie Institution when that Institution has undertaken the initiative."[86]

News of Einstein's appointment and his request for a visa to enter the United States met with resistance from an organization in Brookline, Massachusetts, known as the Woman Patriot Corporation. In December 1932, the group passed a resolution opposing Einstein's entry into the United States on the grounds that he was a communist and a dangerous alien.[87] (Einstein was in fact a socialist.) A *New York Times* editorial poked fun at the group for suggesting that Bamberger and the officers of the IAS be indicted for conspiracy and high treason. The United States Veterans Association put out a statement saying the resolution was "silly . . . nothing short of a national humiliation."[88] A greatly embarrassed State Department gave Einstein his visa. Meanwhile, the Independent Order of B'rith Sholom, a Newark-based organization, "protested against the unfounded and thoroughly unjustifiable attacks" on Einstein.[89] The group adopted a resolution petitioning the New Jersey legislature to extend to Einstein a formal welcome and declaring that the attacks on him "in effect constitute a travesty upon the splendid judgment exercised by Louis Bamberger, Mrs. Felix Fuld, Dr. Abraham Flexner and trustees of the new Institute for Advanced Study."[90]

Despite Einstein's own statements that he had accepted the position, the uncertainty over whether he would actually show up continued almost to the last minute. As late as July 1933, Flexner wrote to Einstein's wife Elsa, "I think you [and your husband] should realize that I have undertaken a great responsibility to Mr. Bamberger and his sister. . . . American newspapers are questioning the nature of Professor Einstein's relation to the Institute. In all fairness to the Bambergers this cannot be. The only way to stop the rumors and confusion is to show up in Princeton on October 2 showing that the connection there is actual."[91] In August he wrote a second letter reminding Einstein of the institute's opening date in German, so there would be no misunderstanding.[92]

In 1932 Einstein had gone to Pasadena to resume his research at the Mount Wilson Observatory; he planned to return to Germany during the summer of 1933 and then start work at the IAS later that year. In March 1933, the Einsteins came east from Pasadena intending to leave by ship from New York Harbor and sail for Antwerp, to avoid landing in Germany. When Hitler had become chancellor the previous January, Einstein had declared that he would never return to Germany as long as the Nazi dictator was in power. He and Elsa were anxious to avoid hotels and the accompanying publicity; so Flexner, as he explained to Bamberger, "acting on something you once said to me . . . invited them to spend a few days quietly in your home in South Orange which they have gladly accepted."[93] Their stay in South Orange was meant to be a secret in order to protect Einstein from the annoying reporters who dogged him. This time Bamberger, who was in Arizona with Mrs. Fuld, wrote back to Flexner himself. His letter reveals his generous nature. "We are happy to learn that the Einsteins will use our South Orange home while they await their departure," he wrote. "I have wired to my secretary to try and cooperate with our house maids and chauffeur to do everything to make the Einsteins comfortable," including keeping their presence strictly confidential.[94]

As it happened, the Einsteins got stuck in Chicago and sent a telegram canceling their visit. Instead, they went straight to New York, where Einstein was supposed to speak at a dinner at the Hotel Commodore in support of Germany's Jews. The couple accepted an invitation from Felix Warburg, who put them up at the Waldorf-Astoria. IAS trustee Florence Sabin attended the banquet and wrote to Flexner to say "that after hearing Professor Einstein I feel that if we had no one else and did nothing else, the Institute would be worthwhile."[95]

A few days before their ship sailed, the Einsteins asked Bamberger's nephew Edgar to drive them to Princeton do a little house hunting in preparation for their move. On the way back to New York, Mrs.

Einstein asked to stop off in Newark. She wanted to buy a fountain pen at Bamberger's as a gift for her son-in-law in Europe. Edgar showed them around the store.[96]

On September 1, 1933, the IAS opened its quarters in Fine Hall, a building that had been designed to accommodate Princeton's mathematicians. Immediately, the Princeton and IAS mathematicians, including Oswald Veblen, Hermann Weyl, and John von Neumann, formed a single congenial group. At the same time, the IAS began contributing $6,000 a year to Princeton University in "appreciation" of having temporary use of the facility. It was Bamberger who provided these funds.[97] He also attended meetings in Princeton as a member of a liaison committee between the IAS and the university. No permanent site for the institute campus had been selected, and there were still no building plans.[98]

On September 22, Abraham Flexner arrived in Princeton with his wife to take up his position as IAS director. Flexner's arrival signaled the start of a long, amiable relationship between the town of Princeton, its university, and the Institute for Advanced Study. "As luck would have it," Flexner wrote Bamberger, "the Institute's 'business' began on the Jewish New Year, which I take to be a good omen"—an uncharacteristic remark from this secularist.[99]

The three years of efforts to convince Albert Einstein to become the head of the institute's school of mathematics culminated with his arrival on October 17, 1933, after elaborate efforts were made to protect him from the crowds waiting to greet him dockside in New York. Einstein's fear of crowds is well documented. In 1921 he had been met by a pack of New York reporters and photographers, whose shouted questions and fierce waving forced him to hold onto his hat and pipe for fear someone would grab them as souvenirs.[100] He got another tumultuous welcome in 1930, when he stopped in New York on his way to Caltech, and he considered remaining aboard his ship for five days rather than face the crowds. The thought of more crowds may have been part of the reason he missed the institute's opening.

Flexner described to Bamberger the scheme that enabled the Einsteins to evade the crowds this time. "You will be interested and amused to know that Mr. Maass arose at daybreak, took a little motor boat, reached Quarantine, met the Einsteins and turned them over to Mr. Farrier and Edgar Bamberger who drove the couple to Princeton post haste."[101] As the *Times* reported, "So sudden and speedy was the departure of Dr. Einstein and his party from Quarantine that a reception committee comprised of Samuel Untermyer, head of a nationwide movement to boycott German-made goods, and New York's mayor John L. O'Brien who was there to offer the 'keys to the city,' were not aware of what was taking place until Einstein was well on his way to Princeton."[102] A week after the Einsteins' arrival in Princeton, Louis and Carrie went to call on them in their new home.[103]

Princeton's officials also welcomed the Einsteins. Princeton University's president, Harold Dodds, reported to Flexner that he and his wife had agreed to submit to a lunch served by Mrs. Einstein of sauerkraut, liver sausage, and other German dishes and that Mrs. Dodds survived the ordeal.[104] Elsa was an efficient and lively woman, who was eager to serve and protect her husband. "He was as pleased to be looked after as she was to look after him."[105] Her guests may have been surprised that she called him "the Professor," or even simply "Einstein," when they were in public.[106]

The moment Einstein arrived in Princeton he was besieged with invitations to speak. The first one came from Edgar Bamberger, who asked him to lecture at the Newark "Y" on any subject he might fancy, on any Monday night during the season.[107] The event would be called the Fuld Memorial Lecture in memory of Felix Fuld.[108] Einstein had to decline, for Flexner had imposed a one-year moratorium on his accepting invitations to speak—anywhere.

Edgar found it necessary to apologize to Flexner for having issued the invitation. "You know that I am the last person to exploit Professor Einstein, in fact, I wish to put myself down now as a charter member of the P.E.P.A. or Professor Einstein Protective Association," he wrote, adding that Louis and Carrie knew nothing about his request.[109] Flexner responded that he didn't feel he could make any exceptions to the no-lecture rule, but (playing it safe) added that he would reconsider if Mrs. Fuld wanted Einstein to speak. He was prepared to acquiesce "in a moment in order to do anything that would make her and Mr. Bamberger happy."[110] He later grudgingly admitted to Mrs. Fuld that interruptions did not affect Einstein's health or his work. He could go to Philadelphia for a dinner and return at one o'clock in the morning without being the worse for wear.[111] Flexner also cautioned Einstein not to talk to the press because the reporters would distort his comments. He worried that Einstein might become "oversaturated," or even worse, that his attention would be diverted from his research.[112]

Flexner's desire to control Einstein's activities may also have been related to his concern that someone from a rival institution might corner Einstein in a social setting and try to tempt him with a better offer, as he himself had done at Caltech. Though acknowledging that "fair exchange was no robbery," Flexner told Edgar Bamberger that if Einstein had a year to sample the idyllic working and living conditions in Princeton, he and Elsa would want to remain.[113]

As part of his moratorium, Flexner opened Einstein's mail and rejected invitations for him to speak. "I have already declined innumerable invitations without even communicating with him," Flexner admitted to Edgar Bamberger.[114] When he discovered this, Einstein was shocked and so angry that he called the IAS a concentration camp. His friend and fellow musician, Emil Hilb, wrote to Flexner angrily objecting to Einstein's isolation. Hilb reminded Flexner that Einstein's great reputation was the very reason he had hired him.[115] Flexner wrote back defending himself, declaring that Einstein "does not understand America and that you have given him unsound advice."[116] In a letter to Herbert Maass, Flexner vigorously denied Hilb's accusation that he was using Einstein for his own purposes. He maintained that he had gone to great lengths to protect Einstein from reporters and also people who made threats on his life, citing two vagrants who had been scouring Princeton in search of Einstein and were arrested and jailed.[117] Controlling all those who wanted access to Einstein was a full-time job.

German sculptor Jacob Epstein, who had created a bust of Einstein, offered to send a replica to the IAS. Flexner was reluctant to accept the gift if it meant a lot of unwanted publicity: "It would be impossible for us to accept the bust unless we were free to keep the fact of its existence and of your generosity a secret until in due course both could be announced and the bust exhibited without any danger of publicity."[118] In fact, the Epstein bust did not come to the institute until 1973. It is displayed in the Common Room in Fuld Hall.[119]

Flexner certainly overstepped his bounds when he rejected an invitation from President Roosevelt and his wife for the Einsteins to meet with them at the White House. Flexner told FDR that he could make no exceptions, explaining that he feared for Einstein's life. "You are aware of the fact that there exists in New York an irresponsible group of Nazis," he wrote. "If the newspapers had access to him or if he accepted a single engagement or invitation that could possibly become public, it would be practically impossible for him to remain in the post which he has accepted."[120] Flexner explained that several attempts had been made to assassinate Einstein while he was living in Germany.[121] One such attack had failed because of the "resourcefulness of Mrs. Einstein," who had invited the gun-waving attacker into her home in Caputh, where the police were waiting.[122]

When Einstein learned that Flexner had refused the president's invitation, he was livid. He assured Mrs. Roosevelt that no invitation had reached him and added, "I want to avoid the ugly impression that I had been negligent or discourteous in this matter."[123] He finally did meet the president when he and his wife were invited to be guests in the White House on January 24, 1934.

Even before settling in Princeton, Einstein had begun a tireless campaign to help Jews and other "enemies" of the Nazi government find positions in universities in Great Britain and outside Europe. He worked with an international network that raised funds and pressured governments to obtain visas for academic refugees, friends, and family.[124] Einstein's political activism worried Flexner. As an avowed pacifist, Einstein was prone to making what Flexner considered politically inopportune statements to the press. Flexner was not insensitive to what was happening in Germany. He told Bamberger that "my own mail for the summer of 1933 was taken up with German friends who have been thrown out of positions and even terrorized; as many as 800 professors — Jews, Liberals, etc. — have been dismissed."[125] But Flexner believed he needed time to establish the institute's reputation and feared that Einstein's speeches at campaign rallies for aid to Jews in Germany and his vocal opposition to Hitler would detract from the important research being done there.[126] Since Einstein was the star of the IAS, however, Flexner had to accept that trying to keep the institute free from these political associations was a losing battle. He felt he had to walk a fine line between Einstein's political activism and the more conservative members of the institute's board of trustees. There is no indication that Bamberger had any of these concerns.

Bamberger and Einstein met next in January 1934 at a music recital featuring Einstein on his violin — an appearance that Flexner had vehemently opposed. Not until he learned that the gala event would be held at the home of New York financier Adolph Lewisohn did he soften his position. Flexner knew that Lewisohn, much like Bamberger, was a lover of classical music, that Lewisohn's home was a perfect venue for Einstein to play his violin, and that the event was an ideal way to please Bamberger. The sponsors and attendees were the cream of German Jewish society: US Treasury Secretary Henry Morgenthau; Arthur Ochs Sulzberger, owner and editor of the *New York Times*; Mrs. David Sarnoff, wife of radio magnate David Sarnoff; the Straus brothers of Macy's; financier Felix Warburg; and of course, Louis Bamberger. Eleanor Roosevelt was there as well. "Proceeds of the event, which is one of the most unusual in the current social season, will be used by Dr. Einstein for the benefit of some of his intimate scientific friends in Berlin," reported the Jewish Telegraphic Agency.[127]

In April 1934, the institute received an anonymous gift of $1 million.[128] No one doubted that Bamberger was the source. He had always intended to add additional amounts to the original endowment as the need arose.[129] No fanfare surrounded his gift. "Mr. Leidesdorf, Mr. Maass, Mr. Bamberger, and I lunched together," wrote Flexner to his wife. "Mr. Bamberger, at the close of the luncheon, calmly turned over to me [a check for] $1 million dollars."[130] Bamberger told the trustees he had made the gift in view of two considerations: that the institute might shortly want to acquire a site; and that the director might feel freer to begin creating the school of economics and politics.[131] Bamberger added, "I desire to put on record my hope that the activities of the School of Economics and Politics may contribute not only to knowledge of these subjects, but ultimately to the cause of *social justice* [emphasis added] which we have deeply at heart."[132]

This gift suggests that Bamberger was satisfied with the IAS's progress to date. Things were going so well that he and Mrs. Fuld decided to relinquish their positions as president and vice president and requested that the institute's bylaws be amended to name them honorary trustees for life, a position that enabled them to participate in all the activities of the board and its committees during their lifetimes. "I assure you that my interest and Mrs. Fuld's interest have become keener and keener as time has passed and that we will do all in our power to promote the objects for which the Institute was founded,"[133] Bamberger wrote. Despite this deep interest, they preferred not to chair committees or add responsibilities to their already busy lives. It was not the first time

Bamberger had used an "honorary" title to describe his role in an organization. It enabled him to exert influence without being the center of attention. Meanwhile, Flexner, continuing his crusade to keep Einstein out of the public spotlight, refused New Jersey governor A. Harry Moore's request to arrange a gala reception to welcome Einstein to the state.[134] At the same time Einstein received a visit from Newark Rabbi Julius Silberfeld, who convinced him that making an appearance in Newark would help draw attention to the plight of Germany's Jews.[135] Einstein said yes.

So it was that on March 25, 1934, Newark and New Jersey finally got a chance to welcome Einstein. An estimated seven to ten thousand "music lovers, admirers of the scientist and sympathizers of the Jews who have been persecuted in Germany" attended an afternoon concert at the Newark Armory. Many hoped that Einstein would play one or two selections on his violin.[136] Tickets cost one to five dollars, and the proceeds went to settling German Jewish refugees in Palestine.[137] Bamberger was listed as an honorary chairman of the event, but there is no record of him or Carrie Fuld attending the concert.[138] Both were now too fragile to be jostled by crowds.

This event required "the most elaborate police precautions ever provided any individual by the city of Newark. A total of 200 Newark police, including a number of detectives and plain clothes men were assigned to guard Einstein and his wife throughout the day."[139] The couple traveled in style from Princeton to Newark in Louis V. Aronson's Rolls Royce and stayed in Aronson's penthouse suite in the Robert Treat Hotel. The governor had appointed Aronson chairman of the welcoming committee. Busy finalizing plans for a lunch for hundreds of dignitaries, he left the job of entertaining Einstein to his son-in-law, Israel Rosengarten, and his grandsons, Richard and Nathaniel ("Buddy") Rosengarten.[140]

Einstein spoke limited English, and the Rosengartens spoke no German. Einstein pulled out his pipe and asked if there were any cigarettes in the room, explaining apologetically that he preferred to crumble cigarettes to smoke in his pipe rather than use pipe tobacco. There were none, so eleven-year-old Richard ran down eight flights of stairs (the elevator wasn't working) to the newsstand in the lobby to buy a pack of Camels, Einstein's favorite brand. The shop owner, however, didn't care who the cigarettes were for and maintained that he had no intention of losing his license by selling cigarettes to a minor. Richard ran back upstairs to report his failure. Since both boys were too young to buy the cigarettes, their father made the same run. Einstein, however, gave no indication that he appreciated these trips up and down the eight flights just in order to please him and in the end decided to smoke his "occasional cigar." Years later Nathaniel recalled that while "Einstein passed out of their lives like a vapor of smoke," the memories of meeting him lasted a lifetime.[141]

That evening a dinner honoring Einstein was held at the Mosque Theater. Its significance to American Jews was such that Rabbi Abba Hillel Silver of Cleveland chartered a commercial airliner by purchasing all the seat tickets so he could get to Newark in time to speak there.[142] Sixty-two New Jersey communities were represented. "Governors of several states, public leaders, scientists, educators and writers" sat on the dais; Mayor Meyer Ellenstein and community activist Michael Stavitsky attended as well.[143] World-famous contralto Ernestine Schumann-Heink flew in from Coronado, California, to sing "The Star-Spangled Banner" and selections from German operas that the organizers thought would please Einstein.[144] Einstein paid the crowd the supreme compliment of wearing a tuxedo, something he had not done even at his daughter's wedding.[145] Bamberger and Carrie Fuld were asked to be members of the dinner committee; however, since their names were not on the list of attendees, it is doubtful that they were there.[146] Nor is there anything to tell us whether Governor Moore publicly acknowledged Louis Bamberger for his role in bringing Einstein to New Jersey.

Einstein addressed the crowd in German, and Rabbi Silberfeld of Newark's Temple B'nai Abraham translated. On Silberfeld's sixtieth birthday he received a letter from Einstein congratulating him on his "cheerful courage in the performance of [his] arduous task."[147] The dinner, like the concert, was enormously successful. It raised a large sum that was used for finding positions in Palestine for Einstein's exiled German colleagues.[148]

It was only a matter of time until rumors of a conflict between Einstein and Flexner reached Bamberger. Einstein objected to Flexner's attempt to monitor his activities and said so. The matter was serious enough that Einstein's wife got involved. She sent Flexner a "frank and candid letter" complaining about his treatment of them. Flexner met with the Einsteins to assure them that he had no desire to limit Einstein's freedom; however, he could not risk compromising the dignity of the IAS and Princeton University "with which we are so closely associated."[149] During a long, serious discussion, Flexner asked the Einsteins to consider that "it is perfectly possible to create an anti-Semitic feeling in the United States" and that he, too, wished to help oppressed Jews in Germany, but (unlike Einstein) "feel it has to be done in quiet and anonymously."[150] As Flexner later reported to Bamberger, Einstein explained that he had received endless "heart-breaking letters mailed from England, Holland, and Belgium from German professors," both Jews and non-Jews, who found Hitler's regime intolerable.[151] In fact, Einstein wrote so many affidavits for visas that his signature on a document lost its value.[152] Like Bamberger, he served as an honorary chairman of fundraising dinners to raise money for German refugees.

The by-now nervous Flexner felt that the last thing he needed was for Einstein to voice misgivings about coming to the IAS. He wrote to Bamberger, "I have had a two-hour talk with Professor Einstein and I wish to assure you and Mrs. Fuld that all the little misunderstandings, which had disturbed him and his wife, have been completely removed."[153] Nevertheless, were it not for the personal relationship that grew up between Bamberger and Einstein, it is possible that Einstein might have left after the term of his initial contract and moved to one of the many universities who wanted him, rather than put up with Flexner and his desire to control his every move. By staying, Einstein assured the future of the institute. His name was the draw for other mathematicians and scholars who wanted to bask in the aura of relativity.

We can only guess about Einstein's feelings regarding Louis Bamberger's support of his position at the institute. German scientists were accustomed to having wealthy Jewish patrons fund their research and give them money. Einstein remarked that "he would consider it reasonable for the Jews themselves to collect the money to support Jewish research workers outside the universities and to provide them with teaching opportunities."[154] Einstein's salary as director of the Kaiser Wilhelm Institutes had been provided through a combination of support from the government and the Koppel Foundation, which was endowed by Leopold Koppel, a Jewish banker in Berlin.[155] From Einstein's point of view, Bamberger was doing what other wealthy Jews had done before him. However, Bamberger far exceeded the German patrons.

Einstein, who paid no attention to such matters, admitted in 1943 that he had mislaid a letter about his retirement and annuity;[156] but Bamberger spent hours going over Einstein's pension report in detail, making sure that his income after retirement would be the same as his institute salary.[157] Years before Einstein thought of retirement, Bamberger insisted that an exception be made for both Einstein and Veblen, enabling them to work until age seventy if they wanted to.[158] The source of Einstein's retirement income, over and above the standard IAS pension, was said to be an anonymous donor—who clearly was Louis Bamberger. At a meeting of the board of trustees on January 25, 1944, Maass and Leidesdorf overheard him saying that he intended to supplement Einstein's retirement income. Although Bamberger died before the paperwork confirming Einstein's pension/salary was signed, the trustees honored his intention and determined that his estate would pay a portion of Einstein's salary for as long as he remained active.[159] Einstein officially retired from the IAS in 1945, but continued his research there until his death in 1955.

What motivated Bamberger to pay such close attention to how Einstein was treated? The answer lay in the fact that they had first come to know of one another in 1925 when Bamberger agreed to represent Newark on the board of the American advisory committee for the founding of the Hebrew University in Jerusalem.[160] Einstein was "involved as a figurehead leader," and much like Bamberger, permitted the use of his name on their letterhead.[161] Concurrently, both men were active in raising funds for displaced Jews in Europe and Russia—Einstein in Germany and Bamberger in Newark.

Once Einstein was settled in at Princeton, he and Bamberger found that they were kindred spirits. Aside from their obvious connection as German Jews, both loved music. Einstein carried his violin wherever he went and could fill an auditorium by agreeing to appear in concert. In December 1933, Flexner wrote Bamberger, "We have asked Professor and Mrs. Einstein to share your box [at the New York Philharmonic] Thursday night of this week, and they have accepted eagerly."[162] It would have been a concert to remember if someone in the audience had discovered that Einstein was in the house. After all, he was one of the most recognizable faces in the world, or at least his mane of white hair was.

Einstein and Bamberger also found common ground in the issue of social justice. For Bamberger social justice was the founding principle of the IAS. His intention was not to lower academic standards, but rather to create a "level playing field" for qualified students. For his part, Einstein once said "striving for social justice is the most valuable thing to do in life."[163] Both men broke with traditional Judaism and became active in the Ethical Culture Society, whose philosophy was based on living in accordance with ethical principles and striving to create a just world. Bamberger had joined the society in 1903.[164] Einstein stated that "without ethical culture there is no salvation for humanity,"[165] a philosophy that would surely have resonated with Bamberger. Einstein and Bamberger's friendship deepened over time. Both were world travelers who were married to their work, but they still found time to enjoy one another's company. Einstein was a frequent guest at Bamberger's summer home on the Shark River in the Jersey shore town of Avon, where he sat scribbling notes and mathematical formulae at Louis's desk.[166] (Their friendship was portrayed in the 1994 movie "I.Q.," an insipid love story and comedy featuring Walter Matthau as Einstein and Charles Durning as Bamberger.)

Neither was interested in public acclaim. Einstein gave orders that his home and office were not to be turned into shrines after he died; Bamberger refused to put his name on the institute's buildings and insisted that once he and Carrie were dead, the office of honorary trustee that had been created for them would cease and no one else would hold this title.[167]

Both were happiest when left alone to pursue their interests and did not understand why their lives were a curiosity to adoring crowds. In general, both thought they were too famous for their own good. They also chose to live far more modestly than they could have. Bamberger's home was far less lavish than those of his wealthy peers, while Einstein had little interest in money other than what was necessary to meet his obligations—although he could have become rich by agreeing to endorse such products as "Relativity Cigars."[168]

One powerful factor in the rapid growth of the IAS was the anti-semitic policies of the Nazi regime, without which the Institute could hardly have attracted Einstein, Weyl, and von Neumann. At the same time, Flexner insisted on being selective in recruiting German mathematicians and scientists for the institute. "I am doing everything in my power to secure opportunities for the German professors who have been displaced," he wrote. "The situation is heart-breaking, but here again the Institute must come first, and we must not do anything except on the basis of sheer merit. . . . It is not easy to live up to these standards, but I have promised Mr. Bamberger and his sister, that I will do so."[169]

As this comment indicates, in this matter he had Bamberger's support. One theory had it that Bamberger created the IAS to provide "a sanctuary for German Jewish refugee scholars, physicists, and scientists."[170] This was certainly not the case. Although Bamberger was intensely aware of the plight of German Jews—and spared no expense to bring relatives of Felix Fuld from Germany to Newark—he would never have sanctioned hiring anyone based solely on their national origin or on political considerations. He knew that an "open-door policy" for unqualified researchers, no matter their country of origin, would have diminished the reputation of the IAS.

"Louis Bamberger was not a scholar but he had an instinct for quality. He did not attempt to influence the judgment of the Director, the Faculty, or the Trustees in details, but he insisted always upon two things—excellence in scholarly work and wise economy in the expenditure of funds."[171]

Initially, Bamberger and Mrs. Fuld resisted hiring Hermann Weyl, a star almost as bright as Einstein, because Weyl continued to waffle over leaving Germany. Bamberger had to be convinced that Weyl was worth hiring; he sent Flexner a telegram saying, "We feel that if Weyl is seriously interested he will come on reasonable terms that you could offer."[172] The fact that Weyl occupied the most famous chair of mathematics in Germany made it easier for Flexner to insist that he be hired. Eventually Weyl joined the IAS faculty, but Bamberger insisted that he not be hired on the same generous terms that had been offered to him originally, and he got his way. To get past any hard feelings, Aydelotte invited Bamberger and Fuld, along with Flexner and his wife, to hear Weyl's first lecture.[173]

By the mid-1930s it had become standard practice for American universities to hire German Jewish scholars and scientists. Ninety-four percent of the intellectuals admitted to the United States between 1930 and the end of World War II, the years Bamberger was active at the institute, were Jewish.[174] Oswald Veblen, who was not Jewish, joined the Emergency Committee in Aid of Displaced Foreign Scholars and became the point person for the relocation of mathematicians to the United States.[175] It was common knowledge that "advocating, in the 1930s, on behalf of European Jewish refugees was a delicate matter."[176] The Great Depression was under way and jobs were scarce for American mathematicians. In addition, antisemitism and xenophobia were prevalent on many campuses. Despite his work in aid of German Jews, Bamberger showed no preferences for hiring them above other nationalities for the IAS. When IAS trustee Frank Aydelotte sent Bamberger information about what other universities were doing for displaced German professors, Bamberger responded that he was "impressed" with their actions, but preferred not to give Jews preference.[177] It was a curious stance for Bamberger to take, particularly since he was active in raising money to help displaced Jews in Europe and particularly Germany.

On the occasion of the institute's fifth anniversary, Bamberger told a reporter that he and Mrs. Fuld were "highly gratified with the results achieved thus far" and that "selecting Princeton is working out splendidly."[178] Regarding the institute's future development, they still expressed a "wait and see" attitude. Flexner knew that Bamberger had "always been skeptical" regarding Flexner's plans to start a school of economics. "Bamberger had said that he had been in doubt as to whether the School of Economics could bring about substantial results."[179] Not until he realized that the results of this experiment might inure to the benefit of the whole world did Bamberger become convinced that the institute was not only justified in undertaking the task, but ought to undertake it.[180] Bamberger assured the board of the cooperation of Mrs. Fuld and himself.

In a comprehensive report sent to Bamberger and Fuld dated July 19, 1937, Flexner traced the history of the IAS and made recommendations. "In course of time, as money was provided and men could be found, the Institute should, in my [Flexner's] judgment, expand as follows: economics and politics, mathematical physics, a school of music, and a school of Oriental Studies."[181] "The budget," he concluded, would, of course, "be discussed for ratification to the Board at its annual meeting." Then he added a line calculated to impress Bamberger: "Thus we could make sure that we are living well within our income, that the schools are consulted as to their needs and that, as far as human foresight can provide, financial problems can be avoided."[182] Finally, they would add "in the near future, a central building and certain increases of salary."[183] The estimated cost for all this was $15 million.

"Now that the weather is about to settle, I would like to arrange a meeting of the Committee on Site," Maass wrote.[184] According to Herbert Maass, the consensus was that "one or two years may be needed before taking any steps in the matter of a site. . . . Then the Institute will determine the site, instead of the site determining the Institute."[185]

With the addition of the School of Economics and Politics and the School of Humanistic Studies, it became evident that a permanent building was necessary. Flexner wrote to trustee Frank Aydelotte, "I am rather fearful that, when the suggestions of the faculty are added up, they are going to require a building far beyond anything that Mr. B. contemplates in point of construction and upkeep."[186] In December 1937, Flexner told Aydelotte that Maass had been in Princeton with two associates to examine a particular parcel of land which was being considered and "both thought the location ideal."[187]

Before land was purchased, the building committee informally agreed to appoint J. Frederick Larson of Hanover, New Hampshire, as the architect and to ask him to work on a plan for a single building that could be constructed for $250,000 or "whatever sum Mr. Bamberger is willing to put into it," as Aydelotte explained to Flexner.[188] In another letter three months later, he told Aydelotte that if the plans and budget were approved by Mr. Bamberger, "I think the Institute is on the way to securing adequate and indeed admirable housing."[189] A revised estimate of $312,000 led Bamberger to ask for time to talk it over with Mrs. Fuld.[190] He understood building overruns, so when construction costs and an endowment were added to the total, he revised his estimate upward to "more like $500,000."[191]

They had their eye on a parcel of land called the Maxwell property, located less than two miles from Princeton University. Flexner sensed that Maxwell "was waiting for us to make him an offer on his property,"[192] but since Bamberger was not in a hurry to build, Flexner put off contacting him. This was an excellent strategy, since Maxwell then called Flexner to say he would take $200,000 for the entire parcel, including his house.[193] Aydelotte felt sure that if Bamberger and Fuld had a chance to study the plan, they would be convinced that the IAS should buy the Maxwell property. They did approve it.

Construction began in late 1938, and in autumn 1939 the institute's faculty and staff moved into Fuld Hall, which was constructed of orange-red brick in a modified Georgian style. It housed separate studies for the faculty and students, as well as a library, a commons, and seminar rooms.[194] Einstein's office was hidden behind an unmarked door to deter visitors from wandering in without an appointment. The cleaning service had strict instructions that no one was permitted to wipe the blackboards for fear that one of Einstein's theories might be erased. Plans to build faculty houses awaited Bamberger's approval.

Claiming ill health, Bamberger and Mrs. Fuld did not attend the dedication ceremonies on May 22, 1939. Their sister Lavinia did the honors. Guests looked on as a time capsule containing photographs of Felix and Carrie Fuld, Louis Bamberger, C. Lavinia Bamberger, Abraham Flexner, and members of the first board of trustees was placed in the cornerstone. Other mementos included photographs of 69 Alexander Street (the early headquarters of the IAS) and of Fuld Hall under construction; IAS *Bulletins* nos. 1–8; letterhead stationery; a bookplate; and a copy of the *New York Times* for that date. "The Institute had to live for ten years in scattered quarters while waiting to see what kind of a building and grounds would ultimately be best adapted to its spirit and its activities," Flexner recalled in his autobiography. When "I knew what was needed, the founders presented us with Fuld Hall, a building ideally adapted to its purposes."[195]

Long before the IAS moved to its new campus, Bamberger was busy building up its library. From time to time opportunities arose to purchase book collections "which happened to be thrown on the market," and Bamberger took these opportunities to donate still more.[196] Thus in 1936 he agreed to find a place to house the Gest Oriental Library Collection, one of the Western world's greatest compilations of Chinese books. He purchased this collection of what was then called "Oriental studies" from McGill University in Canada and arranged for its removal to Princeton. Guion Moore Gest's intention of establishing a collection to be used by North American scholars as a means to further understanding between East and West appealed to Bamberger. His decision to purchase the collection may also have been influenced by Newark Museum's 1924 exhibit "China and the Chinese," which received support from the Chinese government. The acquisition of the collection also coincided with newspaper reports of the Japanese invasion of China, which made American scholars want to know more about Asian history.[197] Roger S. Greene, head of Oriental activities at the Rockefeller Foundation, called it a "goldmine" for researchers, and Bamberger and the Rockefeller Institute gave matching funds of $62,500. It was the first money from an outside source to come to the institute, a departure from Bamberger's original ban on donations other than his own;[198] Flexner's long-standing ties to the Rockefeller Foundation made cooperation with the IAS inevitable. Although Bamberger was responsible for the purchase, the Rockefeller Institute got the credit.

The Gest Library attracted visitors and dignitaries from around the world, including Count Kabayama, director of the Japanese Society of International Cultural Relations. Bamberger and Fuld were invited to attend a luncheon in his honor.[199] The original understanding had been that the collection would be administered as part of the Princeton University Library. In the end, the collection's upkeep was more than the IAS could afford, so it was given to Princeton University, and Bamberger authorized a $500,000 donation from the IAS endowment to support it there. It is currently housed in the Mudd Manuscript Library.[200] In 1940 Bamberger agreed to give an extra $100,000 over four years to support the establishment of a separate library for the institute.[201] Smaller gifts came from his relatives. Bamberger's cousin, Mrs. Carrie Hymes, donated a collection of mathematical books, all classical works in the field, to the institute's library. After Louis and Carrie died, Lavinia Bamberger offered to donate books to the institute from Bamberger's library in South Orange. A delegation of faculty visited Bamberger's home hoping to find a collection of rare books or manuscripts in his library. Instead, they left with a few "sentimental" selections, including histories of countries that Bamberger had visited; a copy of the *Flexner Report* on medical education; a selection from the correspondence of Theodore Roosevelt, whom Bamberger openly admired; and Booker T. Washington's *Up from Slavery*—a total of thirty-five volumes.[202]

As soon as the faculty relocated to the new campus, Flexner announced his retirement. He had already primed Bamberger to expect this. A letter dated July 29, 1939, in which he stated, "I have the feeling that in so far as the Institute is concerned, we have agreed upon a mode of procedure that is dignified and helpful, and that while I will never obtrude my advice, there is nothing I will not do for my successor should he so desire," was a harbinger of things to come.[203] Then, on

August 18, 1939, Flexner wrote to Bamberger that he was resigning.[204] As it turned out, however, Flexner didn't resign of his own choice but was forced out.

Only then did Bamberger discover that the daily operations of the institute were in disarray. He was not aware that there were serious differences of opinion regarding Flexner's running of the institute or that the relationship between the director and some trustees on the one hand, and the faculty on the other, regarding Flexner's leadership, had deteriorated. There were now three essentially autonomous schools—mathematics, economics, and politics—whose members began to meet separately to discuss matters of common interest. They demanded "at least a strong consultative voice in important academic matters."[205] Flexner objected. In his autobiography, published the following year, he asserted that there was no need to hold "dull and increasingly frequent meetings of committees, groups, or the faculty itself,"[206] and said he feared that "once started, this tendency toward organization and formal consultation could never be stopped."[207] In other words, without interference from his professors—who, he noted, complained about anything that took them away from their research —he was free to run the institute as he saw fit. These tensions came to a head when he decided to bypass Bamberger, the trustees, and the faculty with a unilateral decision to fill two permanent appointments to the School of Economics. His arbitrary treatment of Einstein didn't sit well with the institute's trustees either.

Flexner blamed much of his trouble on Veblen. He had received a letter dated August 7, 1939, from trustee Winfield Riefler, describing a dinner attended by professors and trustees who were presumably dissatisfied with Flexner. Flexner responded to Riefler, "I have spent a few days with Mr. Bamberger and Mrs. Fuld. . . . We discussed the Princeton problem and Mr. Bamberger was disgusted when he heard from me for the first time that Veblen called a dinner, of which I [Flexner] had no notice and to which I had not been asked."[208] This dinner appeared to act as a coup to force the seventy-three-year-old director into retirement, particularly since Flexner's announcement that he was retiring came only a couple of weeks after the date of Riefler's letter.

According to Flexner, Bamberger was annoyed when he heard about the dinner. He thought "it was very wrong," and added: "I do not look forward to the coming year with the degree of pleasure with which I have always contemplated it."[209] During their conversation, Bamberger told Flexner, "From time to time, I have heard rumors of trouble among both the Trustees and the faculty. I have no appetite for a situation of this kind following the happy years which we have spent together there. Just what I shall do or how I am not yet clear, but I shall make up my mind, probably this week, and I shall let you know."[210]

Ironically, Flexner's resignation came only a month after Bamberger had written to tell him how pleased he and Carrie were with the job he was doing. "We feel that the Institute is entering a new chapter of its work," Bamberger wrote. "Let us hope that our past success will continue — thanks to you."[211] He and Carrie even gave Flexner a gold watch as a token of their appreciation.

Bamberger blamed himself for not keeping a closer eye on the daily operations, but once he understood the situation, he realized that Flexner had to go. Fortunately, ever the canny businessman, he had ensured that a successor would be ready to take Flexner's place by advising him to train an "understudy."[212] Flexner had already been grooming Frank Aydelotte to be his replacement. Bamberger had Hardin tell Flexner that, "If you act promptly I think the desires expressed in your letter, to save Mr. Bamberger's feelings and to stop dissension among the professors of the Institute, would be realized."[213] Hardin also made sure that Flexner's resignation would be announced quietly, without embarrassing publicity.[214] Bamberger knew he could not monitor the handling of Flexner's resignation from a distance, so he made plans to attend the board meeting on October 9. He also instructed that Frank Aydelotte was to be unanimously elected director as soon as possible, since "any doubt or suspicion as to our complete agreement on Aydelotte as Director would weaken his position and make his conduct of the Institute more difficult."[215] Since Bamberger was a "trustee for life" and had approved the appointment of the board members, he could expect that his selection of Aydelotte would go unchallenged.

On October 29, 1939, an editorial in the *New York Times* praised Flexner as "a militant educator fighting in a democracy for the high things of life and especially for the education of the 'gifted.'" It repeated the story given out by the institute that "Dr. Flexner, who is 74, resigned on the advice of a physician."[216]

On the heels of Flexner's resignation, three board members announced their plans to resign, but were convinced to postpone their resignations until new trustees could be appointed.[217] It may be that they had supported Flexner's leadership, or they may have felt that without him the IAS would be like a ship without a rudder. Nevertheless, Bamberger resisted replacing them right away. He understood the importance of selecting trustees who could work together harmoniously (which is why he put so many family members and close associates on the board). Bamberger also rejected a suggestion that Flexner be named a life or honorary trustee, but without saying why.[218] According to the bylaws, only Bamberger and Mrs. Fuld could be designated as life or honorary trustees, titles that ceased to exist after their passing. Bamberger was a stickler for the rules, so unless the trustees were prepared to change the bylaws, Flexner could not be named.[219]

Fortunately for Flexner, Bamberger was also not interested in trying him in the court of public opinion; he insisted that all internal matters be kept in-house and that no interviews be given. Nevertheless, to put a good face on Flexner's resignation, he requested that a resolution expressing the board's appreciation and admiration of Flexner's work as director be ready for the next meeting. However, there was insufficient time to do this, and some felt it should not be done until Aydelotte became director. As board member Alanson Houghton advised him, "This was putting the cart before the horse."[220] Flexner did not disappear completely. Even after he retired, his name appeared in the minutes of board meetings; he is even listed among those on the executive committee.[221] Keeping Flexner around was a wise move on Aydelotte's part, since he was still engaged in negotiations with the Rockefeller Foundation to secure funding for the School of Economics.[222] Eventually, Flexner moved to New York City. He never forgot his connection to the Bamberger family and their great generosity to him and his entire family. He kept up a regular correspondence with Lavinia Bamberger, who invited the Flexners to visit her in Avon—just like in the "good old days."

Aydelotte had the advantage of already knowing Bamberger. He and his wife Marie had visited Bamberger's summer home in Avon on numerous occasions. The foursome had had dinners and bridge games, which developed into a friendly rivalry, with Louis and Frank losing to Carrie and Marie. They attended concerts together and spent long hours discussing the institute's future. Bamberger enjoyed giving gifts, which he saw as a mark of his appreciation for a job well done. In 1938 he put Aydelotte's name on a list to receive a Schick electric shaver, a new product that Aydelotte said he couldn't afford.[223] This was Bamberger's signal to Aydelotte that he could plan on having Bamberger's support.

When Aydelotte became director, he "realized for the first time that the Institute budget was unbalanced."[224] "Since I have a horror of deficits," Aydelotte wrote later, "and believe that no philanthropic institution ought to spend money which it does not have, about the first thing I did was look around for funds to enable us to balance our budget."[225] In 1940 he succeeded in getting funds from the Rockefeller Foundation. The first grant of $105,000 was for a three-year period on the condition that it would be matched dollar-for-dollar by Bamberger, which it was.[226] The foundation gave another grant in 1943, for $70,000 for work on economics, with the understanding that this too would be matched by Bamberger.[227]

In July 1943 Aydelotte wrote to Bamberger to request permission to conduct a two-year study of the fundamentals of American civilization. Covering English and European thought in the sixteenth and seventeenth centuries, and its reflection in America in the eighteenth century during the formative days of the American union, this study, Aydelotte wrote, "would be broader than mere political history and properly described as the history of thought."[228] His plan was a forerunner of the merging of the School of Economics and Politics and the School of Humanistic Studies in 1949. He asked Bamberger whether, if the Rockefeller Foundation provided half the funds, he and Mrs. Fuld would provide the other half. The subject of American civilization interested Bamberger; it wasn't as theoretical as mathematics or as unpredictable as economics. He immediately responded, "Briefly speaking I am pleased to inform you that we (Mrs. Fuld and I) are agreeable to your proposal."[229] The Rockefeller Foundation also agreed.

As director Aydelotte never forgot that part of his job was to keep Bamberger informed and pleased about how the IAS was functioning. Starting in 1941, he and the trustees arranged to have lunch meetings in Newark to save Bamberger the trip to Princeton.[230] Even after Bamberger died, the next IAS director, J. Robert Oppenheimer, stuck to a policy of keeping Bamberger's remaining relatives informed about the activities of the institute. He hoped they would honor Bamberger's memory by contributing their own money to the IAS. Alas, none of these Bambergers were ever that rich.

World War II brought changes to the IAS. In 1942 Aydelotte notified Bamberger that about "half the usual number of students" would be enrolled.[231] The faculty was reduced to thirty-five, with the prospect that they might be called for war work. He also informed Bamberger that the US Navy attached "great importance to the work which Einstein is doing for them. . . . They send a man to see him every week or two who brings problems and carries back to Washington the results of Einstein's work."[232] Aydelotte was afraid that Einstein's health would suffer if he stayed in Princeton during the summer, but reported to Bamberger that he "looks and seems extremely well."[233]

In the meantime, Aydelotte had to struggle to keep the institute viable. In 1943 he suggested ways to reduce expenditures, such as not replacing retiring professors and reducing or abolishing the stipends that enabled young men to come to the institute. He was reluctant to eliminate the stipends, however, since offering the opportunity to do research was "a great part of the utility of the Institute to the scholarly world."[234] He also considered it essential to preserve a focus on moving forward and reminded Bamberger of his own earlier comment that the institute needed "a mind sensation" or something to reenergize interest in its scholarly offerings.[235] In a letter to Bamberger, he quoted Bamberger's 1912 explanation that he had opened a larger, more modern store because it was "too young to stand still,"[236] adding that the institute too had to move forward or else its attempt to change American education would fail. However, Bamberger refused to allow any discussion of the institute's future plans before his death.[237] He preferred that the trustees decide this after he was gone. Aydelotte was forced to wait until Bamberger died to make any substantive changes.

Although Bamberger had reassured Aydelotte that he and Mrs. Fuld would take care of the institute in their wills, he would not discuss the details.[238] As it turned out, he left most of his estate to the IAS. After his death, even the contents of the South Orange estate, including a lawn mower, tractor, and Mrs. Fuld's beloved garden tools, were sent to Princeton. The metal tools were valuable, since during the war metal items for nonwar use were scarce. As previously mentioned, Aydelotte

requested a dishwasher for the institute's kitchen, but much to everyone's surprise, the Bambergers did not own one.

In 1949 Professor Veblen requested that a Bamberger-Fuld memorial
be created, and the director, Robert Oppenheimer, approved the creation of "Founders Walk," a four-mile trail leading from the edge of the
lawn behind Fuld Hall to the trolley line road and through the woods to
the Raritan Canal.[239] A bench and a rock bearing a bronze plaque with
the founders' names were placed at the beginning of the walk. An inscription on the plaque reads, "Dedicated to Louis Bamberger and his
sister Carrie B. F. Fuld whose vision and generosity made this Institute
for Advanced Study Possible."[240] Veblen didn't like the wording.[241]

Founders Walk was dedicated on October 20, 1950, to commemorate the IAS's fiftieth anniversary. People connected to the early days of
the institute were invited. Dr. Flexner, then living in New York City, did
not attend. He had an appointment in Washington that week. Almost
all others did attend, including Louis Bamberger's good friend Albert
Einstein.

If Bamberger had been granted more time on earth, he would have
seen the institute grow from its first school of mathematics, headed by
Einstein, to include schools of economics, politics, humanistic studies,
natural sciences, and social science, and become "one of the world's
leading centers for theoretical research and intellectual inquiry."[242] To
date a total of thirty-three Nobel laureates in physics, medicine, literature, chemistry, and economics have been faculty members or long-
term visitors since the founding in 1930.

In 2012 the lobby of Fuld Hall was given a long overdue facelift, and
the bronze plaques of Mr. and Mrs. Fuld that had hung in the vestibule
of Fuld Hall for many years were removed and replaced with a new
plaque composed of images of Mr. Bamberger and Mrs. Fuld as well
as text (which had been lacking when the bronzes were on display).[243]
The original bronze plaques are currently on display in cases in the
lobby of the Historical Studies–Social Science Library. There is also a
bronze relief of Bamberger above the library's card catalogue on the
second floor of the Mathematics–Natural Sciences Library in Fuld Hall.
It was gift from Lavinia Bamberger after her brother's death in 1944. In
1945 the Institute purchased an unauthorized portrait of Bamberger by
Henry Wolff to hang over one of the doors of the library, "next to the
place where we plan to put a portrait of Einstein."[244] "Neither one is

a great picture," Aydelotte explained to Edgar Bamberger, "but a hundred years from now our successors will be glad to have them."[245] His decision to hang the two portraits side by side is a reminder that while Albert Einstein made the IAS and Princeton famous, it was Louis Bamberger who provided the bricks, the mortar, and the books.

EPILOGUE
A LIFE WELL LIVED

When Louis Bamberger died in his sleep in March 1944, all of Newark went into mourning. Flags flew at half-mast for three days. Mayor Vincent J. Murphy had Newark city hall draped with mourning colors. L. Bamberger & Co. closed for one day, and its Market Street window displayed photographs of the founder.

"I know you are interested in learning about the [Bamberger] funeral," wrote Jewel, a relative of Felix Fuld, to relatives in Germany. "Altogether there were about twenty-five persons. Mr. Einstein was there and also his lawyer Mr. Hardin and the president of the Museum." (Bamberger's great-niece, Ellen, recalled sitting next to Einstein and thinking it was unusual for a man of his age to attend a funeral wearing no socks.)[1] "It was a very short and plain ceremony. A Rabbi Wice said a few words and everyone recited the Twenty-third psalm. It was all over in a few minutes. Mrs. Fuld did not come downstairs to greet the guests but listened to the service from a convenient spot in an upstairs hallway."[2] Carrie Fuld died four months later.

Two days later Bamberger was cremated at Rosehill Crematory in Linden, New Jersey. His ashes were delivered in a cardboard container to Smith and Smith Funeral Home in Newark, but since no urn had been purchased, they remained there for two days until his nephew Edgar picked them up.[3] After this it is not known what happened to them. Apparently Bamberger had given thought to the disposal of his ashes. A December 6 letter from Aydelotte to Bamberger's sister Lavinia states, "The Trustees were informed of your brother's wishes concerning the disposition of his ashes, and a committee, of which I am a member, was appointed to consult with you as to the best way in which his wishes might be carried out."[4] No such consultation seems to have taken place.

One theory about what was done with Bamberger's ashes was his great-nephew Edgar Bamberger Bing's claim that they were scattered in the Shark River. However, Bamberger was too detail oriented to leave things to chance. Nor would he have left this decision to Carrie, who was ill much of the time. Most likely, Edgar Bamberger made the final decision but never spoke about it, for Louis would have sworn him to secrecy. He thus preserved after death the privacy his uncle had insisted on so strenuously while he lived.

Bamberger's great-nephew Morton Schindel recalled that Bamberger spent his last days at home seated in his favorite chair with a blanket wrapped around his legs, listening to music on his radio while awaiting Schindel's visits. Though Schindel came regularly, he reported no striking confidences. Bamberger would not in any case have spoken ill about the people he did business with. His attitude was that if you had nothing good to say, it was better not to speak. In addition to regular visits from family members, particularly his nephew Edgar, he saw members of Newark's Jewish community, who came to ask for his annual UJA pledge.

Much has been written about the way German Jews helped to set relatives up in business. This was not Louis Bamberger's experience. He may have learned the retail business working for his Hutzler uncles in Baltimore, but there is no evidence that they gave him money to open his Newark store; he used what he had saved from the sale of his half of the business he shared with his brother Julius and the income he earned from his job in New York as a wholesale buyer. The rest came from his partners, Louis Frank and Felix Fuld. He started with three employees and ended with five thousand co-workers on his payroll. It was his amazing business sense, starting with his faith in Newark as a center of commerce, that built his purchase of a small, bankrupt Newark firm into one of the nation's great department stores, to the point where "Busy as Bamberger's" became a household word far beyond the boundaries of New Jersey.

Bamberger was the consummate promoter, who created an advertising department staffed with copywriters, illustrators, and the latest technology. No one knew how to sell a product or convince a shopper that he had her and her family's interests at heart better than he. He drew people in by offering goods and services that probably could have been duplicated locally at Hahne's or Plaut's. But he made his customers' shopping experience so pleasant, with tearooms, restaurants, live fashion shows, and in-house exhibitions, that shoppers spent the entire day at the store. Hundreds still recall the clown ice cream cone. When Bamberger's fellow merchants asked what his secret was, his answer was "volume," which in the retail business meant ordering large quantities of merchandise and selling it all quickly.

How many successful businessmen get to the top of their profession or career without exhibiting a flair for self-promotion? Yet modesty was one of Bamberger's distinguishing characteristics. Although he believed firmly in advertising as part of business, he was known to thank newspapermen for leaving his name and photograph out of their articles.

Bamberger accepted honorary presidencies of charitable organizations, but did not use his largesse to become more famous. Still, when Newark's popular mayor Thomas Raymond died in 1928, Bamberger was tapped as a pallbearer, for by that time he had worked his way into a group of prominent men in Newark who had more to say than anybody else about the decisions that shaped the growth of the city. The following year he was asked to be a pallbearer for Louis Marshall, a towering figure whose death was felt throughout the Jewish world in America and overseas. This connection to Marshall confirms that Bamberger's influence extended well beyond Newark.

Bamberger rarely exhibited emotion and was clearly not sentimental. When he lost his best friend and business partner, Felix Fuld, he did not attend the funeral for fear of exposing himself to unwanted questions from reporters. However, he clearly missed Fuld. He promptly made up his mind that he would not carry on alone and in the summer of that same year sold his business, distributing $1 million among his employees. It is as hard to explain his extreme reticence as it is to understand his demand that his philanthropy remain anonymous. At the same time, he was practical enough to realize that newspaper articles reporting his support of the city's hospitals, his donation of the Newark Museum, and his endowment of the Institute for Advanced Study offered a way to lead by example.

After Bamberger's death, a local Masonic lodge arranged to put his name on a World War II Liberty ship, the SS *Louis Bamberger*. Such ships were named for individuals no longer living, who had made a significant contribution to American life. Since these ships carried more than two-thirds of all cargo leaving the United States, this was a fitting tribute to Bamberger, who had made a living importing and exporting goods to and from ports around the world on cargo ships.

Bamberger was a national and even a world figure. The moment he agreed to endow the Institute for Advanced Study, his name went up in lights in Europe's greatest universities. According to his close friend and attorney, John Hardin, he "became famous the world over and his life for the time was complicated by letters from all over the world inviting him to further philanthropies."[5] But it was not so much Bamberger's decision to endow the institute that makes him a towering philanthropic figure. Rather, it was his ability to envision what Abraham Flexner had in mind when he presented his plan for an educational Utopia and what this would mean to future generations of scholars looking for academic freedom and opportunities for unrestricted research. This endowment was an exceptional commitment for a man who never finished high school. As Porter puts it, "He wanted his fortune used to break new ground, not just follow what was currently fashionable, and to support social experiments that government or private agencies were not likely to fund."[6] He may also have taken into account that you can say things in the context of a cultural institution that you cannot say in the political arena (which could also explain why he steered clear of politics).

It is a testimony to Bamberger's character that Einstein, who knew what it was to be hounded by the press, became his friend. Einstein enjoyed Bamberger's personal style; he wasn't a pushy American looking to capitalize on his friendship with the great scientist. Not only did Einstein attend Bamberger's funeral, but in 1950, when the IAS got around to remembering Bamberger's role in its founding and dedicated a plaque in his memory, Einstein was there, even as Flexner was not.

How then should Louis Bamberger be remembered? Newark historian Charles Cummings aptly describes him as "the personification of the liberal American businessman, who by his strength of character and idealism secured the faith of the American people in private enterprise."[7] His personnel manager and nephew Michael Schapp wrote, "The store itself was an outstanding example of how a big business could be conducted to the approval of its customers and loyal co-workers in the place."[8] Bamberger believed in his business, understood the nature of competition, and subscribed to a high standard of conduct to which he held both his firm and himself—while never taking his eye off the bottom line.

In his will, Bamberger left $520,000 to various Newark institutions, $543,000 to relatives and personal employees, and $19 million, or the bulk of his estate, to the Institute for Advanced Study. Chances are no one will ever know how much money Bamberger gave away in his lifetime. His fifty-acre estate in South Orange is now the site of the East Orange Veterans hospital. At the hospital's entrance is a small stone building with a flat roof that in Bamberger's time was used as a gatehouse, where a security guard monitored the people who came to his home and thus kept his private world secure.

It is regrettable that Bamberger's insistence on keeping his accomplishments as a businessman and philanthropist out of the public eye as much as possible has impoverished the record that the historian depends on. Bamberger himself told his executive secretary, "No one will care what I say; they will only recall what I do."[9] Nevertheless, the record of those actions speaks much of who he was.

NOTES

INTRODUCTION

1. Charles Cummings, "An Enlightened Life of Giving and Selling," *Star-Ledger* (Newark), July 16, 1998, 4.

2. Helen Christine Bennett, "Do the Wise Thing If You Can but Whatever You Do . . . Do Something," *American Magazine*, June 1923, 72.

3. Susan Mintz, e-mail message to the author, January 25, 2008.

4. Marjorie and Al Marcus, in discussion with the author, March 29, 2009.

5. Cummings, "An Enlightened Life of Giving and Selling," 4.

6. M. R. Warner, *Julius Rosenwald: The Life of a Practical Humanitarian* (New York: Harper and Brothers, 1939), x.

7. "Bamberger Terms Gifts 'Debt to City,'" *Newark Sunday Call*, January 22, 1923, 1.

8. Leon Harris, *Merchant Princes: An Intimate History of Jewish Families Who Built Great Department Stores* (New York: Harper and Row, 1979), 308.

9. William Leach, *Land of Desire: Merchants, Power, and the Rise of a New American Culture* (New York: Random House, 1993), 292.10. Linda Forgosh to Edward J. Goldberg, e-mail, July 30, 2010, New York City.

10. "Louis Bamberger Honored as Founder of Store," *Newark Evening News*, December 16, 1942, microfilm.

11. Ibid.

1. BALTIMORE ROOTS, 1855–1887

1. Jerome Levine, "Immigrant Saga" (genealogy research paper, Salisbury University, Salisbury, Maryland, 1990), 2, Bamberger Family Collection, Reisterstown, Maryland.

2. Ibid., 1.

3. Alexandra Lee Levin, *Vision: A Biography of Harry Friedenwald* (Philadelphia: Jewish Publication Society of America, 1964), 23.

4. Malcolm Gladwell, *Outliers* (New York: Little Brown, 2008), 142.

5. Levin, *Vision*, 2.

6. Barbara Tumarkin Dunham, "An American Family: The Bamberger Family," *Philadelphia Inquirer*, May 1976, 1.

7. Lavinia Bamberger to Abraham Flexner, November 8, 1944, container 4, Abraham Flexner Collection, Manuscripts Division, Library of Congress, Washington, DC.

8. Michael J. Lisicky, *Hutzler's: Where Baltimore Shops* (Charleston: History Press, 2009), 17.

9. Ibid.

10. Abraham Shusterman, *The Legacy of a Liberal* (Baltimore: Har Sinai Congregation, 1967), 20.

11. Isaac M. Fein, *The Making of an American Jewish Community: The History of Baltimore Jewry from 1773–1920* (Philadelphia: Jewish Publication Society of America, 1971), 127.

12. Ibid., 129.

13. Ibid., 132.

14. Anton Kaufman, "Leave to Inspect Baltimore Asylum," *Jewish Chronicle*, April 10, 1925, 1.

15. "Hebrews of Newark," *Newark Sunday Call*, June 21, 1896, 46.

16. Levin, *Vision*, 16.

17. Fein, *Making of an American Jewish Community*, 182.

18. Levin, *Vision*, 402.

19. Sherry Gorelick, *City College and the Jewish Poor: Education in New York, 1880–1924* (New York: Shocken Books, 1982), 7.

20. Fein, *Making of an American Jewish Community*, 126.

21. Ibid., 127.

22. Lavinia Bamberger to Abraham Flexner, November 8, 1944, container 4, Abraham Flexner Papers, Manuscripts Division, Library of Congress, Washington, DC.

23. Ibid.

24. Peter M. Ascoli, *Julius Rosenwald: The Man Who Built Sears, Roebuck and Advanced the Cause of Black Education in the South* (Bloomington: Indiana University Press, 2006), 6.

25. Photograph of Felix Fuld standing in front of Baltimore's Chesapeake Rubber Goods Company, circa 1890, inscribed on the back by Fuld's nephew, Bert Berg, on October, 19, 1969, Berg Family Collection, Huntington, New York.

26. Ernest Julian Schmidt, "The Fuld Family" (unpublished manuscript, March 1942, 6), Berg Family Collection, Huntington, New York.

27. "Julius Bamberger Dies in Sanitarium," *Jewish Chronicle*, December 17, 1926, 1.

28. Lavinia Bamberger to Abraham Flexner, November 8, 1944, container 4, Abraham Flexner Papers, Manuscripts Division, Library of Congress, Washington, DC.

29. Ibid.

30. Jan Whitaker, *Service and Style: How the American Department Store Fashioned the Middle Class* (New York: St. Martin's Press, 2006), 67.

31. "Hutzler Relatives Are Left $732,000," *Baltimore Sun*, October 15, 1927, n.p.

32. Leon Harris, *Merchant Princes: An Intimate History of Jewish Families Who Built Great Department Stores* (New York: Harper and Row, 1979), 165.

33. Ibid., 17.

34. Whitaker, *Service and Style*, 12.

35. Robert Hendrickson, *The Grand Emporiums: The Illustrated History of America's Great Department Stores* (Briarcliff Manor, NY: Stein and Day, 1979), 33.

36. Ibid.

37. "Institute Named in L. Bamberger Will," *Princeton Herald*, n.d., 1, container 4, Abraham Flexner Papers, Manuscripts Division, Library of Congress, Washington, DC.

38. Michael J. Lisicky, *Hutzler's: Where Baltimore Shops* (Charleston: History Press, 2009), 19.

39. Harris, *Merchant Princes*, 337.

40. Robert Hendrickson, *The Grand Emporiums: The Illustrated History of America's Great Department Stores* (New York: Stein and Day, 1979), 30.

41. Fein, *Making of an American Jewish Community*, 158.

42. Ibid., 159.

43. Whitaker, *Service and Style*, 67.

2. BUILDING AN EMPIRE, 1892–1911

1. Bennett, "Do the Wise Thing If You Know What It Is," 73.

2. Ibid., 122.

3. Susan Porter Benson, *Counter Currents: Saleswomen, Managers, and Customers in American Department Stores 1890–1940* (Champaign: University of Illinois Press, 1986), 8.

4. Charles J. McGuirk, "Department Stores Forerunner Opened by Jews in Newark," *Newark Ledger*, November 14, 1935, n.p.

5. Ibid.

6. John E. O'Connor and Charles F. Cummings, "Bamberger's Department Store *Charm Magazine* and the Culture of Consumption in New Jersey 1924–1932," *New Jersey History* (fall/winter 1984): 11.

7. Bennett, "Do the Wise Thing If You Know What It Is," 72.

8. Clement A. Price, "Blacks and Jews in the City of Opportunity: Newark, New Jersey 1900–1967" (unpublished paper, meeting of the MetroWest Jewish Historical Society, Whippany, New Jersey, June 1994), 3.

9. Bennett, "Do the Wise Thing If You Know What It Is," 73.

10. Frank I. Liveright, "One of America's Great Stores," typescript, 1956, p. 2, New Jersey Reference Division, Newark Public Library, no. RNJ.658.53 L75.

11. Ibid.

12. Bennett, "Do the Wise Thing If You Know What It Is," 72.

13. Isaac Landman, *The Universal Jewish Encyclopedia* (Skokie, IL: Jewish Publication Society, 2009), 468.

14. Harris, *Merchant Princes*, 4.

15. Hendrickson, *Grand Emporiums*. 130.

16. Ibid., 64.

17. Ibid., 95.

18. Harris, *Merchant Princes*, 114.

19. Hendrickson, *Grand Emporiums*, 71.

20. Ibid., 95.

21. Bennett, "Do the Wise Thing If You Know What It Is," 72.

22. Harris, *Merchant Princes*, 340.

23. Ascoli, *Julius Rosenwald*, 360.

24. Liveright, "One of America's Great Stores," 2.

25. Ibid.

26. "L. Bamberger & Co. Acquired by R. H. Macy for Amount Reported as above $25,000,000," *Newark Sunday Call*, June 30, 1929, 20.

27. "Bamberger's 40 Years of Progress," *Newark Sunday Call*, January 8, 1933, n.p.

28. Bennett, "Do the Wise Thing If You Know What It Is," 72.

29. Cummings, "An Enlightened Life of Selling and Giving," 4.

30. Bennett, "Do the Wise Thing If You Know What It Is," 72.

31. Whitaker, *Service and Style*, 9.

32. Ibid., 8.

33. Ibid., 13.

34. John T. Cunningham, *Newark*, 3rd ed. (Newark: New Jersey Historical Society, 2002), 185.

35. Ibid., 232.

36. Cummings, "An Enlightened Life of Selling and Giving," 4.

37. Cunningham, *Newark*, 203.

38. Leach, *Land of Desire*, 28.

39. Cunningham, *Newark*, 210.

40. Ibid.

41. John Hardin, "Louis Bamberger and Mrs. Felix Fuld," container 4, p. 2, Abraham Flexner Papers, Manuscripts Division, Library of Congress, Washington, DC.

42. Ibid.

43. John Hardin, "Recollections of Mr. Bamberger," New Jersey Trustees box, Institute for Advanced Study Archives, Princeton, New Jersey.

44. Ibid.

45. "We Reminisce a Bit about the Past on the Evening of Our Grand Opening," *Counter Currents*, October 1929, 2.

46. Ibid.

47. Ibid., 1.

48. "Birthdays: Arthur F. Reinhart," *Counter Currents*, March 1928, 7.

49. "A Chat with Mr. Louis Bamberger: Business in the 'Good Old Days,'" *Counter Currents*, November 1928, 10.

50. Ibid.

51. Ibid.

52. "Hebrews of Newark," 46.

53. Ibid.

54. Staff of the Newark Public Library, *Newark's Last Fifteen Years: 1904–1919: The Story in Outline* (Newark: Newark Public Library, 1919), 19.

55. Ibid.

56. Clement A. Price, "Blacks and Jews in the City of Opportunity: Newark NJ 1900–1967" (paper presented at the Jewish Historical Society of New Jersey, Whippany, New Jersey, June 13, 1994), 4, Rutgers University–Newark Special Collections, SNCLY2F144. N6P75 1994.

57. Whitaker, *Service and Style*, 31.

58. Harold S. Wechsler, *Brewing Bachelors: The History of the University of Newark "Origins"* (Newark: Rutgers University Press), 1.

59. Staff of the Newark Public Library, *Newark's Last Fifteen Years, 1904–1919: The Story in Outline* (Newark: Newark Public Library, 1919), 19.

60. "Hill and Cragg," advertisement, *Counter Currents*, October 1929, 1.

61. Leach, *Land of Desire*, 43.

62. Hardin, "Louis Bamberger and Mrs. Felix Fuld."

63. Cunningham, *Newark*, 190.

64. Harris, *Merchant Princes*, xiv.

65. Ibid.

66. "Evolution of the Daily Newspaper," *Jewish Chronicle*, December 24, 1926, 8.

67. Leach, *Land of Desire*, 46.

68. Liveright, "One of America's Great Stores," 4.

69. Ibid.

70. Bennett, "Do the Wise Thing If You Know What It Is," 72.

71. Newspaper clipping, n.d., n.p., Temple Sharey Tefilo-Israel 13-98, box 11, file 1, Jewish Historical Society of New Jersey, Whippany, New Jersey.

72. "A Good Bamberger Story Told by an Old Newark Resident," *Counter Currents*, May 1924, 8.

73. Lavinia Bamberger to Abraham Flexner, November 8, 1944.

74. Liveright, "One of America's Great Stores," 5.

75. Ibid., 6.

76. Ellen Bamberger De Franco to Linda Forgosh, describing Felix Fuld, June 21, 2007, Oakland, California.

77. Liveright, "One of America's Great Stores," 22.

78. "Life Story Like Fiction," newspaper clipping of an obituary that describes Fuld's career, n.d., n.p., Berg Family Collection, Huntington, Long Island.

79. Ellen Bamberger De Franco to Linda Forgosh, November 7, 2007, Oakland, California, private collection of the author.

80. Mildred Levine, telephone interview with the author, April 8, 2015, Reisterstown, Maryland.

81. Ibid.

82. Ellen Bamberger De Franco to Linda Forgosh, March 8, 2008, Oakland, California, private collection of the author.

83. Whitaker, *Service and Style*, 14.

84. Liveright, "One of America's Great Stores," 2.

85. Ibid., 1.

86. Ibid., 5.

87. "Kresge Offers Schindel Post," *Newark Evening News*, December 1, 1929, 1.

88. Morton Schindel, telephone interview with the author, August 7, 2008, Westport, Connecticut.

89. "Edgar S. Bamberger," *Newark Evening News*, June 30, 1952.

90. "Walter S. Moler Called by Death," *Newark Evening News*, October 13, 1928, 1.

91. Ibid.

92. Liveright, "One of America's Great Stores," 6.

93. Ibid.

94. Ibid.

95. "A Page from Our Store History," *Counter Currents*, April 1926, 1.

96. Liveright, "One of America's Great Stores," 7.

97. Ibid.

98. Charles J. McGuirk, "Department

Stores Forerunner Opened by Jews in Newark," *Newark Ledger*, November 14, 1935, n.p.

99. Jackie Berg, in discussion with the author, 2008, Branch Brook Park, Newark, New Jersey.

100. Liveright, "One of America's Great Stores," 4.

101. Ibid.

102. Whitaker, *Service and Style*, 57.

103. Ibid., 68.

104. Seymour Grossman, e-mail to the author, September 29, 2008.

105. "Elbeco," *Counter Currents*, August 1919, 18.

106. Ibid.

107. Liveright, "One of America's Great Stores," 9.

108. American Express Corporate Affairs and Communications, "Inside the Archives: Sailing Safely Home," May 7, 2014.

109. Ibid.

110. Linda Halperin, a former shopper at Bamberger's, showed the author a beaded evening bag made in France in the 1930s with a Bamberger label.

111. Liveright, "One of America's Great Stores," 14.

112. Leach, *Land of Desire*, 280.

113. Ibid.

114. John Hardin Papers, container 4, p. 3, Abraham Flexner Collection, Manuscripts Division, Library of Congress, Washington, DC.

115. "Groundbreaking," *Newark Sunday Call*, February 18, 1911, 1.

116. "A Tunnel between Stores," *Newark Sunday Call*, December 17, 1910, n.p.

117. "Hat Cleaner Sues for Ejection," *Newark Sunday Call*, October 5, 1910, 1.

118. Ibid.

119. "Drives in Rivet for New Store," *Newark Sunday Call*, November 3, 1911, 1.

120. Whitaker, *Service and Style*, 82.

121. Cummings, "An Enlightened Life of Selling and Giving," 4.

122. Dana Egreczky, president of the New Jersey Chamber of Commerce, and Ray Zardetto, Office of Communications, interview with the author, December 14, 2010.

123. Bennett, "Do the Wise Thing If You Know What It Is," 121.

124. Ibid.

3. THE GREAT WHITE STORE, 1912–1921

1. "Fifteen Years Ago Today," advertisement, *Newark Sunday Call*, October 16, 1927, 3.

2. Ibid.

3. "The Greater Store as a Fashion Centre," advertisement, *Bloomfield Citizen*, October 16, 1912, n.p.

4. Ellen Bamberger De Franco, telephone conversation with the author, March 8, 2008.

5. "The Greater Bamberger Store: Formal Opening Next Wednesday," advertisement, *Bloomfield Citizen*, October 12, 1912, n.p.

6. Liveright, "One of America's Great Stores," 15.

7. Milton Riegel, "Making Time under the Bam's Clock," letter to the editor, *Star-Ledger* (Newark), May 15, 1986, n.p.

8. Leach, *Land of Desire*, 60.

9. Whitaker, *Service and Style*, 113.

10. Leach, *Land of Desire*, 104.

11. "Privately View New Big Store," *Newark Sunday Call*, October 15, 1912, 1.

12. Liveright, "One of America's Great Stores," 12.

13. Ibid.

14. Whitaker, *Service and Style*, 94.

15. Leach, *Land of Desire*, 74.

16. "Between Ourselves," *Newark Sunday Call*, November 28, 1915, 3.

17. "Do You Use the 'Red Phones'?" *Counter Currents*, March 1919, 3.

18. Don Karp, e-mail to the author, December 8, 2006.

19. Edward J. Goldberg, Senior Vice President, Government and Consumer Affairs and Diversity Vendor Development, Macy's East, e-mail to the author, July 30, 2010, New York City.

20. "Seventy Five Years in the News," *Around the Clock* (R. H. Macy's in-house publication), December 16, 1967, 8.

21. "Interesting *Counter Currents* Five Years Ago," *Counter Currents*, July 1920, 20.

22. Leach, *Land of Desire*, 119.

23. "To Sponsors — Present and Future," *Counter Currents*, January 1919, 26.

24. Ibid.

25. "Corralling the Finest Art in the Country," *Counter Currents*, October 1920, 13.

26. "What Others Say," *Counter Currents*, June 1919, 13, 14. These are letters from owners of other department stores in America commending Bamberger's on the excellence of the store's employee newsletter.

27. Ibid.

28. "How Far Do We Ship Merchandise Free?" *Counter Currents*, October 1921, 12.

29. "Exhibit Things Newark Makes," *Newark Sunday Call*, February 3, 1913, n.p.

30. "President Starts Exhibition Wheels," *Newark Sunday Call*, February 24, 1914, 1.

31. Ibid.

32. "Between Ourselves," *Newark Sunday Call*, February 21, 1914, 3.

33. "Between Ourselves," *Newark Sunday Call*, February 28, 1915, 3.

34. Ibid.

35. "First Annual Poultry Exhibition," *Newark Sunday Call*, January 4, 1914, 3.

36. Bennett, "Do the Wise Thing If You Know What It Is," 122.

37. "Beginning of the Bamberger Store," *Counter Currents*, June 1919, 6.

38. Whitaker, *Service and Style*, 10.

39. "L. Bamberger & Co. Uses Whole 'Roto' Section," *Newark Evening News*, November 23, 1920, 27.

40. Ezra Shales, *John Cotton Dana and the Business of Enlightening Newark: Applied Art at the Newark Public Library and Museum, 1902–1929* (Ann Arbor, MI: UMI Dissertation Services, 2007), 259.

41. "Between Ourselves," *Newark Sunday Call*, September 1914, 3.

42. "Between Ourselves," *Newark Sunday Call*, January 1, 1915, 3.

43. "Between Ourselves," *Newark Sunday Call*, August 22, 1915, 3.

44. "Between Ourselves," *Newark Sunday Call*, December 6, 1914, 3.

45. "Between Ourselves," *Newark Sunday Call*, January 16, 1916, 3.

46. Ibid.

47. "Between Ourselves," *Newark Sunday Call*, June 7, 1914, 3.

48. "Between Ourselves," *Newark Sunday Call*, August 9, 1914, 3.

49. "Between Ourselves," *Newark Sunday Call*, November 8, 1914, 3.

50. "Between Ourselves," *Newark Sunday Call*, January 3, 1915, 3.

51. Phyllis Levin, Anna Heyman's granddaughter, e-mail to the author, January 21, 2014.

52. David Schechner, interview with the author, December 1, 2006.

53. "Fuld-Bamberger Picture Sparks an 'I Remember,'" *Jewish News*, April 21, 1977, file "Bamberger, deceased," Jewish Historical Society, Whippany, New Jersey.

54. Oscar "Ozzie" Lax, interview with the author, June 22, 2006.

55. "The Important Column — How It Originated and Grew," *Counter Currents*, August 1919, 6.

56. "Tally Figures Never Lie or One Thousand Customers Can't Be Wrong!" *Counter Currents*, May 1929, 12–13.

57. "Between Ourselves," *Newark Sunday Call*, February 7, 1915, 3.

58. Whitaker, *Service and Style*, 132.

59. Leach, *Land of Desire*, 103.

60. Shales, *John Cotton Dana and the Business of Enlightening Newark*, 42.

61. Ibid., 44.

62. Ibid., 272.

63. Robert Hendrickson, *The Grand Emporiums: The Illustrated History of America's Great Department Stores* (Briarcliff Manor, NY: Stein and Day, 1979), 133.

64. "Between Ourselves," *Newark Sunday Call*, February 1916, 3.

65. Leach, *Land of Desire*, 93.

66. Hendrickson, *Grand Emporiums*, 31.

67. Edgar S. Bamberger, "The Weekly Column: Talk No. 8, May 16th Retail Research Association," *Counter Currents*, 4.

68. Bennett, "Do the Wise Thing If You Know What It Is," 81.

69. Leach, *Land of Desire*, 282.

70. Ibid.

71. Whitaker, *Service and Style*, 62.

72. Ibid., 178.

73. Leach, *Land of Desire*, 282.

74. "Between Ourselves," *Newark Sunday Call*, November 12, 1916, 3.

75. O'Connor and Cummings, "Bamberger's Department Store *Charm* Magazine," 4.

76. "Invitation to Attend the 250th Anniversary of Newark from the Committee of 100," B'nai Jeshurun Collection, Jewish Historical Society, Whippany, New Jersey.

77. "Historic Ceremonies and Exercises in Commemoration of the 250th Anniversary of the Founding of Newark, New Jersey in 1666," p. 6, private collection of the author.

78. "Complete List of 4,000 Donors to Newark's 1916 Fund for $250,000," May 9, 1915, p. 15, private collection of the author.

79. Staff of the Newark Public Library, *Newark's Last Fifteen Years*, 21.

80. Henry Wellington Wack, *Newark's 250th Anniversary Celebration* (Newark: Price and Lee, 1916), 18, 19.

81. "Boosts for City Help Business and Win Friends," *Newark Sunday Call*, October 1, 1916, pt. 2, 1.

82. Ibid.

83. "The Greatest Industry Fair Ever Held in Newark Opens Tuesday Morning at 10:30," *Newark Sunday Call*, February 13, 1916, 1.

84. "Prospects Bright for Retail Merchants Week," *Newark Sunday Call*, April 9, 1916, 15.

85. "Community Pays Raymond Tribute," *Jewish Chronicle*, October 12, 1928, 1.

86. "Pennsy Sees Big Future for Newark," *Newark Sunday Call*, June 6, 1915, pt. 2, 1.

87. Whitaker, *Service and Style*, 163.

88. "These Now Wear Salesmanship Pins," *Counter Currents*, June 1922, 8.

89. "Woman's New Field in Department Stores—The Opportunities Awaiting Girls," *Counter Currents*, January 1919, 21.

90. Whitaker, *Service and Style*, 163.

91. Susan Porter Benson, *Counter Cultures: Saleswomen, Managers, and Customers in American Department Stores 1890–1940* (Urbana: University of Illinois Press, 1986), 151.

92. Whitaker, *Service and Style*, 166.

93. "Noted Visitor," *Counter Currents*, February 14, 1925, 8.

94. "A New Club for Newark," *Counter Currents*, December 1921, 5.

95. "New Voters Take Election Day Seriously," *Counter Currents*, October 1920, 5.

96. "Camera Notes Notables Listening to Symphony Notes," *Star-Ledger* (Newark), June 22, 1935.

97. "Store Detective," *Counter Currents*, February 1920, 19.

98. "Marion Eyers the Subject of a Special Article," *Counter Currents*, August 1920, 7.

99. Ibid.

100. "Army and Navy Efficiency Exhibit Opens Tomorrow," *Newark Sunday Call*, April 23, 1916, 4.

101. "Army and Guard Officers to Be at Store Exhibition," *Newark Sunday Call*, April 19, 1916, 5.

102. "The Brewster-Heller Armor Plate Effective against Machine Gun Fire," *Dover Advance*, December 5, 1918, 1.

103. "Our Elevator Operators," *Counter Currents*, February 1929, 2.

104. "Birthdays," *Counter Currents*, October 1924, 6.

105. Ibid.

106. Maxine Olian Apsel, "A 'Pioneer' Recalls Early Black-Jewish Ties in Newark," *Jewish News*, December 24, 1987, 1.

107. "The Orchestra which Provided the Dance Music," *Counter Currents*, February 1924, 12.

108. Ellen Bamberger De Franco to the author, June 22, 2007, Oakland, California.

109. Whitaker, *Service and Style*, 117.

110. "Between Ourselves," *Newark Sunday Call*, May 4, 1919, 3.

111. Ibid., April 28, 1918, 3.

112. Ibid., April 8, 1917, 3.

113. Ibid., June 3, 1917, 3.

114. Liveright, "One of America's Great Stores," 15.

115. Joseph Azzolina, "Ticketing the Bamberger Store," *Counter Currents*, July 1919, 18.

116. "Between Ourselves," *Newark Sunday Call*, February 6, 1916, 3.

117. "Newark Business Meets Fuel Order," *Newark Sunday Call*, January 20, 1918, 1.

118. "We Go Back to a Cover Again," *Counter Currents*, January 1919, 1.

119. "Between Ourselves," *Newark Sunday Call*, September 15, 1918, 3.

120. "Bamberger's to Be $5 Million Company," *Newark Sunday Call*, December 6, 1917, 1.

121. "Thanksgiving Dinners for Camp Dix Boys," *Newark Sunday Call*, November 11, 1917, 3.

122. "Visitors to Camp Dix," *Counter Currents*, January 1918, 5.

123. Staff of the Newark Public Library, *Newark's Last Fifteen Years*, 51.

124. "Between Ourselves," *Newark Sunday Call*, November 4, 1917, 3.

125. "Rooms to Rent," *Counter Currents*, September 1918, 4.

126. "Soldiers Letters," *Counter Currents*, January 1919, 20.

127. "A. M. Brown in France," *Counter Currents*, January 1919, 24.

128. "Paris Shopping Service for Your Boy in France," *Newark Sunday Call*, November 4, 1917, 3.

129. "Between Ourselves," *Newark Sunday Call*, April 28, 1918, 3.

130. "The First Service Roll and the Last One," *Counter Currents*, February 1919, 10.

131. "Jewish Relief Drive on Soon," *Newark Sunday Call*, November 10, 1918, 24.

132. Nathan Strauss and the American Jewish Relief Committee, "To the Co-Workers of L. Bamberger & Co.," July 1, 1918. Letter thanking the store's workers for the four thousand dollars they contributed to the campaign helping to save Europe's Jews.

133. "Welcome for Homecoming Boys," *Counter Currents*, May 1919, 2.

134. "To Co-Workers Formerly in the Service," *Counter Currents*, November 1919, 5.

135. A. Cornell, Savings Division, Treasury Department, to Mr. W. E. Weeks, *Counter Currents*, January 31, 1920 (inside front cover).

136. "Our Greatest Christmas," *Counter Currents*, January 1919, 6.

137. "Newark Honors Its War Dead by Thrilling Parade," *Newark Sunday Call*, November 12, 1922, 15.

138. "Bon Voyage," *Counter Currents*, January 1919, 2.

139. Sanford Epstein, interview with the author, March 5, 2012, Jewish Historical Society, Whippany, New Jersey.

140. Jeanie Gelbart, e-mail to the author, April 8, 2015.

141. "Buy Paris Gowns? Well Not Often," *Newark Sunday Call*, February 23, 1919, 1.

142. Ibid.

143. Ibid.

144. Ibid.

145. Ibid.

146. Alida Michelson, interview with the author, February 14, 2008, Rockville, Maryland.

147. "The Airplane for Commercial Purposes," *Counter Currents*, May 1919, 14.

148. "Commercial Flight Tomorrow May Be First in Country," *Newark Evening News*, April 18, 1919, microfilm.

149. "Forced to Land, Aviator Alights on Building and Rises from It," *Newark Evening News*, August 23, 1919, microfilm.

150. "The Bamberger Store and Vicinity of 'Four Corners' as They Look from Bamberger Delivery Airplane," *Counter Currents*, April 1919, 19.

151. "Merchandise Reaches This City in Aeroplane," *Newark Evening News*, n.d., microfilm.

152. "Seaplane on Shore Trip after Arrival in a Fog," *Newark Evening News*, April 28, 1919, microfilm.

153. "Commercial Aviator Braved Air Risks Successfully, But Neglected Detail of Making Manifest of Goods," *Newark Evening News*, May 15, 1919, microfilm.

154. Bennett, "Do the Wise Thing If You Know What It Is," 73.

155. Mendel Bernstein, e-mail to the author, February 2, 2009.

156. Aero Club badges as seen by Lisa Gil and David Forgosh are on display in the Smithsonian Air and Space Museum in Chantilly, Virginia.

157. Liveright, "One of America's Great Stores," 17.

158. Ibid.

159. Bennett, "Do the Wise Thing If You Know What It Is," 81.

160. "Mr. Bamberger Addresses Big Groups," *Counter Currents*, August 1920, 13.

161. "L. Bamberger & Co. Now Owners of an Entire Block of Central Realty," *Newark Sunday Call*, July 22, 1917, 8.

162. Ibid.

163. "Throngs Attend Opening of New Plaut Addition," *Jewish Chronicle*, November 13, 1925, 1.

164. Karl Rosenberg, ""Do You Know Just How Big We Really Are?" *Counter Currents*, August 1919, 13–14.

165. Harry W. Crooks, "I Didn't Even Know That We Had a Laboratory," *Counter Currents*, June 1919, 15.

166. Edward Anthony, "ELBECO," *Counter Currents*, August 1919, 14.

167. Judy Kulik, e-mail to the author, March 4, 2009.

168. Joseph Azzolina, "Ticketing the Bamberger Store," *Counter Currents*, July 1919, 18.

169. "Waste Paper Is Valuable When There's Enough of It," *Counter Currents*, October 1919, 15.

170. "The Directory Contest," *Counter Currents*, October 1921, 3.

171. Bennett, "Do the Wise Thing If You Know What It Is," 73.

172. "The 600 Co-Workers Who Have Been Here 5 Years or Longer," *Counter Currents*, December 1920, 8.

173. "Boys' Vocational School Holds Exposition in Auditorium," *Counter Currents*, May 1921, 13.

174. "A Great Nation Today Welcomes Its Twenty-Eighth President," *Counter Currents*, March 1921, 7.

175. Ibid.

176. "New Bamberger Building," *New York Times*, October 29, 1922, n.p.

177. "Are You Watching the New Building?" *Counter Currents*, October 1921, 2, 6.

178. Ibid.

4. ONE OF AMERICA'S GREAT STORES, 1922–1929

1. Leach, *Land of Desire*, 280.

2. Bennett, "Do the Wise Thing If You Know What It Is," 72.

3. Anton Kaufman, "Bamberger and Fuld Felicitated at Formal Opening of New Annex," *Jewish Chronicle*, November 3, 1922, 10.

4. "Bamberger & Co. Hosts," *New York Times*, October 31, 1922, n.p.

5. "Fifty Men and Women Who Have Accomplished the Most for Newark," *Newark Sunday Call*, May 21, 1922, pt. 4, 2.

6. "Bamberger & Co. Hosts," *New York Times*, October 31, 1922, n.p.

7. "Bamberger and Fuld Felicitated at Formal Opening of New Annex."

8. Ibid.

9. Ibid.

10. Leach, *Land of Desire*, 264.

11. Bennett, "Do the Wise Thing If You Know What It Is," 75.

12. Ibid., 122.

13. Leach, *Land of Desire*, 299.

14. Liveright, "One of America's Great Stores," 18.

15. "Addition to Big Store Is Formally Dedicated to Public," *Newark Evening News*, October 30, 1922, 1.

16. Ibid.

17. Ibid.

18. Liveright, "One of America's Great Stores," 16.

19. Bill Jaker, Frank Sulke, and Peter Kanze, *The Airways of New York: Illustrated Histories of 156 AM Stations in the Metropol-*

itan Area, 1921–1996 (Jefferson, NC: McFarland, 1998), 151–156.

20. Whitaker, *Service and Style*, 135.

21. Nat Bodian, "Bamberger's in 1929: What Went on Inside the Store," Old Newark Memories, October 9, 2003, accessed on December 22, 2015, http://www.oldnewark.org/mainindex.php. Includes floor plans of the store.www.oldnewark.org/mainindex.php

22. "Radio Chieftains," *American Hebrew*, March 6, 1931, 418.

23. "Gala Program Tomorrow for Opening of WOR," *Newark Sunday Call*, July 23, 1922, 14.

24. Jaker, Sulke, and Kanze, *Airways of New York*, 151–156.

25. "W.O.R.," *Counter Currents*, March 1922, 1.

26. "Louis Bamberger Gives $500,000 for Museum Home," *Newark Evening News*, January 20, 1923, 1.

27. "Louis Bamberger Enjoyed Travel," *Jewish Chronicle*, March 30, 1923, 1.

28. Gene Karlin to the author, August 12, 2008, Union, New Jersey.

29. "Mr. Radiobug Entertains the Kiddies" *Counter Currents*, April 1922, 13.

30. Bodian, "Bamberger's in 1929."

31. "Pioneer Turns U.S. onto Radio," *Sunday Star-Ledger* (Newark), May 23, 1982, 6.

32. Ibid.

33. Ibid.

34. Ibid.

35. Ibid.

36. Ibid., 6.

37. "WOR Daily Crosses the Seas and Delivers Its Bamberger Greeting in Foreign Lands," *Counter Currents*, April 1923, 6.

38. "Radio News," *Counter Currents*, August 1923, 10.

39. "The Inimitable Charlie Himself," *Counter Currents*, October 1923, 7.

40. "Gymnasium Classes via WOR," *Counter Currents*, April 1925, 5.

41. "Rattlesnake Booked to Broadcast from Bamberger Station: Bronx Park Zoo Keeper to Illustrate Talk from WOR," *Newark Sunday Call*, November 2, 1924, 14.

42. "Test for Radio Use of Copyright Music," *Newark Sunday Call*, July 1, 1923, 1.

43. Edward Samuels, "Music and Sound Recordings," in *The Illustrated Story of Copyright*, http://www.edwardsamuels.com /illustratedstory/isc2.htm.

44. Ibid.

45. "WOR Assists in a Spectacular Incident," *Counter Currents*, January 1924, 7.

46. "WOR Makes Record Achievement," *Counter Currents*, February 1926, 3.

47. "Radios Newark Picture: Local Store's London Branch Shown," *Newark Sunday Call*, May 2, 1926, 13.

48. "In First Newark-London Chat: Picture of One Comes via Radio," *Newark Sunday Call*, January 9, 1927, 1, 11.

49. "Air Phone Seen as Aid to Newark's Business," *Newark Sunday Call*, January 9, 1927, 1.

50. "Radios Newark Picture: Local Store's London Branch Shown," *Newark Sunday Call*, May 2, 1926, 13.

51. "New WOR Station Won't Disturb Sets Nearby," *Newark Sunday Call*, February 20, 1927, 6.

52. Ibid.

53. "New WOR Nears Completion," *Newark Sunday Call*, June 5, 1927, 24.

54. Jaker, Sulke, and Kanze, "Introduction," *Airways of New York*, 10.

55. Marianne Macy, *WOR Radio: The First Sixty Years (1922–1982)* (New York: Nightingale Gordon, 1982), 152.

56. "WOR—The Voice of One of America's Great Stores," *Counter Currents*, July 1926, 7–8.

57. Macy, *WOR Radio*, 152.

58. "WOR—The Voice of One of America's Great Stores," 7–8.

59. Morton Schindel, telephone interview with the author, August 8, 2007, Weston, Connecticut.

60. "Carnegie Hall Concerts WOR Feature for Winter," *Newark Sunday Call*, October 23, 1927, pt. 3, 1.

61. Mary and John Callahan, owners of the Estey Organ Museum in Brattleboro, Vermont, confirm the purchase of an Estey organ for Bamberger's home in 1917.

62. "Bamberger's Basement Goes over the Top: Thousands Witness the Opening of Our Popular New Venture," *Counter Currents*, September 1922, 2, 3.

63. Whitaker, *Service and Style*, 45.

64. "The Baby Celebrates Basement Store, Now Three Years Old, a Husky Youngster," *Counter Currents*, September 1925, 1.

65. Leach, *Land of Desire*, 78.

66. Ibid.

67. "Bamberger's Department Store," Charles F. Cummings and John E. O'Connor New Jersey History Fall/Winter 1984, p.4.

68. James H. Madison, "Changing Patterns of Urban Retailing: The 1920s" (essay, Department of History, Indiana University, and Eleutherian Mills-Hagley Foundation), 104.

69. Whitaker, *Service and Style*, 45.

70. "Bamberger's Basement Goes over the Top: Thousands Witness the Opening of Our Popular New Venture," *Counter Currents*, September 1922, 2.

71. "The Bamberger Baby Celebrates," *Counter Currents*, September 1923, 9.

72. "This is the Basement Advertising Department—Plus," *Counter Currents*, October 1923, 4.

73. "Here Are "Bill" Steinke's Impressions of the Big Opening Event as They Appeared in the Newark Ledger," *Counter Currents*, September 1922, 8.

74. Robert Huntingdon, e-mail to the author, Livingston, New Jersey, in which the

former Bamberger employee describes the use of Dobermans to check the store's security at night.

75. "They Sew in Record Time to Win Store's Dress Prizes," *Newark Sunday Call*, June 20, 1926, 10.

76. "500 Thrift Essays," *Newark Sunday Call*, March 1, 1925, 13.

77. "We Garner Our Merchandise from Many Countries," *Counter Currents*, August 1923, 1.

78. "Mr. Egge Is Crowned King Sanitas," *Counter Currents*, June 1923, 8.

79. Dorothy Kosec, e-mail to the author, December 21, 2008.

80. "Dear Sir," *Counter Currents*, April 1926, 7.

81. Edith Churchman, e-mail to the author, January 4, 2009.

82. Leila Deutsch Jacobsen, e-mail to the author, November 27, 2007.

83. George Zeevalk to the author, January 5, 2009, private collection of the author.

84. Leslie Pumphrey, e-mails to the author, January 18, 2014 and January 22, 2014.

85. Janet B. Davidson, e-mail to the author, January 10, 2009.

86. Dorothy Strand to the author, January 12, 2009, Montville, New Jersey, private collection of the author.

87. Bonnie Fand Klane, e-mails to the author, February 1, 2009 and January 22, 2014.

88. Ruth Dargan to the author, June 18, 2007, East Orange, New Jersey, private collection of the author.

89. "Annual Report of Co-Worker's Association," *Counter Currents*, March 1924, 1.

90. "A Message from the President of the Co-Worker's Association," *Counter Currents*, March 1929, 1.

91. Editorial, *Counter Currents*, June 1930, 8.

92. Ibid.

93. "Our New Assembly Hall," *Counter Currents*, September 1923, 5.

94. "The Honor Time System," *Counter Currents*, April 1925, 10.

95. "Birthdays, George Meeker and William Whitley," *Counter Currents*, May 1930, 5.

96. "Bamberger Co. Buys Old Alms House Site," *Newark Sunday Call*, May 5, 1924, n.p.

97. "Further Expansion in 1925," *Counter Currents*, January 1925, 1.

98. Ibid.

99. "Service Station," *Counter Currents*, November 1925, 17.

100. "Reporting Progress on New Service Station," *Counter Currents*, June 1926, 14.

101. "Service Station," *Counter Currents*, December 1926, 7.

102. Nat Bodian, "Bamberger's in 1929: What Went on Inside the Store," Old Newark Memories: Old Newark, October 9, 2003, accessed on January 21, 2016, http://newarkmemories.com/memories/518.php.

103. "Truck 218 to the Rescue!" *Counter Currents*, July 1926, 3.

104. Ibid.

105. "Hats Off to the Boys Who Delivered the Christmas Packages," *Counter Currents*, January 1928, 14.

106. Leach, *Land of Desire*, 369.

107. "The Ideal Home," brochure, trade cat. ref. no. B199 1927, Hagley Museum, Wilmington, Delaware.

108. "Harry A. Braelow, Once Just 'Newsy' Buys 'Ideal Home': Widely Known Bamberger Co. Showplace Changes Hands," *Newark Sunday Call*, December 7, 1924, 8.

109. O'Connor and Cummings, "Bamberger's Department Store," 15.

110. Whitaker, *Service and Style*, 141.

111. Leach, *Land of Desire*, 310.

112. William S. Hunt, editorial, *Newark Sunday Call*, February 10, 1924.

113. Ibid.

114. "'Charm': A New Bamberger Publication to Make Its Debut in February," *Counter Currents*, September 1923, 3.

115. "Bamberger's Department Store, *Charm* Magazine, and the Culture of Consumption in New Jersey, 1924–1932," *New Jersey History* (fall/winter 1984): 1.

116. Sophie Oliver, British researcher, interview on C-span, September 15, 2014, http://www.c-span.org/video/?321524-1 /discussion-1920s-magazines.

117. Dan Turello, "Women, Fashion, and the Transatlantic Avant-Garde," Insights: Scholarly Work at the John W. Kluge Center, blog, September 24, 2014, https://blogs.loc .gov/Kluge.

118. "The First Anniversary of *Charm*," *Counter Currents*, February 1925, 8.

119. "On February 1st New Jersey Will Witness the Publication of the Much Heralded Magazine *Charm*," *Counter Currents*, January 1924, insert 8, 9.

120. "Bamberger's Department Store, *Charm* Magazine, and the Culture of Consumption in New Jersey, 1924–1932," 14.

121. "Gentlemen," *Counter Currents*, August 1927, 11.

122. "*Charm* Magazine Graphically Presented to Co-Workers," *Counter Currents*, July 1928, 3.

123. John Cotton Dana, "A Vision of Newark," *Charm*, February 1929, 2; "City Directory Indicates Gain of 4,320 Newarkers in Year," *Newark Sunday Call*, July 15, 1928, 17.

124. "Bamberger's Department Store, *Charm* Magazine, and the Culture of Consumption in New Jersey, 1924–1932," 25.

125. "Beauty in a Department Store," *Counter Currents*, November 1926, 12.

126. Leach, *Land of Desire*, 168.

127. Whitaker, *Service and Style*, 142.

128. "Seventy-Five Years in the News," *Around the Clock*, December 1967, 9.

129. Whitaker, *Service and Style*, 263.

130. Louis Schindel, letter to the editor, *Sunday Star-Ledger* (Newark), March 11, 1984.

131. Leach, *Land of Desire*, 332.

132. Morton Schindel, telephone interview with the author, 2008.

133. "Newark Store Plans Parade," *Newark Evening News*, 1931, Bamberger Family Collection, Reisterstown, Maryland.

134. Nate Himelstein in Jac Toporek's weekly Weequahic High School newsletter, March 30, 2015.

135. Gretchen Fisher, e-mail to the author, December 12, 2014.

136. "Santa and Ikwa Get 55,000 Letters," *Newark Evening News*, December 17, 1927, 15.

137. Whitaker, *Service and Style*, 118.

138. "Iutuk and Family at Bamberger's, Newark," *Westfield Leader*, December 7, 1927, 11.

139. Morton Schindel, telephone interview with the author, 2008.

140. Ben Kanter, "Fond Memories of Louis Bamberger," letter to the editor, *Star-Ledger* (Newark), 1987.

141. "Iutuk and Family at Bamberger's, Newark."

142. "Store's Herd of Reindeer to Go to High Point Park," *Newark Evening News*, December 22, 1928, 8.

143. "Bamberger's Department Store, *Charm* Magazine, and the Culture of Consumption in New Jersey, 1924–1932," 25.

144. Morton Schindel, telephone interview with author, 2008, Weston, Connecticut.

145. "Music Department Secures Very Old Violins for Display," *Counter Currents*, November 1924, 12.

146. "Display Department," *Counter Currents*, November 1929, 22.

147. "Chopin's Famous Piano to Be

Brought Here," *Newark Evening News*, December 9, 1926, 5.

148. "Business Is Booming," *Counter Currents*, January 1925, 3.

149. "Best Business Year in City's History," Business Survey, *Newark Sunday Call*, January 9, 1927, 16.

150. Ibid.

151. "Welders, as if by Magic Wand, Link Store Buildings into One," *Newark Evening News*, January 16, 1929, 1.

152. "Bamberger Capital Is Raised to $10,000,000," *Newark Sunday Call*, 1926, n.p.

153. "L. Bamberger & Co. Issue Stock," *Counter Currents*, February 1927, 12.

154. "Welders, as if by Magic Wand."

155. "Ceremony as Beam Is Laid," *Newark Evening News*, March 1, 1928, 5.

156. "Welders, as if by Magic Wand."

157. James R. Trotto, e-mail to the author, January 16, 2009.

158. "Plan Ten Million Store Addition," *Jewish Chronicle*, December 24, 1926, 8.

159. "Bamberger's Building Soon to Fill Block," *Newark Sunday Call*, November 28, 1926, 1.

160. "How to See the Greater Bamberger Store," January 2, 2008, accessed on December 23, 2015, http://newarkbusiness.org/photos/stores/display%20image.php.

161. Ibid.

162. Alida Michelson, telephone interview with the author, November 13, 2010.

163. Kanter, "Fond Memories of Louis Bamberger."

164. Richard Weil Jr., president of L. Bamberger & Co., to Paul Shapiro, head of stock in the grocery department, August 18, 1941, private collection of the author.

165. Richard Schlenger to the author, postcard, February 22, 2009, private collection of the author.

166. Fan G. Mulvaney, e-mail to the author, December 29, 2008.

167. Liveright, "One of America's Great Stores," 14.

168. Bodian, "Bamberger's in 1929."

169. Felix Fuld, "Greetings," *Counter Currents*, January 1929, 1.

170. "Bamberger and Co. Reported Sold to R. H. Macy of New York; Store Announces Acquisition Today of Big Newark Institution," *Newark Evening News*, June 29, 1929, 1.

171. Ibid.

172. Liveright, "One of America's Great Stores," 21.

173. "Bamberger and Co. Reported Sold to R. H. Macy of New York."

174. Liveright, "One of America's Great Stores," 21.

175. "Stores Grew Alike from Small Starts," *Newark Sunday Call*, June 30, 1929, 20.

176. "Macy's Buys Bamberger's Newark Store," *New York Herald*, June 30, 1929, 1.

177. Morton Schindel, telephone interview with the author, August 7, 2008.

178. Ellen B. De Franco, e-mail to the author, November 7, 2007.

179. Bea Epstein, interview with the author, December 13, 2009, Jewish Community Center, Livingston, New Jersey.

180. "R. H. Macy & Co. (L. Bamberger & Co.)," *Journal of Industry and Finance* (Newark) (September 1929): 18.

181. "Address of Mr. L. Bamberger," July 1, 1929, private collection of Andrew Schindel, in which Bamberger explains his reasons for selling his store to Macy's. Bamberger gave this speech to his employees from the store's balcony immediately following the sale of his store the day before.

182. Ibid.

183. "Paris Bureau," *Counter Currents*, May 1929, 10.

184. Leach, *Land of Desire*, 168.

185. Ibid.

186. Horace Fuld to Frank Aydelotte, June 17, 1930, Trustees box 4, "Fuld, Mrs. Felix," Institute for Advanced Study Archives, Princeton, New Jersey.

187. "Address of Mr. L. Bamberger."

188. Ibid.

189. Ibid.

190. "Old Employees of Bamberger's Wait Million Checks to Go Out to 235 as a Personal Present from Founder," *Newark Evening News*, September 16, 1929, 1.

191. "Old Employees of Bamberger's Wait Million."

192. "Bamberger's Giving Million 'One of Great Pleasures,'" *Newark Evening News*, September 17, 1929.

193. Ibid.

194. Ibid.

195. "Bamberger Co. Character Will Be Perpetuated," *Newark Evening News*, July 1, 1929, 1.

196. "Additional List of N.J. Salaries Three Newark Concerns File Reports with Federal Trade Commission," *Newark Evening News*, March 1934, 2.

197. Ibid.

198. "Our New Addition Opens," *Counter Currents*, October 1929, 6.

199. "Agriculture Secretary Will Speak at Bamberger Building Dedication," *Newark Evening News*, October 15, 1929, 1.

200. "Our New Addition Opens," *Counter Currents*, October 1929, 6.

201. "Bamberger Co. Character Will Be Perpetuated."

202. Ibid.

203. "Agriculture Secretary Will Speak at Bamberger Building Dedication: Praise from Congelton," *Newark Evening News*, October 15, 1929, 1.

204. "Two Bamberger Officers Resign," *Newark Evening News*, October 8, 1929, 1.

205. "Schindel Rose from Office Boy to Manager of Bamberger Store in Only Job He Held in 29 Years," *Jewish Chronicle*, December 20, 1929, 1, 3.

206. "Store Officials Change Places," *Newark Evening News*, May 2, 1935, 26.

207. "Service to Customers Contest Winners Announced," *Counter Currents*, March 1930, 1.

208. Al Marcus, e-mail to the author, January 21, 2014.

209. "Word from Mr. Bamberger," *Counter Currents*, March 1930, 21.

210. "Steal $2000 At Warehouse," *Newark Evening News*, July 21, 1933, 9.

211. "Bamberger Sees Credit Newark's Not His," *Newark Sunday Call*, December 20, 1942, n.p.

212. Diana M. Howie, "The Legacy of Louis Bamberger," *New Jersey Monthly*, September 1984, 49.

213. Harold Krauss Bamberger, china buyer at Bamberger's, interview with the author, November 17, 2008, Brookside Diner, East Hanover, New Jersey.

214. Connie Warshoff, e-mail to the author, February 9, 2009.

215. Kanter, "Fond Memories of Louis Bamberger."

216. Barry Goldberg recalls Bamberger visiting his mother, Fannie Cohen, in the hospital after her tonsils were removed.

217. Bertha Sossin, letter to the author, February 4, 2009, South Orange, New Jersey, private collection of the author.

218. Laurie Fitzmaurice, e-mail to the author, June 18, 2009.

5. BAMBERGER AS A PHILANTHROPIST

1. Charles F. Cummings, "Knowing Newark," *Star-Ledger* (Newark), July 14, 1997, 4.

2. Laura Porter Smith, *From Sanctuary to Social Responsibility: The History of the Institute for Advanced Study 1930–1933* (PhD diss., Princeton University, 1988), 79.

3. Ibid., 76–77.

4. Walter H. Farrier to Frank Aydelotte, October 13, 1944, Newark, New Jersey.

5. Cummings, "Knowing Newark," 4–5.

6. Ibid.

7. "Jewish Survey to Cover All Phases of Philanthropy Here," *Newark Sunday Call*, September 25, 1927, 24.

8. Orange Bureau of Associated Charities to Mr. L. Bamberger, October 15, 1904, Jewish Historical Society of New Jersey, Whippany, New Jersey.

9. "Minutes, Board of Delegates," Conference of Jewish Charities, Newark, May 4, 1936, Jewish Historical Society of New Jersey, Whippany, New Jersey.

10. William H. Ashby, "Whites Aid Migrating Negroes," *Newark Sunday News*, March 1, 1970, n.p.

11. William B. Gwinnell to Rabbi Solomon Foster, June 1, 1922, Papers of Solomon Foster, Jewish Historical Society of New Jersey, Whippany, New Jersey.

12. Ibid.

13. William H. Ashby, *Tales without Hate* (Metuchen, NJ: Upland Press, 1996), 138.

14. "Council of Social Agencies," Papers of Solomon Foster, Jewish Historical Society of New Jersey, Whippany, New Jersey.

15. Ashby, *Tales without Hate*, 138.

16. Maxine Olian Apsel, "A 'Pioneer' Recalls Early Black-Jewish Ties in Newark," *Jewish News*, December 24, 1987, 1.

17. "Community Chest Is Discussed by Jewish Charities," *Jewish Chronicle*, October 13, 1922, 1.

18. "Community Chest Plan Will Probably Be Tried," *Newark Sunday Call*, April 23, 1922, pt. 2, 1.

19. Rabbi Solomon Foster, "The Jewish Charities and the Community Chest," *Jewish Chronicle*, October 13, 1922, 1, 5.

20. "Jews Will Do Part in Pushing Community Chest Campaign," *Jewish Chronicle*, November 7, 1924, 1.

21. H. D. Burrell to Rabbi Solomon Foster, December 7, 1923, Newark, copy in private collection of the author.

22. Welfare Federation of Newark, "One Hundred Years of Social Work 1836–1936," Jewish Historical Society of New Jersey, Whippany, New Jersey.

23. "Community Chest Approves Budgets of Jewish Bodies," *Jewish Chronicle*, September 12, 1924, 1.

24. "United Way of Essex and West Hudson: A Brief History 1919–1920," brochure text included in *East Orange Veterans' 50th Anniversary and Rededication* booklet (East Orange, New Jersey, 2002).

25. A letter quoted in "Community Charity Appeal Ready Here," *Newark Sunday Call*, November 11, 1923, 1.

26. "Several Large Chest Pledges Are Revealed," *Jewish Chronicle*, November 19, 1937, 1.

27. "Of First Gifts in Chest Drive, Mrs. Fuld Gives $14,000; Bamberger Workers $24,472.00," *Newark Evening News*, January 4, 1923, n.p.

28. "Newark's Chest Campaign Army Being Recruited," *Newark Sunday Call*, October 10, 1937, 11.

29. "Louis Bamberger Last Will and Testament," February 20, 1943, Jewish Historical Society of New Jersey, Whippany, New Jersey.

30. "Newark's Obligation," *Newark Sunday Call*, November 25, 1928, pt. 6, 1.

31. Faith Lurie Grossman, e-mail to the author, February 22, 2009.

32. Gretchen Fischer, e-mail to the author, October 29, 2014.

33. Background statement of trust agreement, January 26, 1987, from Dr. Norma Hymes.

34. "Villages to Be Built in Scouts Gift

Camp," *Newark Sunday Call*, March 20, 1927, 1.

35. Sheldon Denburg, interview with the author, 2008, Jewish Historical Society of New Jersey, Whippany, New Jersey.

36. Quoted in Jac Toporek, Weequahic High School e-mail alumni newsletter, May 21, 2010.

37. Ibid.

38. Ibid.

39. "Rites Friday for Mrs. Fuld," *Star-Ledger* (Newark), July 19, 1944, 16.

40. "Mrs. Fuld Makes Chest Appeal in Her Late Husband's Memory: Calls upon Those Who Co-operated with Leader in Jewish and Non-Jewish Work of Philanthropy to Aid Drive," *Newark Sunday Call*, November 10, 1929, 7.

41. Ashby, *Tales without Hate*, 75–78.

42. Ibid.

43. Cummings,"An Enlightened Life of Selling and Giving," 4

44. Walter H. Farrier to Michael Stavitsky, September 9, 1940, Stavitsky Collection, Jewish Historical Society of New Jersey, Whippany, New Jersey.

45. "Find No Trace of Ring Lost by Mrs. Felix Fuld," *Jewish Chronicle*, November 6, 1925, 1

46. Lavinia Bamberger to Abraham Flexner, November 8, 1944, container 4, Abraham Flexner Papers, Manuscripts Division, Library of Congress, Washington, DC.

47. Ibid

48. E. M. McDuffie to Mrs. Fuld, January 8, 1936, Institute for Advanced Study Archives, Princeton, New Jersey.

49. Ibid.

50. Certificate, Bamberger Family Collection, Reisterstown, Maryland.

51. Ibid.

52. *"Y" Bulletin*, November 14, 1941, Jewish Historical Society of New Jersey, Whippany, New Jersey.

53. "Planting for Distinction," *Cultural Landscape Report*, vol. 2, 77, from Jim Lecky, director of Branch Brook Park, and in Essex County (NJ) Park Commission Archives.

54. Ibid., 78

55. Branch Brook Park Alliance, January 7, 2011, accessed on December 23, 2015, http://www.branchbrookpark.org.

56. "Planting for Distinction," 78.

57. Ibid.

58. "Design for Pupil's Medals to Be Picked Next Week," *Newark Evening News*, January 1928, 5.

59. Ibid.

60. Weequahic Alumni, *Calumet*, no. 37 (fall 2013): 17.

61. Mary Sherot Mandel, e-mail to the author, January 31, 2009.

62. "Bamberger's $500,000 Gift Assures City New Museum: Announcement by Newark Merchant of Half Million Donation Comes as Surprise at Meeting of Trustees," *Newark Ledger*, January 20, 1923, 1.

63. Ibid.

64. "L. Bamberger Philanthropist," *Newark Evening News*, March 11, 1944.

65. "Bamberger Terms Gift 'Debt to City,'" *Newark Sunday Call*, January 22, 1923, 1.

66. *"Mr. Bamberger's Superb Gift," Newark Sunday Call*, January 21, 1923, 1.

67. Rabbi Solomon Foster, "Louis Bamberger, Philanthropist," editorial, *Jewish Chronicle*, January 26, 1923.

68. Cummings, "Knowing Newark," 4.

69. *Newark Museum Annual Report 1909–1910*, p. 13, Newark Museum Archives, Newark, New Jersey.

70. "Newark Museum Annual Meeting Minutes," April 29, 1913, Newark Museum Archives, Newark, New Jersey.

71. "Bamberger Terms Gift 'Debt to City,'" 2.

72. Ibid.

73. Ibid.

74. Trustees of the Newark Museum Association to Louis Bamberger, January 20, 1923, Newark Museum Archives, Newark, New Jersey.

75. "Louis Bamberger Gives $500,000 for Museum Home," *Newark Evening News*, January 20, 1923, 2.

76. "Bamberger Gives $500,000 for Museum Building," *Jewish Chronicle*, January 26, 1923, 12.

77. "Louis Bamberger Gives $500,000 for Museum Home," *Newark Evening News*, January 20, 1923, 2.

78. Louis Bamberger, "To the Trustees of the Newark Museum Association," January 19, 1923, Newark Museum Archives, Newark, New Jersey.

79. Ibid.

80. "Gift Is Complete Surprise," *Newark Sunday Call*, January 21, 1923, 2.

81. Ibid.

82. "Bamberger Terms Gift 'Debt to City,'" 2.

83. Stuart Goldblatt, Macy's executive, interview with the author, New York City.

84. Solomon Foster Manuscript Collection, MG 1350/8, New Jersey Historical Society, Whippany, New Jersey.

85. "Mr. Bamberger Turns the First Sod for the Newark Museum," *Counter Currents*, March 1924, 3.

86. Edward P. Alexander, *Museum Masters: Their Museums and Their Influence* (Walnut Creek, CA: Rowman Altamira, 1995).

87. Shales, *John Cotton Dana and the Business of Enlightening Newark*, 278.

88. "John Cotton Dana Described as Evangel of Modern Craftsmanship," *New York Herald Tribune*, reprinted in *Newark Sunday Call*, September 16, 1928, pt. 6, 1.

89. Shales, *John Cotton Dana and the Business of Enlightening Newark*, 42.

90. Ibid., 277.

91. "Report to the Board of Trustees of the Newark Museum Association," January 29, 1924, Newark Museum Archives, Newark, New Jersey.

92. "Date to Be Selected Soon for Newark Museum Endowment Fund Drive," *Newark Sunday Call*, April 20, 1924, pt. 3, 24.

93. "Report to the Board of Trustees of the Newark Museum Association," January 29, 1924, New Museum Archives, Newark, New Jersey.

94. "Date to Be Selected Soon for Newark Museum Endowment Fund Drive."

95. Ibid.

96. "Work of Newark Museum Attracts Nation-Wide Attention," *Newark Sunday Call*, June 1, 1924, 13.

97. "Cornerstone of the Museum Is Laid," *Counter Currents*, May 1925, 1.

98. Ibid.

99. "Foster Delivers Benediction at Laying of Museum Cornerstone," *Jewish Chronicle*, May 22, 1925, 1.

100. "Newark Mayor Praises Jewish Donor of Structure," *Jewish Telegraphic Agency*, March 19, 1926.

101. Ibid.

102. "Opening of New Newark Museum," *Counter Currents*, March 1926, 1.

103. "Cornerstone of the Museum Is Laid," *Counter Currents*, May 1925, 2.

104. "Newark Museum Draws 8,000 Visitors in 4 Days," *Newark Sunday Call*, March 21, 1926, 14.

105. Ibid.

106. Ibid.

107. Ibid.

108. Blueprints from 1927 for an addition to the Newark Museum were discovered by Newark Museum archivist Jeffrey Moy. The blueprints were in the basement of the museum and were addressed to John Cotton Dana at his home in Vermont. They

were plans for a proposed science museum, which Bamberger was thinking of building with a breezeway leading from the main building to the addition. Jarvis Hunt was to be the architect.

109. "Bamberger's $500,000 Gift Assures City New Museum," *Newark Ledger*, January 23, 1923, 2.

110. Ulysses G. Dietz, interview with author, 2008, on the subject of silver items given to the Newark Museum by Bamberger.

111. "Minutes," Newark Museum Board of Trustees, October 21, 1930, Newark Museum Archives, Newark, New Jersey.

112. "Machine Models at Museum Here Will Be Repaired," *Newark Sunday Call*, May 23, 1937, 20.

113. "L. Bamberger Holds Two Museum Posts," *Jewish Chronicle*, February 12, 1926, 1.

114. "Few Like Bamberger Are Found Today," *Jewish Chronicle*, September 23, 1934, 1.

115. "Newark Mayor Praises Jewish Donor of Structure," *Jewish Telegraphic Agency*, March 19, 1926.

116. Arthur Frederick Egner, Foreword to *Louis Bamberger: A Record of His Benefactions to His Community and His Country* (Newark, NJ: Newark Museum, 1934).

117. Beatrice Winser to Louis Bamberger, June 28, 1940, Newark Museum Archives, Newark, New Jersey, copy in the private collection of the author.

118. Ibid.

119. "Launch Bamberger," *New York Sun*, November 30, 1944, Trustees box 2, Institute for Advanced Study Archives, Princeton, New Jersey.

120. M. R. Werner, *Julius Rosenwald, The Life of a Practical Humanitarian* (New York: Harper and Brothers, 1939), 323.

6. BAMBERGER, THE FACE OF NEWARK'S JEWS

1. Jacob Billikopf to Mrs. Fuld, February 7, 1928, Trustees File, Institute for Advanced Study Archives, Princeton, New Jersey.

2. "L. Bamberger, Philanthropist," *Newark Evening News*, March 11, 1944, n.p.

3. "Degree of Doctor of Science to Be Conferred upon Louis Bamberger by Newark Technical School Tonight," *Jewish Chronicle*, June 17, 1927, 1.

4. Whitaker, *Service and Style*, 46.

5. "Map of Newark Showing Areas Where Different Nationalities Predominated: Estimated Foreign Population in 1911," Jewish Historical Society of New Jersey, Whippany, New Jersey.

6. Alan V. Lowenstein to William B. Helmreich, June 25, 1997, 3, Jewish Historical Society of New Jersey, Whippany, New Jersey.

7. William B. Helmreich, *The Enduring Community: The Jews of Newark and MetroWest* (New Brunswick: Transaction, 1999), 86.

8. Ibid.

9. Ellen De Franco to the author, June 21, 2007, Oakland, California.

10. "Felix Fuld Given Impressive Tribute at Testimonial Dinner: Is Nominated by Foster as Leader of Jersey Jewry," *Jewish Chronicle*, November 14, 1924, 7.

11. Hebrew Benevolent and Orphan Asylum Society, "Donations in Kind," in annual report, February 1, 1900–1901 (Newark, NJ: Baker Printing),12, Jewish Historical Society of New Jersey Archives, Whippany, New Jersey.

12. Allan Kane, interview with the author, May 4, 2007.

13. Dee Gulkin Sherman, e-mail to the author, January 18, 2014.

14. Ibid.

15. Hebrew Benevolent and Orphan

Asylum Society, "Donations in Kind," *Annual Meeting, January 20, 1903*, in *Annual Reports 1887–1911* (Newark: W. H. Skurts, 1888), 17, Jewish Historical Society of New Jersey Archives, Whippany, New Jersey.

16. Hebrew Benevolent and Orphan Asylum Society and United Hebrew Charities, "Bamberger Serves on Committee of Arrangements, and Reception Committee for Golden Jubilee," *50th Annual Report, January 31, 1911*, in *Annual Reports 1887–1911* (Newark: W. H. Skurts, 1888), 67, Jewish Historical Society of New Jersey Archives, Whippany, New Jersey.

17. Jack J. Dann, "Wilson at 1911 Golden Jubilee," *Jewish News*, October 1961, n.p.

18. "Is Honored," *Jewish Chronicle*, April 10, 1925, 1.

19. "New Orphan Asylum Name Is Announced," *Jewish Chronicle*, August 10, 1928, 1.

20. Jane Wallerstein, *Path of Service: A History of the Jewish Counseling and Service Agency of Essex County and Its Predecessor Agencies, 1861–1961* (Newark, NJ: Jewish Counseling and Service Agency, 1962), n.p., Jewish Historical Society of New Jersey Archives, Whippany, New Jersey.

21. Arthur Kligman, interview with the author, 2011.

22. Florence Blume, "From the Student Council," *Temple Tidings* (Temple B'nai Jeshurun weekly newsletter), May 27, 1927, 4.

23. "Louis Bamberger, Philanthropist," New Jersey Historical Society Manuscript Collection, MG 1350/8, Whippany, New Jersey.

24. Ibid.

25. "Felix Fuld Gives $2500 for Archaeological Operations in Palestine," *Jewish Telegraphic Agency*, June 17, 1928.

26. Cyrus Adler to Felix Fuld, February 4, 1927, collection of the author.

27. Rabbi Foster to Louis Bamberger,

n.d., New Jersey Historical Society Manuscript Collection, MG 1350/9, New Jersey Historical Society Archives, Newark, New Jersey.

28. "Felix Fuld Given Impressive Tribute at Testimonial Dinner," 7.

29. "Bamberger Gives $1,000 for Jewish Education Work," *Jewish Chronicle*, May 4, 1923, 1.

30. Abraham Flexner to Louis Bamberger, January 16, 1935, Trustees box 2, Institute for Advanced Study Archive, Princeton, New Jersey.

31. Meyer C. Ellenstein, "Yeshiva College Scholarship Fund Dinner Committee," *Jewish Chronicle*, December 15, 1935, pp. 6–7, Solomon Foster Papers, MG 1350, New Jersey Historical Society Archives, Newark, New Jersey.

32. Roth, *American Pastoral*, 13.

33. "Thirteen Organizations in Conference of Jewish Charities," *Jewish Chronicle*, November 14, 1924, 1.

34. "Minutes of Executive Committee of the Conference of Jewish Charities," November 30, 1925, box 1, folder 4, p. 3, Jewish Historical Society of New Jersey Archives, Whippany, New Jersey.

35. Ibid., 1.

36. Ibid.

37. A brochure, "The First Fifty Years," celebrates the founding of the Essex County Federation. Jewish Historical Society of New Jersey Archives, Whippany, New Jersey.

38. "In Pushing Community Campaign, Louis Bamberger Predicts," *Jewish Chronicle*, November 7, 1924, 1.

39. Ibid.

40. "Minutes of Board of Delegates of the Conference of Jewish Charities," June 2, 1925, box 1, folder 4, 3000 series, Jewish Historical Society of New Jersey Archive, Whippany, New Jersey.

41. "Minutes of Meeting of Board of Del-

egates of the Conference of Jewish Charities," September 29, 1925, box 1, folder 4, 3000 series, Jewish Historical Society of New Jersey Archive, Whippany, New Jersey.

42. Ibid.

43. "Minutes of Board of Delegates of the Conference of Jewish Charities," October 7, 1926, box 1, folder 5, Jewish Historical Society of New Jersey Archive, Whippany, New Jersey.

44. "Minutes [of] Meeting [of the] Conference of Jewish Charities," November 27, 1922, p. 3, box 1, folder 1, Jewish Historical Society of New Jersey Archive, Whippany, New Jersey.

45. Newark to Conduct Single Drive for $600, 000," Jewish Telegraphic Agency, January 24, 1926.

46. "Nearly Half of Newark's Combined Campaign Quota Raised at Opening Dinner," Jewish Telegraphic Agency, May 24, 1926.

47. "'Organized Effort to Capture Jewish Vote Resented Here': Felix Fuld Says Race as Unit Does Not Support Any Party," *Newark Sunday Call*, November 2, 1924, pt. 2, 3.

48. Ibid.

49. Ibid.

50. Ibid.

51. Ibid.

52. "Felix Fuld Writes His Reasons to Mr. Bruno for Opposing the Bible Bill," n.d., n.p., Berg Family Collection, Huntington, Long Island.

53. Ibid.

54. "News Brief," Jewish Telegraphic Agency, November 10, 1926, n.p.

55. "Republican Merchants Meet," *Herald Tribune*, October 2, 1936, n.p.

56. "Bamberger Concern Neutral in Politics, W. J. Wells States," *Newark Evening News*, November 1, 1936, n.p.

57. "Louis Bamberger Declares for Roosevelt," *Jewish Chronicle*, October 30, 1936, 1.

58. John Hardin in "Recollections of Mr. Bamberger," Trustees box 2, Institute for Advanced Study Archives, Princeton, New Jersey.

59. William B. Helmreich, *The Enduring Community: The Jews of Newark and MetroWest* (New Brunswick, NJ: Transaction Publishers, 1999), 52.

60. "Jews Ask Big Building Fund," *Jewish Chronicle*, May 3, 1920, 1.

61. "Shall All These Smaller New Jersey Cities and Towns Put Newark to the Blush?" n.d., n.p., Donald Rubinoff scrapbook, Jewish Historical Society of New Jersey Archives, Whippany, New Jersey.

62. "Jews Ask Big Building Fund," *Jewish Chronicle*, May 3, 1920, 1.

63. "Half Million Dollar Campaign for Jewish Youth of City Begins in May," *Jewish Chronicle*, March 28, 1920, 1.

64. "Jewish Drive Opening Guns Net $200,000," *Jewish Chronicle*, May 11, 1920, 1.

65. Ibid.

66. "Minutes [of] Special Meeting of the Trustees of Young Men's and Young Women's Hebrew Association," December 4, 1921, series 2200, box 1, folder 2, Jewish Historical Society of New Jersey Archives, Whippany, New Jersey.

67. Michael A. Stavitsky, "The 'Y' in Retrospect," in *Twentieth Anniversary Celebration 1924–1944*, 26–29, brochure, Jewish Historical Society of New Jersey Archives, Whippany, New Jersey.

68. Ibid., 27.

69. Louis Bamberger to Aaron Lasser, April 27, 1940, series 2200, box 1, file 6, Jewish Historical Society of New Jersey Archives, Whippany, New Jersey.

70. "Minutes [of] Conference of Jewish Charities," June 2, 1925, box 1, folder 4, Jewish Historical Society of New Jersey Archives, Whippany, New Jersey.

71. "Minutes [of] Board of Trustees: 'Newark YM-YWHA 1921–1922,'" May 3, 1922,

series 2200, box 1, folder 2, Jewish Historical Society of New Jersey Archives, Whippany, New Jersey.

72. Unsigned letter to Miss H. Kleinberg @ L. Bamberger & Co., June 26, 1920, Jewish Historical Society of New Jersey, Whippany, New Jersey.

73. "These Dreams," *Counter Currents*, May 1920, inside cover.

74. Ruth Grossman, "High Street YMHA Ends 30-year Era, but the Memories Will Linger On," *Star-Ledger* (Newark), 1954, n.p., George Kahn biography file, series 2001, "YM-YWHA Building 1952–1968," box 1, folder 10, Jewish Historical Society of New Jersey Archives, Whippany, New Jersey.

75. *Twentieth Anniversary Celebration 1924–1944*, 6, brochure, Jewish Historical Society of New Jersey Archives, Whippany, New Jersey.

76. "Surprise Donation Mark Affair of Young Hebrews," *Jewish Chronicle*, May 20, 1925, 1.

77. "Golden Jubilee of New Jersey 'Y' Camps Commemorates 50 Year History of Dedicated Service to Our Youth," *New Jersey "Y" Camper Golden Jubilee Special Edition*, 3, souvenir journal, Jewish Historical Society of New Jersey Archives, Whippany, New Jersey.

78. "State 'Y' Federation Elects Louis Bamberger Honorary Head," *Jewish Chronicle*, October 24, 1930, 2.

79. Excerpt from Harry Lebau's history of Elizabeth's Jews, "The Perfect Cipher," Ruth Lebau Brewster, collection box 1, looseleaf binder, Jewish Historical Society of New Jersey Archives, Whippany, New Jersey.

80. "Library Notes," *"Y" Bulletin*, December 31, 1943, 1.

81. "It Was a Joy a Hundred-fold," *Jewish News*, June 9, 1977, n.p.

82. Dore Schary, *Heyday* (Boston: Little, Brown, 1979), 16.

83. Rabbi Solomon Foster, "The New Jewish Center," editorial, *Jewish Chronicle*, May 16, 1924, 4.

84. Ibid.

85. Ibid.

86. Helmreich, *Enduring Community*, 138.

87. Grossman, "High Street YMHA Ends 30 Year Era."

88. "Bamberger Sends $5000," Jewish Telegraphic Agency, May 9, 1934.

89. "Minutes of Meeting of "Y" Board of Trustees," June 24, 1940, box 1, folder 6, Jewish Historical Society of New Jersey Archives, Whippany, New Jersey.

90. "Minutes [of the] YM-YWHA Board of Directors 1941–1945," March 22, 1945, box 1, folder 8, Jewish Historical Society of New Jersey Archives, Whippany, New Jersey.

91. Alan M. Kraut and Deborah A. Kraut, *Covenant of Care: Newark Beth Israel and the Jewish Hospital in America* (New Brunswick, NJ: Rutgers University Press, 2007), 75.

92. "Success Is Seen in Beth Israel's Drive for Funds," *Newark Sunday Call*, January 29, 1928, 18.

93. "Break Ground for Beth Israel Hospital," *Jewish Chronicle*, August 20, 1936, 1.

94. "Initial Gifts to Beth Israel Are Well over $700,000," *Jewish Chronicle*, May 16, 1924, 1.

95. "Success Is Seen in Beth Israel's Drive for Funds," *Newark Sunday Call*, January 29, 1928, 18.

96. Bernard Miller to Beth Israel's Board of Directors, August 14, 1934, box 29, Jewish Historical Society of New Jersey Archives, Whippany, New Jersey.

97. Kraut and Kraut, *Covenant of Care*, 99.

98. Ibid., 77.

99. "Success Is Seen in Beth Israel's Drive for Funds," *Newark Sunday Call*, January 29, 1928, 18.

100. Kraut and Kraut, *Covenant of Care*, 77.

101. "Prominent Warsaw Zionist, Krejnin, Commits Suicide," Jewish Telegraphic Agency, October 14, 1927, n.p.

102. "Tribute to Ben Selling," Jewish Telegraphic Agency, May 19, 1927, n.p.

103. Minutes [of] Board of Directors Beth Israel Hospital," July 20, 1934, 2, box 29, Jewish Historical Society of New Jersey Archives, Whippany, New Jersey.

104. Ibid., 3.

105. Ibid.

106. Ibid.

107. Kraut and Kraut, *Covenant of Care*, 96.

108. "Beth Israel Hospital Report Shows Year of Economy, Progress, and Debt Clearance," *Jewish Chronicle*, January 31, 1936, 1.

109. "Last Will and Testament of Louis Bamberger," February 20, 1943, p. 3, Jewish Historical Society of New Jersey Archives, Whippany, New Jersey.

110. "Last Will and Testament of Carrie B. F. Fuld," May 31, 1944, p. 4, Jewish Historical Society of New Jersey Archives, Whippany, New Jersey.

111. "Few Closer to Life of Newark," *Newark Evening News*, n.d., n.p.

112. Kraut and Kraut, *Covenant of Care*, 103.

113. "The Felix Fuld Memorial," *Counter Currents*, May 1929, 10.

114. "Half Staff Newark Flags for Felix Fuld," *Atlantic City New Jersey Press*, January 23, 1929, n.p., Berg Family Collection, Huntington, Long Island.

115. Kraut and Kraut, *Covenant of Care*, 83.

116. "Late Merchant and Philanthropist Eulogized before 2,500," *New York Herald Tribune*, February 6, 1929, n.p.

117. "An Appeal to the Jews of Newark," a circular distributed by the committee hosting the mass meeting at the Odeon Theater with keynote speaker Louis Marshall, chairman of the American Relief Committee, is in the author's collection.

118. "$40,000 Pledged for Jewish Relief," *New York Times*, April 30, 1917, n.p.

119. "Leaders in New Jersey's Jewish Relief Drive," *Star Eagle*, October 17, 1919, n.p.

120. "Newark and New Jersey Reading to Play Big Part in Nationwide $14 Million Campaign for Relief," *Jewish Chronicle*, January 20, 1922, 1.

121. "Newark Jewry, Lauded for Work in Big Relief Drive, Continues in Campaign to Reach Goal," *Jewish Chronicle*, March 10, 1922, 1.

122. "Minutes [of] Executive Committee of the Conference of Jewish Charities," November 30, 1925, series 3000, box 1, folder 4, Jewish Historical Society of New Jersey Archives, Whippany, New Jersey.

123. "Newark to Conduct Single Drive for $600,000," Jewish Telegraphic Agency, January 24, 1926, n.p.

124. "Nearly Half of Newark's Combined Campaign Quota Raised at Opening Dinner," Jewish Telegraphic Agency, May 24, 1926, n.p.

125. "Fund to Aid Jews Stricken in Europe Gets Flying Start," *Newark Sunday Call*, April 18, 1926, n.p.

126. "Russian Government Will Match Colonization on Large Scale, Official Announcement Says, Gives Further Details of New Organization," Jewish Telegraphic Agency, June 4, 1928, n.p.

127. Isaac Fein, *The Making of an American Jewish Community: The History of Baltimore Jewry from 1773–1920* (Philadelphia: Jewish Publication Society of America, 1971), 150.

128. "Bamberger Farm School Delegate," *Jewish Chronicle*, May 28, 1926, 1.

129. "$15,000,000 Drive to Be Conducted

by Farm School," *Jewish Chronicle*, June 11, 1926, 1.

130. "Plan Campaign to Raise Funds for Homeland," *Jewish Chronicle*, May 18, 1923, 1.

131. "Several Hundred Representative Jews from All Over U.S. to Attend," Jewish Telegraphic Agency, October 14, 1928, n.p.

132. "Weizmann Calls Special Meeting to Discuss Situation in Palestine," *Jewish Chronicle*, May 1928, 1.

133. "Body of Louis Marshall Arrives on Leviathan Today: Funeral Tuesday," Jewish Telegraphic Agency, September 23, 1929.

134. "Newark to Aid Suffering Victims of Palestine Atrocities," *Jewish Chronicle*, September 6, 1929, 1.

135. Ibid.

136. "Wolber Backs Drive to Assist German Jews," *Newark Sunday Call*, June 18, 1933, 6.

137. "Large Gift to Jewish Relief," *Newark News*, June 7, 1933, n.p.

138. "Launch Drive Here on Monday for Relief of Jews of Germany; Louis Bamberger Gives $25,000," *Jewish Chronicle*, June 9, 1933, 3.

139. Ibid.

140. "Jewish Leaders Begin Campaign for Relief Fund," *Newark Star Eagle*, June 1933, n.p.

141. "Y.M.H.A. Urges Ban on Berlin Olympiad," *Newark Star Eagle*, November 12, 1934, Michael A. Stavitsky Collection, Jewish Historical Society of New Jersey, Whippany, New Jersey.

142. Warren Grover, *Nazis in Newark* (New Brunswick: Transaction, 2003), 122.

143. Ibid.

144. Ibid., 121.

145. Ibid.

146. Ibid., 242.

147. Ibid., 243.

148. Ibid., 244.

149. "Newark Soon Launches Drive for $50,000 Seminary Fund," *Jewish Chronicle*, December 21, 1923, 1.

150. Jacob De Haas, ed., *The Encyclopedia of Jewish Knowledge* (New York: Behrman's Jewish Book House, 1934).

151. "Bamberger's Valuable Book Collection Goes to Seminary Library," Jewish Telegraphic Agency, November 2, 1927.

152. Oscar "Ozzie" Lax, interview with the author, June 22, 2008.

153. Donald Rubinoff, grandson of Abraham J. Dimond, interview with the author, March, 19, 2009.

154. Frank Liveright to Rabbi Solomon Foster, November 9, 1911, Papers of Solomon Foster, box 1, correspondence 1911, folder 4, Jewish Historical Society of New Jersey Archives, Whippany, New Jersey.

155. "Push Jubilee Plan of Progress Club," *Jewish Chronicle*, October 28, 1921, 1.

156. "Between Ourselves," *Newark Sunday Call*, February 20, 1921, 3.

157. "Minutes [of] Mountain Ridge Country Club Collection," February 8, 1927, box 1, folder 4, Jewish Historical Society of New Jersey Archives, Whippany, New Jersey.

158. Ibid., April 7, 1938, box 1, folder 15.

159. Ibid., June 17, 1939, box 1, folder 16.

160. "Fuld Memorial Unveiled as Country Club Opens," *Jewish Chronicle*, June 26, 1931, 1.

161. Alan V. Lowenstein to William B. Helmreich, June 25, 1997, Jewish Historical Society of New Jersey, Whippany, New Jersey.

162. Leon Harris, *Merchant Princes: An Intimate History of Jewish Families Who Built Great Department Stores* (New York: Harper and Row, 1979), 241.

163. "Progress Club, Half Century in Existence Observes Birthday in Fitting Celebration," *Jewish Chronicle*, January 27, 1922, 1.

164. "Message from President Scheck," *Jewish Chronicle*, May 23, 1930, 2.

165. "Progress Club Notes," *Jewish Chronicle*, May 23, 1930, 8.

166. "Progress Club Suits Action to Its Name: New Building Stands as Achievement of Local Jewry," *Jewish Chronicle*, May 29, 1931, 22.

167. "Congratulations and Best Wishes," *Jewish Chronicle*, May 23, 1930, 9.

168. "Aronson Sees Progress Club Providing Wholesome Influence in Community," *Jewish Chronicle*, February 5, 1932, 2.

169. "Minutes Ledger Progress Club," February 3, 1913, 118.

170. "Social Event," *Newark Sunday Call*, January 4, 1914, 6.

171. "Novel Features Are Planned for Hebrew Ball," *Newark Sunday Call*, January 23, 1916, 8.

172. "Aronson Donates $10,000 in Drive Inaugurated to Help Progress Club Pay Off Mortgage Debt of $150,000," *Jewish Chronicle*, November 9, 1934, 1.

173. "New Progress Club Stone Set in Place," *Jewish Chronicle*, October 4, 1929, 1.

174. "Progress Club, Half Century in Existence," 1.

175. "Progress Club Mortgage Foreclosed, Group Calls Meeting to Decide Future," *Jewish Chronicle*, November 29, 1936, 1.

176. "Minutes 'Y' Board of Trustees," February 9, 1943, box 1, folder 8, Jewish Historical Society of New Jersey Archives, Whippany, New Jersey.

7. "MAECENAS OF ALL THE ARTS"

1. "Hazomir Choral Group Annual Concert," *Jewish Chronicle*, April 22, 1927, 1, 6.

2. "John Hardin Recalls Louis Bamberger," Abraham Flexner Papers, container box 4, "Bamberger, Louis 1939–1944," Manu-

scripts Division, Library of Congress, Washington, DC.

3. "Uzal H. McCarter Endorses Campaign to Preserve Jefferson's Mansion," *Jewish Chronicle*, May 24, 1925, 1.

4. "10 Jews on New Jersey Committee for Bi-Centennial," *Jewish Chronicle*, July 10, 1931, 1.

5. "Governor Names 10 Jews to Jersey Washington Fete Body," Jewish Telegraphic Agency, July 9, 1931.

6. Anthony DePalma, "Exodus," *New Jersey Monthly*, September 1985, 89.

7. "Louis Bamberger to Receive Second Honorary Degree," *Newark Sunday Call*, June 12, 1927, 8.

8. "Degree of Doctor of Science to be Conferred upon Louis Bamberger by Newark Technical School Tonight," *Jewish Chronicle*, June 17, 1927, 1.

9. "Louis Bamberger to Receive Second Honorary Degree," *Newark Sunday Call*, June 12, 1937, 8.

10. Harold S. Wechsler, "Brewing Bachelors: The History of the University of Newark," *Paedagogica Historica: International Journal of the History of Education* 46, nos. 1–2 (2010): 229–249.

11. "N.U. to Seek Million Fund," *Newark News*, February 17, 1937, n.p., microfilm.

12. Dr. Frank Kingdon, "N.U. to Seek Million Fund," *Newark News*, February 17, 1937.

13. "Last Will and Testament of Louis Bamberger," February 20, 1943, Jewish Historical Society of New Jersey Archives, Whippany, New Jersey.

14. "John Hardin," Abraham Flexner Papers, container box 4, "Bamberger, Louis 1939–1944," Manuscripts Division, Library of Congress, Washington, DC.

15. Editorial, *Newark Sunday Call*, February 17, 1924, n.p.

16. Joseph Stroock to Dr. Stephen S. Wise, May 12, 1937, Emma Gottheil

Collection (1917–1938), box 110, folders 4 and 5, American Jewish Historical Society, New York City.

17. Ulysses G. Dietz, interview with the author, 2008, Newark Museum, Newark, New Jersey.

18. Helmreich, *The Enduring Community*, 85.

19. Mark Finston, "Jersey 'Writes Off' Debt with History," *Star-Ledger* (Newark), October 27, 1983, n.p.

20. *Proceedings of the New Jersey Historical Society Annual Meeting*, October 23, 1944, 11, New Jersey Historical Society Archives, Newark, New Jersey.

21. "Bamberger Sees Credit Newark's Not His," *Newark Sunday Call*, December 20, 1942, n.p.

22. "Historical News of Interest," *Proceedings of the New Jersey Historical Society* 15 (1930): 372, New Jersey Historical Society Archives, Newark, New Jersey.

23. "Some Valuable New Light on the History of Newark," *Newark Sunday Call*, July 8, 1923, pt. 2.

24. Editorial, *Newark Sunday Call*, February 17, 1924, n.p.

25. "Minutes [of the] New Jersey Historical Society Annual Meeting," *Proceedings of the New Jersey Historical Society* 14 (1929): 159, New Jersey Historical Society Archives, Newark, New Jersey.

26. Nat Bodian, "Newark Memories," www.OldNewark.org.

27. "The Local Historian and New Jersey History," in *Proceedings of the New Jersey Historical Society*, April 1938, 132, New Jersey Historical Society Archives, Newark, New Jersey.

28. *"Y" Bulletin*, November 18, 1927, Jewish Historical Society of New Jersey Archives, Whippany, New Jersey.

29. Michael Meyer, "The German-Jewish Legacy in America" (Paul Lecture, Jew-

ish Studies Program, Indiana University, Bloomington, 2010), 6.

30. John C. French, "Otto Sutro and Music in Baltimore-Maryland," *Maryland Historical Magazine* 47 (1952): 260–62.

31. John Elwood, Estey Organ Museum, e-mail to the author, December 6, 2013.

32. Edgar S. Bamberger, "My Trip Abroad" diary, February–June 1936, p. 19, Bamberger Family Collection, Reisterstown, Maryland.

33. Ibid., 19.

34. "Newark Music Festival Opens Tomorrow," *Newark Sunday Call*, May 3, 1925, pt. 3, n.p.

35. "Newark Music Festival," program, 1918.

36. "Enrico Caruso Successful Performance," *Newark Sunday Call*, May 11, 1919, 11.

37. "Festival a Huge Success," *Newark Sunday Call*, May 25, 1919. Pt. 3, 14.

38. "Patrons Support Music Festival," *Newark Sunday Call*, December 21, 1919, 1.

39. Leach, *Land of Desire*, 140.

40. "Many to See Performance in Aid of Hebrew Orphan Home," *Newark Sunday Call*, October 31, 1920, 2.

41. "Music Festival Chorus of 500 Voices Will Be Broadcast Tomorrow by WOR," *Newark Sunday Call*, May 11, 1924, 21.

42. "Broadcast Newark's Largest Band on the Air Tomorrow," *Newark Sunday Call*, July 20, 1924.

43. Newark Music Foundation to Solomon Foster, December 20, 1926, Solomon Foster Collection, Jewish Historical Society of New Jersey Archives, Whippany, New Jersey.

44. "Foster Originates Move for Newark Music Foundation," *Jewish Chronicle*, January 21, 1927, 1.

45. Ibid.

46. "Music Foundation Files Corpora-

tion Papers Tomorrow," *Newark Sunday Call*, May 13, 1927, 28.

47. "Newark Music Foundation," brochure, n.d., New Jersey Historical Society Manuscript Collection, MG 2 F. This brochure lists the names of donors in support of the Music Foundation.

48. "Newark Music Festival's Concert Patrons Listed," *Newark Sunday Call*, May 14, 1939, sect. 2, 1.

49. H. G. Michelson, "Fifteenth Music Festival Opens Tomorrow Night," *Newark Sunday Call*, April 28, 1929, 23.

50. Ibid.

51. "Carnegie Hall Concerts WOR Feature for Winter," *Newark Sunday Call*, October 23, 1927, radio sect., n.p.

52. "Newark Studio of WOR Opens September 16," *Newark Sunday Call*, September 8, 1929, pt. 3, 1.

53. "WOR Announces Plans for Fall Radio Programs: Wintertime Features on Schedule Now in Making," *Newark Sunday Call*, August 28, 1929, n.p.

54. "Louis Bamberger 80 Wednesday," *Star-Ledger* (Newark), May 12, 1935, n.p.

55. Ibid.

56. "The Outlook for Music Widened by Scholarships," *Newark News*, November 23, 1928, 13.

57. "Opening the Door," *Newark Sunday Call*, Editorial and Magazine Features, pt. 6, February 6, 1927, 1.

58. Ibid.

59. "Tuesday Last Day to Enroll for Bamberger Scholarships in Music," *Jewish Chronicle*, November 12, 1926, 7.

60. "Bamberger Music Scholarships Given Violinists and Pianists," *Newark Evening News*, April 26, 1930, 5.

61. "Award Music Scholarships," *Newark News*, February 1, 1928, 5.

62. "In the Realm of Music," *Newark Sunday Call*, March 19, 1933, pt. 3, 4.

63. "Youth Must Be Served!," *Newark Sunday Call*, February 20, 1927 1, 8.

64. "Girl Unable to Use Legs Piano Contestant," *Newark Evening News*, February 1, 1928, 5.

65. "Scholarships in Music Changed," *Newark News*, November 12, 1928, 6.

66. "37 Winners Named in First Auditions for Scholarship," *Newark Sunday Call*, April 6, 1930, 1, 17.

67. "Distinguished Judges for Auditions," *Newark Sunday Call*, March 4, 1928, 21.

68. H. G. Michelson,"Fifteenth Music Festival Opens Tomorrow Night," *Newark Sunday Call*, April 28, 1929, 23.

69. "In the Realm of Music," *Newark Sunday Call*, December 11, 1932, 5.

70. "Fuld Estate to Be Scene of Concerts Committee Reception," *"Y" Bulletin*, June 8, 1933, n.p.

71. Ibid.

72. "Stadium Concerts," *Newark Sunday Call*, July 12, 1936, pt. 3, 1.

73. Burt Ironson, e-mail to the author, March 20, 2014.

74. H. G. Michelson, "In the Realm of Music," *Newark Sunday Call*, March 16, 1930, n.p.

75. Ibid.

76. Ibid.

77. Ibid.

78. "Mrs. Fuld Plans to Carry on in Music Projects," *Newark Sunday Call*, January 27, 1929, Burrelle's Press Clipping Bureau, New York.

79. *"Y" Bulletin*, June 8, 1933, front cover.

80. Helen S. Meyer to Solomon Foster, January 2, 1925, Solomon Foster Collection, "High Street Music 1925–1980," Jewish Historical Society of New Jersey Archives, Whippany, New Jersey.

81. "'Buddy' Katchen Acclaimed by 1,300 at Debut Here," *Jewish Chronicle*, February 5, 1937, 1.

82. "Mrs. Felix Fuld Honorary Head of Debut Recital," *Newark Sunday Call*, December 27, 1936, sect. 2, 8.

83. "Julius Katchen, Concert Pianist and Brahms Specialist, Is Dead," *New York Times*, April 30, 1969, n.p.

84. "In the Realm of Music," *Newark Sunday Call*, January 17, 1932, pt. 3, 9.

85. Sarah Doppelt, telephone interview with the author, November 12, 2006. At age twelve, Doppelt was one of the first youngsters to play the violin in the "Y" orchestra.

86. "Crippled Children to Benefit by Mosque Opera," *Newark News*, December 24, 1934, n.p.

87. "A Dream Comes True," *Newark Evening News*, December 27, 1934, n.p.

88. "Opera Benefit Net Is $2,048," *Newark Evening News*, January 1934, 2.

89. Ibid.

90. "Capacity Audience to Attend 'Madame Butterfly' at Mosque," *Newark Sunday Call*, January 19, 1936, 10.

91. "Hails Opera: Have Guests," *Newark Evening News*, December 24, 1934, microfilm.

92. "Capacity Audience to Attend 'Madame Butterfly' at Mosque," *Newark Sunday Call*, January 19, 1936, 10.

93. "Concert Tickets Are Put on Sale," *Newark News*, November 14, 1936, 3.

94. "44 Masterpieces of 5 Nations in Jersey's Greatest Art Show," *Newark Sunday Call*, September 29, 1940, 12.

95. Charles F. Cummings, "An Enlightened Life of Giving and Selling," *Star-Ledger* (Newark), July 18, 1997, 4.

8. BAMBERGER, EINSTEIN, AND THE INSTITUTE FOR ADVANCED STUDY, 1930–1944

1. Frank Aydelotte to Abraham Flexner, November 4, 1933, general box, "Ast–Ay," file "Aydelotte, F., 1930–37," Institute for Advanced Study Archives, Princeton, New Jersey.

2. "Bamberger Gives $5,000,000 for Study," *New York Times*, June 8, 1930, box American Co.–Ann., file "Ann. 1930–1934," Institute for Advanced Study Archives, Princeton, New Jersey.

3. "Louis Bamberger and Mrs. Fuld Give $5,000,000 to Establish Institute of Advanced Learning," *Newark Evening News*, June 8, 1930, 1.

4. "Flexner Gives Views on New Institute Here," *Jewish Chronicle*, July 18, 1930, 1.

5. "Opening of School on Bamberger Gift Is Some Time Off," *Newark Sunday Call*, October 12, 1930, 16.

6. Ibid.

7. "Medical College for This City a Possibility," *Newark Sunday Call*, October 24, 1915, 8.

8. Ascoli, *Julius Rosenwald*, 177.

9. Abraham Flexner to Louis Bamberger, June 16, 1931, Trustees box 2, "Bamberger, L. 1930–1936," Institute for Advanced Study Archives, Princeton, New Jersey.

10. Abraham Flexner, *I Remember* (New York: Simon and Shuster, 1940), 358.

11. George Dyson, *Turing's Cathedral* (New York: Vintage Books, 2012), 29.

12. Louis Bamberger to Abraham Flexner, May 5, 1930, Trustees box 2, "Bamberger, L., 1930–31," Institute for Advanced Study Archives, Princeton, New Jersey.

13. *Organization and Purpose: Bulletin No. 1*, December 1930, 20, Institute of Advanced Study Archives, Princeton, New Jersey. *Bulletin No. 1* explains Bamberger's reasons for endowing the IAS.

14. Abraham Flexner to Oswald Veblen, July 14, 1933, Stern Chronological files, Institute for Advanced Study Archives, Princeton, New Jersey.

15. Armand Borel, "The School of Mathematics at the Institute for Advanced Study,"

3, January 3, 2008, accessed on January 5, 2016, http://www.princeton.edu/mudd /finding_aids/mathoral/pmcxbor.htm.

16. Abraham Flexner to Louis Bamberger, August 1, 1933, Trustees box 2, "Bamberger, L., 1930–38," Institute for Advanced Study Archives, Princeton, New Jersey.

17. Abraham Flexner to Louis Bamberger, October 21, 1930, Trustees box 2, "Bamberger, L. 1930–38," Institute for Advanced Study Archives, Princeton, New Jersey.

18. Louis Bamberger to Abraham Flexner, April 11, 1932, Stern Chronological files, box/tab "1900–5/1932," p. 1, Institute for Advanced Study Archives, Princeton, New Jersey.

19. "Report of the Director," in "Minutes of the Annual Meeting of the Institute for Advanced Study," October 13, 1931, 16, Trustees box 2, Institute for Advanced Study Archives, Princeton, New Jersey.

20. George Dyson, *Turing's Cathedral* (New York: Vintage Books, 2012), 31.

21. "Bamberger Tract Probably Site of College," *Newark Sunday Call*, June 8, 1930, 2.

22. Louis Bamberger to Trustees, April 11, 1932, Stern Chronological files, box/tab "1900–1935/1932," Institute for Advanced Study Archives, Princeton, New Jersey.

23. The original letter sent and signed by Louis Bamberger and Carrie Fuld to prospective trustees June 4, 1930, inviting them to serve on the board of trustees of the Institute for Advanced Study is in the author's collection.

24. Dyson, *Turing's Cathedral*, 24.

25. Frank Aydelotte to Lewis Weed, May 9, 1940, Stern biographical files, box A–C, file "L. Bamberger," Institute for Advanced Study Archives, Princeton, New Jersey.

26. Frank Aydelotte to Lewis Weed, April 29, 1941, Stern biographical files, box "A–C,"

file "L. Bamberger," Institute for Advanced Study Archives, Princeton, New Jersey.

27. Louis Bamberger to Abraham Flexner, December 3, 1930, Trustees box 2, "Bamberger, L. 1930–36," Institute for Advanced Study Archives, Princeton, New Jersey.

28. Abraham Flexner to Frank Aydelotte, February 27, 1935, general box, "Ast–Ay," file "Aydelotte, Frank, 1930–37," Institute for Advanced Study Archives, Princeton, New Jersey.

29. Abraham Flexner to Frank Aydelotte, February 5, 1935, general box, "Ast–Ay," file "Aydelotte, Frank, 1930–37," Institute for Advanced Study Archives, Princeton, New Jersey.

30. Abraham Flexner to Louis Bamberger and Mrs. Fuld, February 11, 1931, Trustees box 2, file "Bamberger, L., 1930–36," Institute for Advanced Study Archives, Princeton, New Jersey.

31. Esther S. Bailey to Louis Bamberger, January 19, 1931, Trustees box 2, "Bamberger, L. 1930–36," Institute for Advanced Study Archives, Princeton, New Jersey.

32. Abraham Flexner to Louis Bamberger, October 11, 1932, Stern Chronological files, box "1900–1935," Institute for Advanced Study Archives, Princeton, New Jersey.

33. Louis Bamberger to Abraham Flexner, January 14, 1936, Trustees box 2, file "Bamberger, L., 1930–36," Institute for Advanced Study Archives, Princeton, New Jersey.

34. Abraham Flexner to Mrs. Fuld, June 6, 1936, Trustees box 4, "Fuld, Mrs. F.," Institute for Advanced Study Archives, Princeton, New Jersey.

35. "Dr. Abraham Flexner to Speak," *"Y" Bulletin*, December 21, 1931, 2000 series, box 3, file 3–3, Jewish Historical Society of New Jersey Archives, Whippany, New Jersey.

36. Louis Bamberger to Abraham

Flexner, February 20, 1932, Trustees box 2, "Bamberger, L. 1930–36," Institute for Advanced Study Archives, Princeton, New Jersey.

37. Allyn Jackson, "The IAS School of Mathematics," *Notices of the AMS* 49, no. 8 (Sept. 2002): 901.

38. Abraham Flexner to Anne Flexner, June 23, 1931, Abraham Flexner Papers, container 4, Manuscripts Collection, Library of Congress, Washington, DC.

39. Flexner, *I Remember*, 392.

40. Dyson, *Turing's Cathedral*, 23.

41. Ibid.

42. Ibid.

43. Ibid.

44. Ibid., 24.

45. Steve Batterson, "The Vision, Insight, and Influence of Oswald Veblen," *Notices of the AMS* 54, no. 5 (May 2007): 612–13.

46. Ibid., 613.

47. Dyson, *Turing's Cathedral*, 24.

48. Abraham Flexner to Louis Bamberger, January 16, 1935, Trustees box 2, "Bamberger, L., 1930–36," Institute for Advanced Study Archives, Princeton, New Jersey.

49. Louis Bamberger to Abraham Flexner, January 18, 1935, Trustees box 2, "Bamberger, L., 1930–36," Institute for Advanced Study Archives, Princeton, New Jersey.

50. "Report of the Director," appendix, Abraham Flexner to Trustees, "Confidential," September 26, 1931, 12, Institute for Advanced Study Archives, Princeton, New Jersey.

51. Ibid.

52. Dyson, *Turing's Cathedral*, 25.

53. "Docket for Regular Meeting of the Trustees of the Institute for Advanced Study," January 11, 1932, 2, Institute for Advanced Study Archives, Princeton, New Jersey.

54. Abraham Flexner to Louis Bam-

berger, July 26, 1932, Trustees box 2, "Bamberger, L., 1930–36," Institute for Advanced Study Archives, Princeton, New Jersey.

55. Laura Smith Porter, "Louis Bamberger and the Concept of Community," in *From Intellectual Sanctuary to Social Responsibility: The Founding of the Institute for Advanced Study 1930–1933* (Ann Arbor, MI: UMI, 1988), 4.

56. Alexander Leitch, *A Princeton Companion* (Princeton: Princeton Legacy Library, 1978) is a reference book on Princeton University.

57. "New Bamberger Institute Would Please Princeton," *Newark Sunday Call*, October 2, 1932, 8.

58. Helen Dukas, interview with the author, March 22,1956, Stern Chronological files, box "1900–1935," sect. "pre-1929," Institute for Advanced Study Archives, Princeton, New Jersey.

59. Dyson, *Turing's Cathedral*, 27.

60. Walter Isaacson, *Einstein: His Life and Universe* (New York, Simon and Schuster, 2007), 395.

61. Ibid.

62. "Report of the Director [of the] Institute for Advanced Study," marked "Confidential," December 28, 1931, 2, Institute for Advanced Study Archives, Princeton, New Jersey.

63. Robert Millikan at the California Institute of Technology to Abraham Flexner in New York, Pasadena, California, July 25, 1932, Stern Chronological files, box "1900–1935," Institute for Advanced Study Archives, Princeton, New Jersey.

64. Ibid.

65. Isaacson, *Einstein*, 397.

66. Abraham Flexner to Albert Einstein, July 12, 1932, Stern Chronological files, box/tab "1900–1935/1932," Institute for Advanced Study Archives, Princeton, New Jersey.

67. Abraham Flexner to Louis Bam-

berger, August 30, 1932, Trustees box 2, "Bamberger, L., 1930–36," Institute for Advanced Study Archives, Princeton, New Jersey.

68. "Institute for Advanced Study Headed by Flexner," *New York Times*, October 11, 1932, 18.

69. Abraham Flexner to Louis Bamberger, "Buildings and Grounds," March 1, 1932, Stern Chronological files, box "1900–1935," Institute for Advanced Study Archives, Princeton, New Jersey.

70. Edgar Bamberger to Abraham Flexner, February 24, 1932, Trustees box 2, "Bamberger, Edgar, 1930–1943," Institute for Advanced Study Archives, Princeton, New Jersey.

71. Herbert Maass, "Mr. Maass," Trustees box 2, "Bamberger, L., 1943," n.p., Institute for Advanced Study Archives, Princeton, New Jersey. This article discusses how the Institute for Advanced Study came into being.

72. Abraham Flexner to Percy Straus, April 9, 1932, Stern Chronological files, box/tab "1900–1935/1932," p. 2, Institute for Advanced Study Archives, Princeton, New Jersey.

73. "Einstein Will Head School Here, Opening Scholastic Center," *New York Times*, October 11, 1932, 18.

74. Edwin Brody, interview with the author, 2008, conducted at the Jewish Historical Society of New Jersey, Whippany, New Jersey.

75. *Alumni Weekly*, October 14, 1932, Princeton University Archives, Princeton, New Jersey.

76. Albert Einstein to Abraham Flexner, June 14, 1932, Stern Chronological files, box/tab "1900–1935/1932," Institute for Advanced Study Archives, Princeton, New Jersey.

77. Laura Smith Porter, "Albert Einstein and the Politics of Science," in *From Intel-lectual Sanctuary to Social Responsibility*, 269.

78. Abraham Flexner to Frau Einstein, July 6, 1933, Stern Chronological files, box/tab "1900–1935/1932," Institute for Advanced Study Archives, Princeton, New Jersey.

79. Abraham Flexner to Carrie Fuld, July 20, 1933, trustees Box 4, "Fuld, Mrs. F.," Institute for Advanced Study Archives, Princeton, New Jersey.

80. Ibid.

81. Ibid.

82. Abraham Flexner to Louis Bamberger, August 22, 1932, Trustees box 2, "Bamberger, L., 1930–1936," Institute for Advanced Study Archives, Princeton, New Jersey.

83. Abraham Flexner to Louis Bamberger, July 18, 1932, Trustees box 2, "Bamberger, L., 1930–1936," Institute for Advanced Study Archives, Princeton, New Jersey.

84. Abraham Flexner to Louis Bamberger, August 30, 1932, Trustees box 2, "Bamberger, L., 1930–1936," Institute for Advanced Study Archives, Princeton, New Jersey.

85. Louis Bamberger to Abraham Flexner, August 26, 1932, Trustees box 2, "Bamberger, L., 1930–1936," Institute for Advanced Study Archives, Princeton, New Jersey.

86. Abraham Flexner to Louis Bamberger, October 11, 1932, Trustees box 2, "Bamberger, L., 1930–1936," Institute for Advanced Study Archives, Princeton, New Jersey.

87. "Einstein Sails for Job in Jersey, Forgives Official Who Vexed Him," *Newark Sunday Call*, December 11, 1932, 18.

88. Raymond Fosdick to Abraham Flexner, December 6, 1932, Stern Chronological files, box/tab "1900–1935/1932," Institute for Advanced Study Archives, Princeton, New Jersey.

89. "Petition New Jersey Legislature for

Formal Welcome to Professor Einstein," Jewish Telegraphic Agency, December 14, 1932.

90. Ibid.

91. Abraham Flexner to Frau Einstein, July 6, 1933, Stern Chronological Files, box 1900–1935, tab 1932, Institute for Advanced Study Archives, Princeton, New Jersey.

92. Abraham Flexner to Albert Einstein, August 8, 1933, Stern Chronological files, box/tab "1900–1935/1932," Institute for Advanced Study Archives, Princeton, New Jersey.

93. Abraham Flexner to Mrs. Felix Fuld, telegram, Biltmore Hotel, Phoenix, March 10, 1933, Trustees box 4, "Fuld, Mrs. F.," Institute for Advanced Study Archives, Princeton, New Jersey.

94. Louis Bamberger to Abraham Flexner, March 11, 1933, Trustees box 2, "Bamberger, L., 1930–1936," Institute for Advanced Study Archives, Princeton, New Jersey.

95. Abraham Flexner to Mrs. Fuld, March 16, 1933, Trustees box 4, "Fuld, Mrs. F." Institute for Advanced Study Archives, Princeton, New Jersey.

96. "Einsteins Come to Newark to Shop," *Newark Evening News*, March 18, 1933, is in a scrapbook containing newspaper clippings, awards, and photographs of Edgar Bamberger's career. It was assembled by his granddaughter, Mildred Levine, who keeps the scrapbook at her home in Reisterstown, Maryland.

97. "Einstein Will Begin Labors at Institute," *Newark Sunday Call*, October 15, 1933, n.p.

98. "Einstein Will Head New School Here," *New York Times*, October 11, 1932, 18.

99. Abraham Flexner to Louis Bamberger, September 22, 1933, Trustees box 2, "Bamberger, L, 1930–1936," Institute for Advanced Study Archives, Princeton, New Jersey.

100. Peter Michelmore, *Einstein: Profile*

of the Man (New York: Dodd Mead, 1962), 59.

101. Abraham Flexner to Mr. Bamberger and Mrs. Fuld, October 17, 1933, Trustees box 2, "Bamberger, L., 1930–1936," Institute for Advanced Study Archives, Princeton, New Jersey.

102. "Einstein Arrives; Pleads for Quiet; Whisked from Liner by Tug at Quarantine," *New York Times*, October 18, 1933.

103. "Mrs. Felix Fuld and Her Brother, Louis Bamberger of Centre Street South Orange Will Motor to Princeton," *Newark Sunday Call*, October 22, 1933, Edgar Bamberger's scrapbook, Bamberger Family Collection, Reisterstown, Maryland. Copy courtesy of Mildred "Bunny" Levine, Edgar Bamberger's granddaughter.

104. Abraham Flexner to Mrs. Fuld, March 6, 1934, Trustees box 4, "Fuld, Mrs. F.," Institute for Advanced Study Archives, Princeton, New Jersey.

105. Isaacson, *Einstein*, 247.

106. Ibid.

107. Edgar Bamberger to Abraham Flexner, June 27, 1933, Trustees box 2, "Bamberger, L., 1930–1943," Institute for Advanced Study Archives, Princeton, New Jersey.

108. Ibid.

109. Ibid.

110. Abraham Flexner to Edgar Bamberger, July 6, 1933, Trustees box 2, "Bamberger, Edgar, 1930–1943," Institute for Advanced Study Archives, Princeton, New Jersey.

111. Abraham Flexner to Mrs. Fuld, March 6, 1934, Trustees box 4, "Fuld, Mrs. F.," 2, Institute for Advanced Study Archives, Princeton, New Jersey.

112. Abraham Flexner to Herbert Maass, October 13, 1933, Stern Chronological files, box/tab "1900–1935/1933," Institute for Advanced Study Archives, Princeton, New Jersey.

113. Abraham Flexner to Edgar Bamberger, July 6, 1933, Trustees box 2, "Bamberger, Edgar 1930–1943," Institute for Advanced Study Archives, Princeton, New Jersey.

114. Ibid.

115. Emil Hilb to Abraham Flexner, New York City, November 30, 1933, Stern Chronological files, box/tab "1900–1935/1933," p. 1, Institute for Advanced Study Archives, Princeton, New Jersey.

116. Abraham Flexner to Emil Hilb, December 4, 1933, Stern Chronological files, box/tab "1900–1935/1933," p. 2, Institute for Advanced Study Archives, Princeton, New Jersey.

117. Abraham Flexner to Herbert H. Maass, December 4, 1933, Stern Chronological files, box/tab "1900–1935/1933," Institute for Advanced Study Archives, Princeton, New Jersey.

118. Abraham Flexner, in response to a cable from Hiram J. Halle, London, November 26, 1933, Stern Chronological files, box/tab "1900–1935/1933," Institute for Advanced Study Archives, Princeton, New Jersey.

119. Erica Mosner, IAS archival assistant, e-mail to the author, August 11, 2014.

120. Abraham Flexner to Franklin D. Roosevelt, November 21, 1933, Roosevelt Papers, Franklin D. Roosevelt Library, Hyde Park, New York.

121. Ibid.

122. "Resourcefulness of Frau Einstein Prevents Murder of Scientist," *Jewish Chronicle*, February 13, 1925, 1.

123. Albert Einstein to Eleanor Roosevelt, November 21, 1933, Roosevelt Papers, Franklin D. Roosevelt Library, Hyde Park, New York.

124. Jewish Historical Society of Greater Washington (DC), "Object of the Month," e-mail to the author, September 5, 2012. The e-mail features a note from Albert Einstein

written in 1938 pressuring governments to obtain visas for German scientists to come to America.

125. Abraham Flexner to Mr. Bamberger and Mrs. Fuld, August 23, 1933, Trustees box 2, "Bamberger, L., 1930–1936," p. 2, Institute for Advanced Study Archives, Princeton, New Jersey.

126. Smith Porter, *From Intellectual Sanctuary to Social Responsibility*, 259.

127. "Einstein at Fiddle in Benefit Concert," Jewish Telegraphic Agency, January 14, 1934.

128. "$1,000,000 Gift Aids Flexner Institute," *New York Times*, April 25, 1934, n.p.

129. Louis Bamberger to Dr. Abraham Flexner, "Louis Bamberger Invites Dr. Abraham Flexner to Serve as a Trustee," June 4, 1930, Trustees box 2, "Bamberger, L., 1930–1936," Institute for Advanced Study Archives, Princeton, New Jersey. This is the letter Bamberger sent to individuals he asked to become trustees of the IAS, which included Abraham Flexner. The author has the original letter sent to E. Bamberger, hand-signed by L. Bamberger and C. Fuld, in her private collection.

130. Abraham Flexner to Anne Flexner, June 23, 1931, container 4, Flexner Papers, Manuscripts Collection, Library of Congress, Washington, DC.

131. Louis Bamberger to the Trustees of the Institute for Advanced Study, April 23, 1934, Trustees box 2, "Bamberger, L., 1930–1936," Institute for Advanced Study Archives, Princeton, New Jersey.

132. Ibid.

133. Louis Bamberger, President, to the Trustees of the Institute for Advanced Study, January 9, 1933, Stern Chronological files, box "A–Cl," tab "Bamberger," p. 2, Institute for Advanced Study Archives, Princeton, New Jersey.

134. Abraham Flexner to Frau Einstein,

October 25, 1933, Stern Chronological files, file/tab "1900–1935/1932," Institute for Advanced Study Archives, Princeton, New Jersey.

135. Ibid.

136. "10,000 to Greet Einstein Sunday," *Jewish Chronicle*, March 23, 1934, 1.

137. "Rabbi Lauds Einstein as an Advocate of Justice," *Jewish Chronicle*, March 30, 1934, 1.

138. "Newark Prepares for Event," Jewish Telegraphic Agency, March 14, 1934.

139. "Einstein Guest of State Here Today; Police Complete Plans to Handle Crowd at Reception," *Newark Sunday Call*, March 25, 1934, 12.

140. Nathaniel S. ("Buddy") Rosengarten, "How Can You Forget Albert Einstein?" unpublished manuscript, April 2001, Jewish Historical Society of New Jersey Archives, Whippany, New Jersey.

141. Ibid.

142. "Who Paid? Newark or Cleveland?" *Jewish Chronicle*, March 30, 1934, 1.

143. "New Jersey Acclaims Einsteins in Huge Newark Reception," Jewish Telegraphic Agency, March 26, 1934, 1.

144. "Einstein Reception Gains Support Throughout State," *Newark Sunday Call*, March 18, 1934, 11.

145. "Garb at Wedding Minor, Is New Einstein Theory," *Newark Sunday Call*, November 30, 1930, n.p.

146. "New Jersey Acclaims Einsteins in Huge Newark Reception," Jewish Telegraphic Agency, March 26, 1934.

147. "Einstein Lauds Silberfeld on His Sixtieth Milestone," *Jewish Chronicle*, April 3, 1936, 1.

148. "New Jersey Acclaims Einsteins in Huge Newark Reception," Jewish Telegraphic Agency, March 26, 1934.

149. Abraham Flexner to Frau Einstein, November 15, 1933, Stern Chronological files, file/tab "1930–1935/1932," Institute for Advanced Study Archives, Princeton, New Jersey.

150. Ibid.

151. Abraham Flexner to Louis Bamberger, September 26, 1933, Trustees box 2, "Bamberger, L., 1930–1936," Institute for Advanced Study Archives, Princeton, New Jersey.

152. "Einstein in Princeton: Scientist, Humanitarian Cultural Icon," Historical Society of Princeton exhibition, March 5, 1995.

153. Abraham Flexner to Louis Bamberger, December 11, 1933, Trustees box 2, "Bamberger, L., 1930–1936," Institute for Advanced Study Archives, Princeton, New Jersey.

154. Smith Porter, *From Intellectual Sanctuary to Social Responsibility*, 269.

155. Ibid.

156. Albert Einstein to Frank Aydelotte, August 9, 1943, Directors, Aydelotte box 3, "Financial Flexner File: Financial Pensions 2," Institute for Advanced Study Archives, Princeton, New Jersey.

157. Frank Aydelotte to Albert Einstein, February 12, 1944, Directors, Aydelotte box 3, "Financial Flexner File: Financial Pensions 2," Institute for Advanced Study Archives, Princeton, New Jersey.

158. Frank Aydelotte to Herbert Maass, May 2, 1944, Trustees box 2, "Bamberger, Louis," Institute for Advanced Study Archives, Princeton, New Jersey.

159. Ibid.

160. "Opening of Hebrew University to Be Observed Here Wednesday," *Newark Sunday Call*, March 29, 1925, 8.

161. Isaacson, *Einstein*, 522.

162. Abraham Flexner to Louis Bamberger, December 11, 1933, Trustees box 2, "Bamberger, L., 1930–1936," Institute for Advanced Study Archives, Princeton, New Jersey.

163. Isaacson, *Einstein*, 433.

164. Dr. Marc A. Bernstein, archivist, New York Society for Ethical Culture, e-mail to the author, June 30, 2008, New York City.

165. Proclamation, Office of the Mayor of the City of New York, 1951, on the occasion of the Ethical Culture Society's seventy-fifth anniversary.

166. Edgar B. Bing, interviews with the author in Bing's home, 2008–2010, Avon-by-the-Sea, New Jersey.

167. Herbert Maass to Abraham Flexner, April 7, 1933, "General By-Laws," Stern Chronological files, box/tab "1900–1935/1933," Institute for Advanced Study Archives, Princeton, New Jersey. This letter identifies the status of Bamberger and Fuld as honorary members of the IAS Board of Trustees.

168. Michelmore, *Einstein*, 12.

169. Abraham Flexner to Frau Einstein, July 6, 1933, Stern Chronological files, box/tab "1900–1935/1932," Institute for Advanced Study Archives, Princeton, New Jersey.

170. Gordon Bishop, "Gems of New Jersey: Einstein = mc2," *Star-Ledger* (Newark), September 30, 1984, 5.

171. Trustees of the IAS, draft resolution paying tribute to Louis Bamberger, 1944, box 2 "Bamberger, L., 1943–n.d.," Institute for Advanced Study Archives, Princeton, New Jersey.

172. Louis Bamberger to Abraham Flexner, telegram, Canadian National Telegraphs, July 19, 1933, Trustees box 2, "Bamberger, L., 1930–1936," Institute for Advanced Study Archives, Princeton, New Jersey.

173. Frank Aydelotte to Abraham Flexner, October 16, 1933, general box, "Ast–Ay," file "Aydelotte, Frank, 1930–1937," Institute for Advanced Study Archives, Princeton, New Jersey.

174. Gertrude Dubrovsky, "Exiles in Paradise: Princeton's Intellectual Emigres, 1930–1950," *New Jersey Historical Commission Newsletter*, February 1987, 5, 6.

175. Batterson, "The Vision, Insight, and Influence of Oswald Veblen," 615.

176. Ibid.

177. Frank Aydelotte to Abraham Flexner, August 18, 1933, general box, "Act–Ay," file "Aydelotte, Frank, 1930–1937," Institute for Advanced Study Archives, Princeton, New Jersey.

178. "5-Year Progress of Institute Is Gratifying to Bamberger," newspaper clipping n.d. 1935 is in Trustees file, Box 4, "Fuld, Mrs. F," Institute for Advanced Study Archives, Princeton, New Jersey.

179. Abraham Flexner to Louis Bamberger, June 23, 1939, p. 3, container 4, Abraham Flexner Papers, Manuscripts Collection, Library of Congress, Washington, DC.

180. Ibid.

181. Abraham Flexner to Louis Bamberger and Mrs. Fuld, July 18, 1937, p. 12, container Four, Abraham Flexner Papers, Manuscripts Collection, Library of Congress, Washington, DC.

182. Ibid., 13.

183. Ibid.

184. Herbert Maass to Edgar S. Bamberger, Re: The Institute for Advanced Study, March 28, 1933, Institute for Advanced Study Archives, Princeton, New Jersey.

185. Herbert Maass to IAS Trustees, April 11, 1932, Stern Chronological files, box/tab "1900–1935/1932," Institute for Advanced Study Archives, Princeton, New Jersey.

186. Abraham Flexner to Frank Aydelotte, November 4, 1937, general box, "Ast–Ay," file "Aydelotte, Frank, 1930–1937," Institute for Advanced Study Archives, Princeton, New Jersey.

187. Abraham Flexner to Frank Aydelotte, December 6, 1937, general box,

"Ast–Ay," file "Aydelotte, Frank, 1930–1937," Institute for Advanced Study Archives, Princeton, New Jersey.

188. Frank Aydelotte to Abraham Flexner, June 24, 1938, Trustees box 1, "Acheson–Aydelotte," file no. 3195, "Aydelotte, Frank 1930–1939," Institute for Advanced Study Archives, Princeton, New Jersey.

189. Abraham Flexner to Frank Aydelotte, September 23, 1938, Trustees box 1, "Acheson–Aydelotte," file no. 3195, "Aydelotte, Frank, 1930–1939," Institute for Advanced Study Archives, Princeton, New Jersey.

190. Abraham Flexner to Frank Aydelotte, September 26, 1938, Trustees box 1, "Acheson–Aydelotte," file no. 3195, "Aydelotte, Frank, 1930–1939," Institute for Advanced Study Archives, Princeton, New Jersey.

191. Herbert Maass to Abraham Flexner, June 14, 1938, Stern Chronological files, box "A–Cl," file "Bamberger," Institute for Advanced Study Archives, Princeton, New Jersey.

192. Frank Aydelotte to Abraham Flexner, September 26, 1938, Trustees box 1, "Acheson–Aydelotte," file no. 3195, "Aydelotte, Frank 1930–1939," Institute for Advanced Study Archives, Princeton, New Jersey.

193. Abraham Flexner to Frank Aydelotte, September 20, 1938, Trustees box 1, "Acheson–Aydelotte," file no. 3195, "Aydelotte, Frank 1930–1939," Institute for Advanced Study Archives, Princeton, New Jersey.

194. "Scholars in New Home," *New York Times*, October 2, 1939, n.p.

195. Flexner, *I Remember*, 394.

196. "Minutes of Joint Meeting of Executive and Finance Committees," June 15, 1936, p. 5, Institute for Advanced Study Archives, Princeton, New Jersey.

197. Abraham Flexner to Louis Bamberger, August 5, 1936, Trustees box 2, "Bamberger, L. 1930–1936," Institute for Advanced Study Archives, Princeton, New Jersey.

198. Abraham Flexner to Louis Bamberger, June 24, 1936, Trustees box 2, "Bamberger, L., 1930–1936," Institute for Advanced Study Archives, Princeton, New Jersey.

199. Frank Aydelotte to Louis Bamberger, April 4, 1940, Trustees box 2, "Bamberger, L., 1937–1942," Institute for Advanced Study Archives, Princeton, New Jersey.

200. Nancy Lee Swann, sinologist and archivist for the Gest Collection, December 7, 2009, accessed on January 6, 2016, http://www.umass.edu/wsp/resources/profiles/swann.html.

201. "Report of the Director, Rockefeller Bamberger Fund," May 13, 1940, p. 6, general box 58, file "Rockefeller-Bamberger Fund, 1939 and 1940," Institute for Advanced Study Archives, Princeton, New Jersey.

202. Frank Aydelotte to Lavinia Bamberger, November 14, 1944, general box, "Ba–Bh–Barn," file "Bamberger, C. Lavinia," Institute for Advanced Study Archives, Princeton, New Jersey.

203. Abraham Flexner to Mr. Bamberger and Mrs. Fuld, July 29, 1939, container 4, Manuscripts Collection, Library of Congress, Washington, DC.

204. Edgar Bamberger to Abraham Flexner, August 18, 1939, Trustees box 2, "Bamberger, E. 1930–1943," Institute for Advanced Study Archives, Princeton, New Jersey.

205. Armand Borel, "The School of Mathematics at the Institute for Advanced Study," December 12, 2014, p. 1, accessed on January 6, 2016, http://www.princeton.edu/mudd/finding_aids/mathoral/pmcxbor.htm.

206. Flexner, *I Remember*, 366.

207. Ibid.

208. Abraham Flexner to Winfield Riefler, August 7, 1939, Institute for Advanced Study Archives, Princeton, New Jersey.

209. Abraham Flexner to Louis Bamberger, in Winfield Riefler's letter, August 7, 1939, Institute for Advanced Study Archives, Princeton, New Jersey.

210. Ibid.

211. Louis Bamberger to Abraham Flexner, July 19, 1938, Trustees box 2, "Bamberger, L., 1937–1942," Institute for Advanced Study Archives, Princeton, New Jersey.

212. Abraham Flexner to Louis Bamberger, August 1, 1933, Trustees box 2, "Bamberger, L., 1930–1936," Institute for Advanced Study Archives, Princeton, New Jersey.

213. John Hardin to Abraham Flexner, August 9, 1939, Stern Chronological files, box "A–Cl," file "Bamberger," Institute for Advanced Study Archives, Princeton, New Jersey.

214. Ibid.

215. Ibid.

216. "Dr. Abraham Flexner Lauded for Services to High Education," *New York Times*, October 29, 1939.

217. Frank Aydelotte to Lewis Weed, May 9, 1940, Stern Chronological files, box "A–Cl," file "Bamberger," Institute for Advanced Study Archives, Princeton, New Jersey.

218. Louis Bamberger to Frank Aydelotte, November 21, 1939, Trustees box 2, "Bamberger, L., 1937–1942," Institute for Advanced Study Archives, Princeton, New Jersey.

219. Ibid.

220. Alanson B. Houghton to Louis Bamberger, October 5, 1939, Stern Chronological files, box "A–Cl," file "Bamberger," Institute for Advanced Study Archives, Princeton, New Jersey.

221. Erica Mosner, e-mail to the author, September 30, 2014, Princeton, New Jersey.

222. Abraham Flexner to Raymond Fosdick, February 9, 1939, general box 58, file "Rockefeller Foundation 1934–1942," Institute for Advanced Study Archives, Princeton, New Jersey.

223. Frank Aydelotte to Louis Bamberger, June 24, 1938, Directors box 1, "A-Building," file "Bamberger, Louis," Institute for Advanced Study Archives, Princeton, New Jersey.

224. Frank Aydelotte to Robert A. Oppenheimer, March 23, 1949, Directors "Aydelotte" box, "Oppenheimer-Z" (box 6), file "Rockefeller Bamberger Fund," Institute for Advanced Study Archives, Princeton, New Jersey.

225. Ibid.

226. Ibid.

227. Ibid.

228. Frank Aydelotte to Mr. Bamberger, July 23, 1943, Trustees box 2, "Bamberger, L., 1943," Institute for Advanced Study Archives, Princeton, New Jersey.

229. Louis Bamberger to Dr. Aydelotte, September 4, 1943, Trustees box 2, "Bamberger L., 1943," Institute for Advanced Study Archives, Princeton, New Jersey.

230. Frank Aydelotte to Mr. Bamberger, July 23, 1943, Trustees box 2, "Bamberger, L., 1943," Institute for Advanced Study Archives, Princeton, New Jersey.

231. Louis Bamberger to Frank Aydelotte, September 4, 1943, Trustees box 2, "Bamberger, L., 1943," Institute for Advanced Study Archives, Princeton, New Jersey.

232. Frank Aydelotte to Louis Bamberger, August 27, 1943, Trustees box 2, "Bamberger, L.," Institute for Advanced Study Archives, Princeton, New Jersey.

233. Ibid.

234. Ibid.

235. Frank Aydelotte to Mr. Bamberger, July 23, 1943, p. 2, Trustees box 2, "Bamberger, L., 1943," Institute for Advanced Study Archives, Princeton, New Jersey.

236. Ibid.

237. Ibid.

238. Ibid.

239. "Report of the Director," October 11, 1944, Stern biographical files, box "A–Cl," file "Bamberger," Institute for Advanced Study Archives, Princeton, New Jersey.

240. Mrs. Leary to Mr. Bradley, November 4, 1949, general box, "Ba–Bh," file "Bamberger Fuld Memorial Walk Dedicated October 20, 1950," Institute for Advanced Study Archives, Princeton, New Jersey.

241. Ibid.

242. Institute for Advanced Study, "Mission and History," accessed on January 24, 2016, https://www.ias.edu/about/mission-and-history.

243. Erica Mosner, e-mail to the author, August 12, 2014, Princeton, New Jersey.

244. Frank Aydelotte to Edgar Bamberger, June 16, 1945, Trustees box 2, file "Bamberger, Edgar 1944–," Institute for Advanced Study Archives, Princeton, New Jersey.

245. Ibid.

EPILOGUE

1. Ellen Bamberger De Franco to the author, June 28, 2007, Oakland, California, collection of the author.

2. Fuld family relative, Jewel (no last name), to "Dearest Dr.," Berg Family Collection, Huntington, Long Island. This letter describes the memorial service conducted for Louis Bamberger at his home in South Orange on March 13, 1944. A copy of the letter is in the author's collection.

3. Joanne La Greca, Rosehill Crematory supervisor, e-mail to the author, March 6, 2014, Linden, New Jersey.

4. Frank Aydelotte to Lavinia Bamberger, December 6, 1944, general box, Institute of Advanced Study Archives, Princeton, New Jersey.

5. John Hardin, "Recollections of Mr. Bamberger," Trustees box 2, "Ba–Bh," file "Bamberger," folder "Bamberger, C. Lavinia," Institute of Advanced Study Archives, Princeton, New Jersey. This is among a series of recollections written by IAS trustees, most of whom were appointed by Bamberger (usually family or business associates), who were asked to give their feelings on and opinions of Bamberger—how he inspired them and what they learned from working for and with him.

6. Smith Porter, *From Intellectual Sanctuary to Social Responsibility*, 4.

7. Charles F. Cummings, "Knowing Newark," *Star-Ledger* (Newark), July 14, 1997, 4.

8. Michael Schapp, "Mr. Schaap Recalls Bamberger," Trustees box 2, Institute for Advanced Study Archives, Princeton, New Jersey.

9. Walter H. Farrier to Frank Aydelotte, October 13, 1944, general box, "Fall–Flem," file "Farrier, Walter H.," Institute for Advanced Study Archives, Princeton, New Jersey.

INDEX